Human Rights as Social Construction

Most conceptions of human rights rely on metaphysical or theological assumptions that construe them as possible only as something imposed from outside existing communities. Most people, in other words, presume that human rights come from nature, God, or the United Nations. This book argues that reliance on such putative sources actually undermines human rights. Benjamin Gregg envisions an alternative; he sees human rights as locally developed, freely embraced, and indigenously valid. Human rights can be created by the average, ordinary people to whom they are addressed. And they are valid only if embraced by those to whom they would apply. To view human rights in this manner is to increase the chances and opportunities that more people across the globe will come to embrace them.

Benjamin Gregg teaches social and political theory at the University of Texas at Austin. He is the author of *Thick Moralities, Thin Politics: Social Integration Across Communities of Belief* (2003) and *Coping in Politics with Indeterminate Norms: A Theory of Enlightened Localism* (2003). His articles have appeared in *Political Theory, Review of Politics, Theory and Society, Polity, Ratio Juris, Comparative Sociology,* and *International Review of Sociology.*

D0878730

Human Rights as Social Construction

BENJAMIN GREGG

University of Texas at Austin

CAMBRIDGE
UNIVERSITY PRESS

CAMBRIDGE UNIVERSITY PRESS
Cambridge, New York, Melbourne, Madrid, Cape Town,
Singapore, São Paulo, Delhi, Mexico City

Cambridge University Press
The Edinburgh Building, Cambridge CB2 8RU, UK

Published in the United States of America by Cambridge University Press, New York

www.cambridge.org
Information on this title: www.cambridge.org/9781107612945

First published 2012
Reprinted 2012 (twice)
First paperback edition 2013

A catalogue record for this publication is available from the British Library

Library of Congress Cataloguing in Publication Data
Gregg, Benjamin Greenwood.
Human rights as social construction / Benjamin Gregg.
  p. cm.
Includes bibliographical references and index.
ISBN 978-1-107-01593-7 (hardback)
1. Human rights – Social aspects. I. Title.
JC571.G7825 2011
323.01 – dc23 2011025073

ISBN 978-1-107-01593-7 Hardback
ISBN 978-1-107-61294-5 Paperback

For Keqin, Nicholas, and Saskia

Contents

vii

Acknowledgments

How does one write an acknowledgment? The "writer exploits the authorial channel to convey – nay, to broadcast – a personal message in a voice different from the one he will immediately take up. A Durkheimian twist. As if the self-demanding labor of doing the book gave the writer the privilege and obligation to show publicly that he has a separate, private life and is committed to it, while at the same time those who make up this life have a right to be so recognized. One is reminded of the presence of hand-held wives when husbands accept success or defeat in their effort to win an election" (Goffman 1974:298, n. 68).

In that spirit, I am grateful for the critical feedback generously provided by Kathleen Higgins, Gary Jacobson, the late David Sciulli, and above all Ross Zucker, with whom I have debated political theory ever since our paths crossed at Yale decades ago; by insightful audiences at the Universität Bern, the Europa Universität Viadrina, the University of Nebraska at Lincoln, and the University of Texas at Austin School of Law; by discussants and critical audiences at various meetings of the American Political Science Association, the Midwest Political Science Association, and the Political Studies Association of the United Kingdom; and by the judicious anonymous reviewers for Cambridge University Press. I also thank the Humboldt Universität zu Berlin, and my host Klaus Eder, for hospitality during a research visit devoted to sociological theory. I am grateful as well to Keqin Gregg for guidance in Chapter 8's discussion of genetics; to Laura Tendler for editing both sensitive and aesthetic; to Peggy Rote for managing production with patience and efficiency, in equal measure; to Nicholas Gregg, who designed the cover image for a narrative not easily limned in figural terms; to Catherine Zinser of the Blanton Museum of Art for counsel on Netherlandish engravings with Parmigianinesque vocabularies; and to my generous and thoughtful editor, Robert Dreesen.

In other news: Chapter 3 originally appeared, in a different version, as "Anti-Imperialism: Generating Universal Human Rights out of Local Norms" in *Ratio Juris* 23, no. 3, pp. 289–310, © 2010 by Wiley-Blackwell. Used with kind permission of Wiley-Blackwell. Chapter 4 originally appeared, in a different version, as "Individuals as Authors of Human Rights: Not Only Addressees" in *Theory and Society* 39, no. 6, pp. 631–61, © 2010 by Springer. Used with kind permission of Springer. Chapter 6 originally appeared, in a different version, as "Translating Human Rights into Muslim Vernaculars" in *Comparative Sociology* 7, no. 4, pp. 415–33, © 2008 by Brill. Used with kind permission of Brill. Chapter 7 originally appeared, in a different version, as "Deploying Cognitive Sociology to Advance Human Rights" in *Comparative Sociology* 9, no. 3, pp. 279–307, © 2010 by Brill. Used with kind permission of Brill.

Introduction

Human Rights as Local Constructions of Limited but Expandable Validity

Jeremy Bentham's pungent critique of one conception of rights – rights valid independently of all institutions, and valid regardless of whether they are recognized by anyone – remains more quotable than any other, even after 170 years or so: "*Natural rights* is simple nonsense; natural and imprescriptible rights, rhetorical nonsense, – nonsense upon stilts" (Bentham 1843:501). Aimed at the revolutionary French Assembly's *Déclaration des droits de l'Homme et du Citoyen* of 1789, his critique follows directly from his premise: rights are the "child of law: from *real* laws come *real* rights; but from *imaginary* laws, from laws of nature... come *imaginary* rights" (Bentham 1843:523). How has Bentham's claim fared after so many years? On the one hand, the ancient legacy of natural and imprescriptible rights retains its attraction today, most powerfully in the notion of human rights. Perhaps Bentham might sense at least some vindication in the fact that, as a matter of empirical observation, we find in the world today, as ever, no agreement as to whether human rights exist or even can exist – and if they exist, of what provenience, let alone what rights those might be in particular, and which are fundamental, and which secondary. For the social constructionist approach I take, provenience is a matter of history and contingency rather than, say, necessary truths discoverable by man if not eternal verities revealed to the elect.[1] And as a matter of contingent fact, there are no generally accepted histories of the idea of human rights or even of movements for human rights; there are instead more than a few competing histories. To take but one recent example: Samuel Moyn asserts that the

---

[1] By "social constructionism" I refer to a sociological and philosophical tradition that finds one significant expression in Berger and Luckmann (1966) and another in Searle (1995). This book hopes to contribute to this tradition.

human rights idea emerged, at least in its current status in global political discourse, only in the 1970s rather than, say, with the moral intuitions of venerable and primordial religions, or in the American and French Revolutions, or with the post-Holocaust United Nations(UN) in the 1940s, or with the *Universal Declaration of Human Rights* in 1947. In Moyn's account, human rights emerged as the next great utopia following the exhaustion, if not failure, of various earlier utopias from which morally needy idealists now sought to distance themselves. Such utopias span quite an arc, from anticolonialist nationalism to communism to humanism to hopeful visions of the nation-state: "Born of the yearning to transcend politics, human rights have become the core language of a new politics of humanity that has sapped the energy from old ideological contests of the left and right" (Moyn 2010:227).

What Moyn does not contend, but what his account (like other recent accounts)[2] suggests, is that the history of human rights, indeed the very idea of human rights, all too frequently is a projection onto the past of one or the other contemporary understanding, assumption, or preoccupation in realms moral, legal, religious, or philosophical. But where Moyn sees the weakness of the human rights idea as merely one more utopian politics, I see possibilities for a human rights politics whose purchase and practice might be magnified powerfully along all the dimensions I develop in each of my nine chapters. In each I view human rights as social constructions. I take their constructedness as a license to recommend their local fabrication, if possible by their addressees themselves, ultimately in ways that would transform the nation-state into a human rights state. I go far beyond Moyn, who cannot identify an advisable human rights politics other than to urge its "minimalist" quality: that advisable politics be built around a small core of claims such that human rights "cannot be all things to all people" (Moyn 2010:227). But a minimalist core by itself implies nothing about content; in particular, it provides no guidance on questions such as: Which norms and why those? What conception of the "good life" do they presuppose? By itself, a core, minimalist or otherwise, says nothing about how human rights might be brought about in the everyday life of countless individuals diverse in belief and practice. Fearing a politics of impossible goals and unrealizable expectations, or a politics diluted conceptually by moralism and rendered impotent practically, Moyn offers no model of a politics of human rights, even of the realist vision he vaguely favors: one that would prevent "catastrophe through minimalist ethical norms"

---

[2] In later chapters I discuss those of Quataert (2009) and Hunt (2007).

rather than build "utopia through maximalist political vision" (Moyn 2010:226) – more a "general slogan or worldview or ideal" than a "recipe for the displacement of politics" through the "moral transcendence of politics" (Moyn 2010:227). This book embraces politics, eschews moral transcendence, but still provides a distinct vision of human rights.

Human Rights as Politics: Social Construction Without Theology or Metaphysics

I articulate that vision by reconceiving human rights as social construction, and I construct human rights as valid initially only for communities that embrace them. Human rights can be "grown" locally by their addressees themselves. They would carry an exceptional motivating power, for theirs would be a validity that is indigenous rather than imposed from without or coerced from within. My vision contrasts starkly with much human rights thinking that insists that such rights can be valid only if that validity is immediately universal, indeed a priori. Such thinking tends toward the otherworldly, either metaphysical or theological. I analyze both at length, showing that universal human rights so conceived are demonstrably unattainable, whereas my realistic, locally sensitive, small-bore, quotidian alternative allows for the expansion of validity across diverse cultures and political communities even as it takes account of the unique and particular features of any local environment and any concrete milieu. It allows for human rights universally valid if validity is constructed as mundane, this-worldly, and contingent: as something achieved not given or revealed. By avoiding treacherous metaphysical or theological assumptions, it avoids the hornet's nest of problems they entail. Consider, for example, what might seem to be the single claim most likely to find immediate agreement, everywhere: the widespread idea of a human right to life. Does it mean a right of a human embryo to the life it has? Would "the life it has" mean a right to be free of genetic manipulation? Might it mean a right of an embryo in vitro to be implanted into a uterus, if a right to life means a right to an uncertain and precarious opportunity for life, to conditions that allow for further development? Is a right to a *chance* of life (borne by an embryo in vitro) also a right to be free of genetic manipulation? At just what cell stage might the embryo possess this right? As I show, answers plausible and in that sense capable of wide embrace in the twenty-first century are much more likely to be socially constructed than supernatural.[3] And theological or

---

[3] Chapter 9 addresses human rights in the context of genetic manipulation.

metaphysical assumptions would provide human rights foundations that are nothing short of otherworldly. We nature-bound humans, evolved organisms that we are, may be sorely tempted to regard a supernatural basis as the strongest, most objective or secure one possible precisely because it is not dependent on the human beings to whom it is addressed and to whom it would apply. This way of thinking tellingly betrays a deep suspicion about the capacity of humankind for moral behavior. For it suspects that a norm that applies to human beings yet is not created by them is, *for that reason*, "better" or "stronger" or "truer" than norms of some nonhuman, indeed preternatural provenience.

My counterargument asserts two things: first, that transcendental norms can only be a figment of imagination and, second, that human beings are *not* cast adrift morally if norms do not exist independently of human culture and imagination. Indeed, the moral self-ennoblement of human beings is precisely that of humankind giving itself norms of social and political behavior. And it does so precisely by means of social construction. Humankind's task is then to construct, for itself, in its manifold communities across immense differences in history, culture, experience, level of socioeconomic development, and so forth, a compelling code of behavior for human beings – and, over time, compelling beyond the local venues where in each instance it begins. That task requires us to struggle with the daunting challenges of a naturally evolved species of unparalleled cognitive capacity, emotional sensitivity, and psychological fragility.

This book attempts that postmetaphysical, post-theological moral self-ennoblement in terms specific to human rights. Those terms refer to a particularly ambitious form of behavioral norm: one that would obtain initially only within the community that freely embraces it yet aspires to obtain across the profound confines, more cognitive than geographical, that separate human communities and divide many communities within themselves. The theological and metaphysical sources I reject have always already been challenged (and with time increasingly challenged) by natural science and, to a lesser extent, by social science. Both these ways of looking at the world offer resources for moving toward behavioral norms of wide validity. For example, natural science understands members of the human species as so similar that the DNA of any particular member can represent, at a biological level, all members, bar none. Here we have one possible basis on which a kind of normative universalism might be constructed: all members of the species are equal members. My approach is not at all natural scientific but rather proceeds mainly along dimensions philosophical, sociological, anthropological, and jurisprudential (and, in one chapter, even neurobiological). That those dimensions offer bases for binding norms of wide validity should be clear in each and every chapter.

The Term "Human Rights"

In speaking of "human rights," I refer usually to the *idea* of human rights. To be sure, for human rights theory and practice alike, it matters a great deal just *how* human rights are specified individually as well as in relation to each other (for example, moral norms in particular are likely here and there to conflict with each other). I develop the idea of human rights as a kind of rhetorical vehicle, open to different contents and capable of transporting different conceptions of human rights as well as varying lists of basic and secondary human rights. The human rights idea is contingent along several dimensions, and I propose a pragmatic approach to dealing with these contingencies.[4] Thus I argue that human rights are best understood in terms of the pragmatic imperative for desired results, as distinguished from, say, an epistemological imperative for objective truth. For example, an inventory of human rights composed of those behaviors likely to be widely challenged is pragmatic; there is nothing to be gained practically by including behaviors of little concern to most people.

When I speak of the "human rights idea," the reader should imagine, at least as propositions, some of the more capacious of the alleged rights against the modern nation state, such as rights to life, safety, and personal liberty; to belief, expression, and conscience; and to privacy and property. What I do not primarily intend are alleged rights no less capacious but of a different order: rights to a "decent" standard of living, say, or to the integrity and perseveration of distinct and fragile cultural groups.

And when I refer to the human rights idea, the reader should also imagine negative rights, that is, rights to be protected from something, rights to be free of interference by others. Negative rights constrain the state (among other institutions and organizations) in its treatment of the individual. My project does not preclude human rights as positive rights, that is, rights to something, rights that require more than noninterference, for example to a decent standard of living. The goal of developing as wide a validity as possible, ideally one eventually global, allows for negative rights much more than for positive ones because almost any right

---

[4] Elsewhere I develop a pragmatic social theory, on which I draw in this book, to deal with the indeterminacy of social norms (Gregg 2003a) as well as problems of social integration in normatively pluralistic communities (Gregg 2003b).

entails an obligation.[5] First, those persons or institutions against which one has a right are obligated not to interfere with that right. And as the number of persons who possess a particular right increases, the number of persons on whom it poses obligations increases correspondingly. A regime of universal human rights would entail a regime of universal human obligations; today for everyone everywhere to take that kind of responsibility, and to accept being held accountable, remains as distant a goal as can be imagined. However difficult it might be to justify and practice negative rights, the discursive justification and practical application of positive rights is significantly more difficult. Consider: a universal negative right to life and personal safety would entail each person's obligation to respect the life and safety of all other persons. That obligation is much more easily realized than a universal positive right to a certain standard of living, which would entail the obligation of all persons to secure an adequate standard for all other persons. But against whom, for example, does the individual enforce the rights specified in Article 25 of the *Universal Declaration of Human Rights*: "Everyone has the right to a standard of living adequate for the health and well-being of himself and of his family including food, clothing, housing and medical care and necessary social services, and the right to security in the event of unemployment, sickness, disability, widowhood, old age or other lack of livelihood in circumstances beyond his control"?

Overview

I articulate this approach in four parts. Part I includes the first three chapters. The first two explain why (and how) I reject traditional otherworldly foundations for human rights. The third chapter develops my alternative: human rights as this-worldly norms initially of local not universal validity.

Part II comprises Chapters 3 and 4 and explores two unacknowledged but promising resources for constructing a this-worldly foundation for

---

[5] But obligations rarely imply rights. Whereas the obligation to pay taxes might be thought to imply a right to vote on the legislators who enact taxes, the obligation to care for one's child need not imply that one has a right to decide the nature of that care, even as many communities leave such decisions to the parents or other caregivers. John Searle posits obligations that do not entail the obligated persons' rights: he speaks of a "universal human right to be helped by others in desperate situations when one is unable to help oneself and when others are so situated as to be able to help one," but also in circumstances in which people are "unable to fend for themselves. Thus infants and small children have a right to care, feeding, housing" and "people who are incapacitated due to injury, senility, illness, or other causes also have absolute rights to care," as a right "necessary for the maintenance of any form of human life at all" (Searle 2010:193–194).

human rights: the cultural and political dynamics of a human rights-capable personality, and the neuropsychological dynamics of human rights-supportive emotions.

Part III brings together Chapters 6 and 7, each of which draws on sociological insights to show how the human rights idea might be "grown" in local soils.

Part IV, composed of Chapters 8 and 9, sketches two long-term concerns of human rights as social construction, issues that may define the future of the project for human rights: the possible transmutation of the nation state, and the potential transformation of our species-wide conception of human nature, biologically understood.

Now in somewhat greater detail: Chapter 1 analyzes two competing accounts of human rights: as a theological expression of a supernatural realm (a major and abidingly influential account) and, alternatively, as a socially constructed artifact. I reject the theological approach on several fronts: on the one hand, anthropology casts doubt on theological grounds for a universal embrace of human rights; on the other hand, social constructionism is much less culturally exclusive than religious faith, and it better allows for the moral agency of individual rights bearers. My social constructionist approach offers a prudential logic of mutual benefit, valid for all persons with respect to each person's capacity for culture, and the promise of his or her formation in processes of enculturation.

Chapter 2 is a pendant to Chapter 1, addressing the other venerable and enduring effort to ground, understand, and interpret human rights: metaphysics. I identify crippling difficulties of this approach and offer a political alternative: we humans *can* pull ourselves up morally by our own normative bootstraps. Central to this effort is Georg Simmel's notion of "webs of affiliations." I show that non-normative "webs" can integrate members normatively across their normative differences. Affiliation of this sort can still deliver human rights.

Chapter 3 argues for human rights as culturally particular and valid only locally such that human rights might be spread without cultural imperialism. And it argues that recognition of the incommensurability of different cultures need not entail an uncritical tolerance of just about anything. Recognition actually allows for a critical, objectivating stance toward other communities or cultures: locally valid human rights *can* possess a critical capacity as well as promote a community's self-representation in ways allowing for diversity.

Chapter 4 shows how human rights might be "self-authored." Self-authorship has three features: it emerges through collective political action; it has a critical capacity; and it can be borne by nonidiosyncratic norms. To author one's own human rights requires a personality structure of "assertive selfhood" as well as a "field of recognition," that is, a social structure supportive of assertive selfhood. Whereas personality structure concerns the *internal* or psychological disposition of the individual insofar as it motivates his or her political behavior, social structure concerns the *external* or institutional arrangements of political community.

Chapter 5 deploys neurobiology and developmental anthropology to advance the human rights idea in terms of emotional affect, specifically in terms of a fictive kin relationship in its rich emotionality. Given the behaviorally motivating force of emotions and the fact that affect is universally shared by humans, fictive kin relationships could contribute directly and powerfully to the global promotion of two core requirements of human rights: altruism and reciprocity.

Chapter 6 draws on the example of Islamic communities to show how interpreters might develop human rights *within* their own culture even as they promote extralocal ideas and practices. Local interpreters can do so despite points of significant conflict between the local culture and the human rights idea, and they *need* to do so in ways that resonate with the local culture but also challenge it. Because they possess a "dual consciousness," cultural and political translators can be outside intermediaries and, at the same time, local participants.

To any local culture, Chapter 7 develops a cognitive approach as distinguished from a normative one. Chapter 7 advances human rights as *internal* to any given community's culture. Human rights can be advanced internally by means of "cognitive reframing," as I show with respect to two empirical examples: female genital mutilation in Africa and child prostitution in Asia.

Chapter 8 argues that a naturalistic conception of human life and society is consistent with the possibility of constructing universal human rights. A naturalistic conception interprets biological membership in terms of a cultural category. This chapter also addresses the question of where human rights so conceived might "begin": only as a person after birth, someone socially recognized, or at any prior point along that developmental pathway leading from sperm and ova to an unmistakable human being?

Chapter 9 questions the widespread conviction that human rights must be based on one or another notion of "human dignity." It bases them instead on positive law because human rights can only be available in concrete, particular political communities. As long as any given political community is contingent and particular, so too are human rights. They can only be had through politics. Yet politics of this sort is unlikely in the fundamental political organization of the world today: the nation state. My alternative is the "human rights state." It would recognize and enforce human rights at local levels, by local norms, but guided by an inclusionary logic as distinguished from the exclusionary logic of the sovereignty-fixated nation state. That is, the human rights state assigns the status of "unmistakable human being" to all biological humans, but now in the political sense of claiming that each person is entitled to a right to have rights, to the existence of human rights.

The Coda briefly addresses this question: What might be lost by taking a social constructionist approach to human rights? Responding to this question also allows me to recapitulate what is gained.

My effort to reconceive human rights as social construction builds on perspectives developed in earlier work. One would improve conditions for normative agreement within heterogeneous communities, and across different communities, by reframing contentious issues in terms more "normatively thin" than "normatively thick."[6] The other shows how justice and rights might be generated at local levels of political communities, indeed in ways sensitive to the particular circumstances of any given community or subcommunity.[7] Localism can achieve some of the key goals of a very different approach – justice conceived as universally valid – without the severe and debilitating problems that beleaguer all universalist approaches. This book applies each of these perspectives to the problems and promise of the project for human rights. It also advances the argument of each beyond the earlier state of discussion.

---

[6] *Thick Moralities, Thin Politics* (Gregg 2003b).
[7] *Coping in Politics with Indeterminate Norms* (Gregg 2003a).

PART I

THIS-WORLDLY NORMS: LOCAL NOT UNIVERSAL

1

Human Rights

Political Not Theological

Part I lays out three arguments for conceiving of human rights norms as valid locally and contingently (where "valid" refers to beliefs or practices that members of community recognize and identify with). These arguments contest the common approach of viewing human rights as universally valid a priori. Chapter 1 argues for human rights norms as distinctly "political," that is, as this-worldly social constructions. It challenges the widespread notion that human rights are theological in source. Chapter 2 continues this argument against otherworldly sources for human rights norms, but now disputing the familiar claim that human rights are metaphysical in foundation. Chapter 3 then shows how human rights norms, even if *initially* valid only locally and contingently, nonetheless over time could, by means sketched out in this book, move asymptotically toward a validity that, as a matter of empirical description, would approach universality. Validity of this sort might be achieved through the various kinds of politics that I delineate from a range of perspectives in Chapters 3 through 9.

I begin with a question about normative foundations: Whence human rights? (1) I ask this question with practical intent: Would any particular answer entail practical consequences for their recognition or practice – with one response more likely to spread, the other to hinder, the idea of human rights? I say yes and compare two competing accounts of human rights: as a theological expression of a supernatural realm and as a socially constructed cultural artifact. (2) I then develop several arguments against the theological approach. In advocating for the universal embrace and practice of human rights, an argument from sacredness is weaker than a social constructionist account for several reasons: (a) anthropology casts doubt on theological grounds invoked for a universal embrace of human rights; (b) social constructionism is less culturally exclusive than are religious faiths; and (c) social constructionism better allows for the moral agency of individual rights bearers. (3) I articulate my alternative account as a prudential logic of mutual benefit that is (a) universalistic in an empirical sense, given the capacity for culture and the process of enculturation, (b) yet relativistic as instantiated in any given culture. (c) The two dimensions may be combined by creating, over time, the universal validity of an originally particularistic cultural commitment: human rights as political not theological. I conclude by showing how my approach grounds human rights "politically" rather than by political fiat: as a politics of agency, not as a theology. (4) Finally, socially constructed human rights constitute a politics of agency that responds (a) to the absence of agency in politics by fiat; (b) as a moral language; and (c) as a language that facilitates groups and communities giving rights to themselves.

Competing Approaches to Human Rights: Socially Constructed as Distinguished from Theologically Given

To possess defensible rights is no guarantee against abuse and oppression, but defensible rights appear to decrease the likelihood of victimization. What exactly makes a right defensible? In part its embrace by persons affected or concerned. To embrace the idea of human rights, one need not ground it. A plausible account as to why human rights are valid could be relevant for practical purposes if one account rather than another might better persuade people to embrace them. I consider two very general approaches: supernatural explanations of the source and validity of the human rights idea and socially constructed explanations. By *supernatural* I mean forces (and their sources) somehow beyond nature and not subject to nature. In other words, one might approach human rights either "theologically" or "politically."[1] For example, a Christian argument for human rights may claim that human beings are created *imago dei*, as images of God or reflexes of divine law. Human rights so conceived are grounded normatively in their dependence on a deity, one often conceived as possessing consciousness and desire. Religious belief typically invokes a notion of *sacredness*, sacredness that extends to human beings and grounds human rights. Communities of such belief may advocate justice and criticize authoritarian beliefs, institutions, and practices. They

---

[1] To be sure, other possibilities abound, including various combinations. For analytic purposes I consider two very distinct options. Further, I consider theological forms of supernaturalism in this chapter and metaphysical forms in Chapter 2.

may solidarize with victims and combat injustice. Even if they misconstrue the kind of normative foundation that can make human rights possible, that misconstrual need not impede human rights–friendly behavior. But sometimes that misconstrual might so impede, and in such cases my alternative is more promising and less problematic.

To assert, theologically, that human beings are sacred is to assert their innate or natural dignity or value, and to aver that this quality entails human rights. Such rights are conceivable in a variety of ways. All of them confront the problem that Richard McKeon (1949:35) identified in the *Universal Declaration of Human Rights* as it was being drafted: "what is meant by these rights, and these differences of meanings depend on divergent basic assumptions, which in turn lend plausibility to and are justified by contradictory interpretations of the economic and social situation, and finally lead to opposed recommendations concerning the implementation required for a world declaration of human rights."[2] This is the problem posed by any norm that is indeterminate with respect to meaning and proper application.[3] But indeterminacy is less of a problem for social constructionism than for theology inasmuch as no one making otherworldly claims can reassure him- or herself that the addressees share the speaker's intended meaning. Claims that are this-worldly offer greater resources for such reassurance, for example empirical experience.

Beyond this issue of how to secure successful communication among people is the issue of how to ensure successful action within one's social environment. Here, too, the supernatural is rather taxing; it is never the "cheapest" or "most efficient" means to successful action, such as achieving goals. Consider efficiency: a person's exchange with one or more gods guarantees nothing to him or her and often enough it disappoints anyone seeking rewards, whether in empirical contexts or nonempirical ones, whether now or in the future. And consider the "cost" of a tense relationship in which the "degree of distinctiveness, separation, and antagonism in the relationship between a religious group and the 'outside' world" might be described as a kind of tension (Stark 2000:281). The higher someone's level of tension with his or her sociocultural environment, the "more expensive it is to belong to a religious group" and the "more exclusive, extensive, and expensive is the level of commitment required

---

[2] To be sure, likely no list of many different rights (and no list of ultimate human goods) can be free of internal conflicts. Rights to liberty can be in tension with rights to equality or security; for example, a right to private property easily conflicts with a right to distributive justice. Various theories order different rights according to moral priority but none of these theories is held consensually.

[3] I suggest a way of coping politically with indeterminate norms in Gregg (2003a).

by a religious group" (Stark 2000:282). Given a "reciprocal relationship between expense and the value of the rewards of membership," the more "expensive" the faith, the "higher its average level of member commitment" (ibid.). But the more "expensive" a faith, the fewer members it is likely to have. Rodney Stark and Roger Finke (2000:281) suggest as much: churches stand in relatively lower tension with their surroundings whereas sects, in relatively higher tension. Churches are larger than sects and more stable. By analogy to this distinction between "sect" and "church," a theological approach to human rights is more sectlike than churchlike. And as an instable and self-marginalizing approach to spreading the human rights idea, it is more taxing than social constructionism.

Michael Perry's argument from sacredness shows why.[4] Human rights require a specifically theological foundation because, according to Perry, they follow from humans' inherent, inalienable sacredness. From this quality derives the moral capacity of all human beings, their moral equality with each other, and their ethical obligation to one another. That is, they can be moral only through a sense of the sacred. That is why Perry must fear what he takes to be the moral vacuity of this-worldly norms: "If one believes neither in god nor, therefore, in the . . . sacredness of every human being, but does believe that our evolved nature is fulfilled by becoming persons who love one another, then one believes that to act contrary to one's nature is to violate . . . what? Evolution? To speak of 'violating' evolution is surely to speak metaphorically: How does one 'violate' evolution?" (Perry 2007:25). To violate someone's "human nature" is to violate the "sacredness of every human being" (ibid.). Moral worth cannot be socially constructed because the mundane world of time and space, matter and force cannot itself generate moral claims. Rather, such claims depend on a dimension that transcends the world of mundane experience. As a basis for human rights, moral worth is transcendental in Pope John XXIII's (1961) sense of human beings "transcending" nature. Such an argument is unlikely to resonate with persons who do not share its particular theological presuppositions – that is, with a majority of the world's peoples.

To be sure, not all theologies are captured by the argument from sacredness. Nor is Perry's account representative of all theologically foundationalist accounts of human rights; no single account is. But Perry's

---

[4] Perry's work has a limited focus: on debates specific to the American context. The earliest work of UNESCO (1949) is broader, as is Glendon's (2001), but to elucidate the argument from sacredness, Perry's work offers itself more directly than these others.

captures quite a span of theological approaches. Jeffrie Murphy (1988:239), for example, claims that the "liberal theory of rights requires a doctrine of human dignity... that cannot be... detached from a belief in God or at least from a world view that would be properly called religious in some metaphysically profound sense." Similarly, only by resort to the supernatural can Raimond Gaita (1991) claim that human beings are ends in themselves, worthy of unconditional respect and possessing inalienable dignity and rights. According to Jean Hampton (1998:120), the "fundamental wrong done, when the inherent dignity of any human being is not respected – when any human being is violated – is not that our local ('Eurocentric') sentiments are offended"; rather, the "very order of the world – the normative order of the world – is transgressed." My critique of the argument from sacredness reaches beyond Perry's version of the argument.

Arguments Against a Theological Approach to Human Rights

In advocating the universal embrace and practice of human rights, an argument from sacredness is weaker than a social constructionist account for three reasons: (a) anthropology casts doubt on theological grounds for a universal embrace of human rights; (b) social constructionism may be less culturally exclusive than are religious faiths; and (c) social constructionism better allows for the moral agency of individual rights bearers.

(a) Like other social sciences, anthropology adopts a social constructionist approach to human culture, including culture in the form of normative beliefs and practices. In an anthropological approach, human rights offer an example of historically contingent normative culture. Cultural anthropology in particular is a science of differences, even as it may sometimes face political imperatives to stress what is shared across diverse cultural borders. As the UN drafted its human rights declaration in 1947, the American Anthropological Association (AAA), dedicated to the study of profound and enduring cultural difference, disputed the notion of rights valid across all cultural boundaries (even as many cultures overlap at points, and even as all cultures to various extents are hybrids). The AAA sought to discourage the drafting committee accordingly, querying the UN Human Rights Commission that drafted the *Universal Declaration*: "How can the proposed Declaration be applicable to all human beings and not be a statement of rights conceived *only* in terms of values prevalent in the countries of Western Europe and America?" For "what is held to be a human right in one society may be regarded as anti-social by another people, or by the same people in a different period of their history" (AAA 1947:539, 542). The nub of this critique is that a rights claim is a cultural claim, because rights are cultural artifacts; and that as cultural artifacts, rights are valid only for the cultures in which they resonate, that is, for the local community alone. In other words, cultural "validity" is always local; hence no culture is universally "valid," even as many artifacts, despite their origins at specific times in specific cultural regions, today have achieved more or less universal embrace. These include natural science, modern medicine, various types of engineering, and various technologies (but note: these are artifacts not woven of *normative* tissue, unlike human rights and other moral claims). If cultural validity is local, then some human rights claims will conflict with some aspects of some of the cultures beyond the particular one making a particular claim about human rights.

Fifty years later the AAA officially embraced the idea of human rights, finding the idea compatible with "anthropological principles of respect for concrete human differences, both collective and individual, rather than the abstract legal uniformity of Western tradition" (AAA 1999). AAA's 1999 statement coheres with its 1947 statement: it maintains that irreducible cultural differences exist no less than tensions between such differences and the uniformity of *any* system of normative rules (including human rights). But now the AAA argued that human rights norms can be reconciled with irreducible cultural differences among different communities. Tellingly, it neglected to say just how (likely it was unable to say just how).

Both statements imply that cultural difference might be treated as a human right insofar as it affects identity at the levels of both individuals and groups. It does so in two ways: first, a particular culture might claim that its members have a right to be free of the oppression of foreign cultural imposition. It might also claim that it has a right to preserve differences inherited from its past. Second, a particular culture might assert that its members have a right to be free of the oppression of internal cultural imposition. It might claim a right to change or cast off inherited differences and to create new ones; such a right to difference would be open-ended. I would emphasize that both senses of a right to cultural difference are compatible with human rights understood as political not theological.

The question remains: What are the prospects for the idea that someday all political communities might reach consensus on the individual's innate, rights-generating identity simply as a human being? In this chapter I compare a social constructionist version of this idea with a theological one. Claude Lévi-Strauss (1983:329) offers one historically influential social constructionist version. He asserts that a "concept of an all inclusive humanity" that makes "no distinction between races or cultures" appeared only "very late in the history of mankind and did not spread very widely across the face of the globe.... For the majority of the human species, and for tens of thousands of years, the idea that humanity includes every human being on the face of the earth does not exist at all. The designation stops at the border of each tribe, or linguistic group, sometimes even at the edge of a village. So common is the practice that many of the peoples we call primitive call themselves by a name which means 'men'"; in other words, they claim that the "other tribes, groups, and villages do not partake in human virtue or even human nature" (ibid.).

To be sure, more or less all political communities today appear ready to recognize all "tribes" as members of *Homo sapiens sapiens.* The question for this chapter is: Do they do so for reasons specifically theological? The argument I address – that all persons are sacred and, as such, possess human rights – is more peculiar culturally (in Lévi-Strauss's sense) than are the claims of modern biology. After all, the human genome is more than 95 percent identical with that of the chimpanzee; further, each individual human's genome is 99.9 percent identical with that of every other human. But natural scientific insight is unlikely the primary determinant of how many persons today view the world. Rather, sustained personal experience, such as increased interaction (above all economically) with people very different from oneself in various spheres of everyday life (particularly in more metropolitan areas, but also throughout the global market and popular culture), may well persuade more people than theology or natural science that "all tribes" belong to the species *Homo sapiens sapiens.*

(b) If socially constructed human rights are a cultural parochialism, they unavoidably constitute a very particular cultural understanding. Cultural understandings of human rights might be socially constructed in any number of ways. Some are likely to conflict with others. According to social constructionism, no particular construction is "natural," "necessary," or "objective." But in principle any particular construction could find universal embrace.

In short, social constructions are not necessarily exclusive, but every religion is. Any particular religious faith can define itself only by excluding many persons in the world, namely persons of other faiths as well as persons without religious convictions. Even Buddhism or Unitarianism, in their generous openness to persons of many different theological views, has an identity only if it understands itself in some ways as distinct from other faiths.[5]

Thus, in the perpetually luxuriant growth of different conceptions of the supernatural, any construal of one particular theology as objective and valid for all persons must surely appear, from the standpoints of the legions of excluded faiths, as a cultural particularism masquerading as universalism: as a cultural artifact claiming to be independent of all culture. Perry, for example, roots his claims about cosmology and biology in a very particular theology that he presents as universally true and culturally transcendent. His argument presupposes a belief in the New Testament God as guarantor of human sacredness. Presumably he regards this particular deity as the only "true" or "real" one within a broad field of competitors.

Consequently, any theological approach to human rights that "consists of explanations that justify and specify terms of exchange with Gods, based on reasoning about revelations" as "communications believed to come from Gods" (Stark 2004:14), will persuade some, even many, persons of other faiths (as Islam and Christianity show). But no one religion has ever persuaded the majority of all persons.[6] Here we see the particularism of any given faith; particularism becomes parochialism in the context of seeking to persuade others in different cultures and in diverse polities. Consider, for example, the argument from sacredness: "If every human being is sacred in the objective sense, then, in violating the Bosnian Muslim, the Bosnian Serb does not merely violate what some of us attach great value to; he violates the very order of creation" (Perry 2007:28). Here the adjective "objective" marks as wholly independent of human culture something that Perry takes to be an incontrovertible fact of sacredness. Talk of the "sacred order of creation" endows human

---

[5] For it, too, competes to maintain current adherents and to attract new adherents. It does so perhaps at a disadvantage because "exclusive religious organizations offer more valuable and apparently less risky religious rewards" than nonexclusive groups (Stark 2000:283).

[6] To be sure, some religions, including Christianity and Islam, have taken root in a wide variety of cultures (and the future of Christianity in particular lies in Africa and Latin America, no longer in the West where it developed, let alone in the Middle East where it began). But that spread remains partial. Even major religion is always one of several major religions, none of which is held by even a majority of the world's peoples, and in that sense each remains parochial for every other faith.

depravity with an otherworldly cast. It does so in the sense that the word "Auschwitz" has come to symbolize something – however inchoate – more than injustice toward particular men, women, and children. It symbolizes a "violation of who God is, of what the universe is, and, in particular, of who we human beings are" (Perry 2007:27). And yet never have human cultures agreed (among themselves or within themselves) on exactly what human beings (to say nothing of God and the universe) are – whether in philosophy, anthropology, or even areas of biology. By contrast, social constructionism might appear as a particularism to some persons of faith, but a particularism never as particular as any rival faith or as any argument grounded in revelation or in rival revelatory traditions.

(c) Protection of rights validates individual and collective moral agency. Yet human rights, extended to populations without their free consent, violate the addressees' moral autonomy. By *extend* I mean "to impose," as distinguished from "to argue for" (simply arguing in favor of the rights of those who have not yet done so for themselves does not itself violate their moral autonomy). Human rights interventions should be undertaken only with the consent of their addressees. Exceptions to this norm could be justified in cases of gross and irreparable physical harm, such as assaults on life in the shape of genocide, for example on the grounds that coercion may preserve life and therewith its potential for moral agency.

Intervention is exceedingly problematic. On the one hand, the interveners are never selected by the victims; they are never selected by those whose rights they would defend. Unclear is what right the interveners might have to act on behalf of others: to "represent" them. On the other hand, the interveners might encourage or facilitate the emergence of the moral agency of those on whose behalf they intervene, perhaps against some group of *insiders* who have prevented the "aggrieved" or "benighted" group from achieving moral autonomy to this point. This question is mirrored in the UN Charter; it urges states to freely embrace human rights yet it also rejects outside intervention into states as well as interference in their internal affairs. As a matter of historical fact, since the creation of the UN, no interventions have ever commanded an international consensus just as support for the coercive imposition of human rights norms has never been consensual.

Consensus is agreement, and agreement can facilitate agency. To impose on someone or on some group may be to deny that person's or group's agency, even if what is being imposed is attractive: the ascription of moral worth to the addressee, for example. John Stuart Mill

(1984:118) claimed that "nations which are still barbarous have not got beyond the period during which it is likely to be for their benefit that they should be conquered and held in subjection by foreigners." Mill implies that a "barbarous" group that benefits from foreign conquest today might eventually cease to "need" conquest when it becomes like the conqueror, that is, no longer "barbarous." Mill's foreigner, who presumes to represent the best interests of the locals today, evidently may still believe that tomorrow the locals could become capable of adequately representing their own best interests. But Mill cannot concede that, say, colonized peoples may prefer immediate political and legal agency in the form of sovereignty, indigenous rights, and indigenous institutions of enforcement. He cannot concede that they may prefer these things to protective representation proffered by outsiders – even human rights–oriented outsiders.[7]

The alternatives I consider in this chapter – the theological and the social constructionist approach – might, despite their differences, still respond similarly to the following question: How do we know when to defer to local practice and when to override it? First, a community that discriminates against some of its members in ways that do not constitute persecution, and in ways accepted by those discriminated against, should be respected in its choice and organization. How much respect, then, and for how long, should human rights advocates afford local cultures that, say, discriminate against women? If "discrimination" here means "to assign a subordinate position within religious practices," and if those affected also embrace this position, outsiders should respect this form of inequality even if it appears to violate a human rights understanding of equality.

Further, theological and social constructionist approaches might also respond similarly to the following assertion: that human rights are ill understood when understood to delegitimize, in wholesale fashion, a traditional culture. The issue raises itself where that which the outside observer takes to be oppression is regarded differently by the local participants: not as oppression but as some social or personal good – as claimed,

---

[7] Some well-intentioned imposers might construct the imposed upon as persons unable to represent themselves, as persons who can only be represented by others, or as passive observers even of decisions that affect them directly. To represent the "aggrieved" or "benighted" as incapable of moral autonomy is to manipulate them in the very way they are represented. Self-selected representatives may assume a patronizing stance toward the represented, like the outsider telling locals what their moral worth is because "they cannot represent themselves" ("cannot" in the sense of "incapable of"), because "they can only be represented by others" (Marx 1975:307).

for example, by communities that practice female genital cutting.[8] The participants would preserve traditions and practices that non-local human rights advocates would end. Theological and social construction-ist approaches might agree that some forms of belonging may be more important to the participants than individualistic liberties (for example, freedom of speech, conscience, and assembly; choice of marriage part-ners; or matters of childbearing).

But would theological and social constructionist approaches to human rights draw the same line between acceptable and unacceptable interven-tion? Could the former argue as easily as the latter for respecting only those cultural elements, and embracing only those religious practices, that are compatible with and supportive of, say, a woman's health, health care, and education, as well as her welfare in marriage, in the work-place, and in other spheres of daily life? After all, this argument entails a certain distance from those cultures and religions (or an objectivat-ing stance toward them). That distance or stance likely will challenge some religions and some theologies (and challenge some more than others). Some age-old religions perpetuate various forms of age-old obe-dience that reinforce hierarchical social arrangements and understand-ings, such as the systematic subordination of women. Secularism and relativism, both compatible with a social constructionist approach, are less wedded to received customs and mores. And a socially constructed notion of human rights is less encumbered than a theological one by tradition when asking: Is a given practice a human rights abuse if the addressees of that practice do not regard it as such?

Human Rights as Political Not Theological

I have argued for human rights conceived as particular cultural creations socially reinforced through other cultural inventions. These include the kinds of cultural preferences found in various traditions. One preference would be cosmopolitan political thought extending back to the epistles of the apostle Paul.[9] Another would be individuals' cultural expectations of defensible civil rights. A third would be cultural mores that express this or that form of reciprocity, such as if I do not wish to be abused in mind or body, I could imagine that neither do you. Reciprocity so understood is a distinctly prudential notion: anyone capable of suffering physical pain

---

[8] For a non-Millian, social-constructionist approach to such communities, see Chapter 6.
[9] Compare Jennings (2005).

or social humiliation will understand why others would reject pain and humiliation for themselves. Prudential reciprocity motivates behavior along the lines of mutual benefit. Of any action we may ask whether we ourselves would object to being its addressee. We cannot imagine anyone wishing to be subjected to rightlessness, degradation, torture, or murder. Likely everyone may regard such subjections as noxious for anyone on the receiving end, including those who perpetrate them.

Prudential reciprocity is pragmatist in that it privileges, above questions of ultimate foundation, human rights conceived in terms of what they might do in practical terms for particular persons in specific circumstances. A pragmatist account regards human rights as something good even if they are not supported by a compelling theory. After all, the violator of human rights does not violate them because he or she regards them as lacking a normative foundation (or a particular normative foundation).

This pragmatist point does not register in the theological claim that if humans are seen as merely the contingent result of cosmological, chemical, or evolutionary chance rather than supernatural plan, then "whether I kick your face in or support you charitably, the universe is as indifferent to that as whether another galaxy blows up tonight" (Prager and Glover 1993:4). Such an argument entails the unlikely assumption that a person or community not in possession of universal moral principles (whatever their foundation) is *for that reason* indifferent to human suffering or injustice. No one is indifferent to his or her own physical pain or social humiliation and may be assumed, in many or most cases, to be capable of sensitivity to the plight of persons victimized through pain or humiliation (although such sensitivity does not imply that the person in question therefore will not inflict pain or humiliation but only that the inflictor knows what he or she is doing). To be sure, this common insight, even with its prudential underpinnings of mutual benefit, hardly entails that all groups and individuals will always refrain from doing unto others what they would not want done unto themselves. But this insight may entail as much for some groups and some persons at least some of the time, and if so, it offers a basis for advocating human rights. It also allows that people may be prudentially motivated to embrace human rights.

This prudential logic of mutual benefit is (a) universalistic along one dimension and (b) relativistic along another. (c) The two dimensions might be combined by creating, over time, the universal validity of an originally particularistic cultural commitment to human rights as political not theological.

(a) As a process, enculturation is a universal phenomenon in the sense that different communities and diverse societies share similar processes of enculturation. In each case, this process generates very particular communities. Enculturation is a prime means by which culture is transmitted from human to human. Both as individuals and as group members, in part consciously and in part not, people acquire the norms and perspectives of their various communities as they become more or less integrated within a society's weave of social relations.

Enculturation proceeds by socialization. For example, cultural identity derives in part from the individual's socialization into particular cultural communities. Socialization is integration, one that allows each of us to "belong" to ourselves and, at the same time, to others, that is, to our own groups and communities. On the one hand, the individual's intentions, desires, and feelings may result in part from his or her individuation, inasmuch as individuation occurs through socialization. On the other hand, we can "belong" to each other in political community by means of social solidarity. And the energies of social solidarity, animated by a human rights consciousness, might plausibly motivate belief and behavior resonant with human rights. In this case, solidarity would refer to a human rights consciousness as a facet of the individual's moral identity; it would involve the individual's assumption that he or she must answer to socially generalized expectations.

Our individual embrace of human rights may be reinforced by institutions such as the local legal order, public education, or popular culture. In a legal order, the individual's possession of any right "depends on receipt of a special sort of social recognition and acceptance" of his or her juridical status (Michelman 1996:203). That status occurs within a "specific juridico-civil community of consociates who stand in a relation of reciprocal duty to one another" (Benhabib 2002b:549). Yet no legal order can fully institutionalize ethical relationships; for social integration to take place, forms of social solidarity quite beyond legal bonds are also needed.

(b) This universal capacity to create culture leads to products of relative cultural validity and resonance. Some cultural particularity – many of the local understandings, practices, and norms that constitute a culture – is not wholly unique in origin but the result of processes of enculturation more or less similar to each other (or that overlap). These processes of social and cultural production might be regarded as general attributes of human species-being, "quite compatible with a pragmatic cultural relativism that understands specific cultural differences as the products of activities that mediate universal human capacities to contextually varying circumstances" (Turner 1997:278).

By *relativism* I mean that justifiable belief or warrantable assertion is a matter of how you reason. And how you reason is a function of what modes of reasoning are available or familiar to you: the "idea that what makes a theory or an interpretation good or bad depends on the purposes you might reasonably want it to serve" (Stout 1988:299). Social constructionism identifies cultural validity as man-made. And it identifies cultural claims as relative in the ways that all human artifacts are: in terms of time, place, context, and validity for any given community. In this sense, the autonomous, human rights–supporting individual is no less a cultural invention.

And in this sense, every such cultural product is relative, even human rights. This quality hardly precludes a critical capacity: "Since relativism does not imply tolerance, moral criticism remains a viable option for the relativist" (Renteln 1988:68). In other words, that a criticism does not have universally shared foundations or presuppositions does not of itself render it impotent, implausible, or unpersuasive.[10]

(c) Socialization into the socially constructed authority of human rights likely would differ from socialization into the theological authority of human rights. (And socialization may dispense with religion even as religion cannot dispense with socialization.) Socialization into the authority of human rights, as a socially constructed commitment to the rights of others, is always open to debate and disagreement. From a religiously oriented socialization that posits eternal and universal human rights norms a priori, a social constructionist understanding of human rights as valid in the end only for those individuals and communities that freely accept them, and accept them on grounds themselves socially constructed, cannot follow.

At this point one might wonder: Why even call such rights "human rights"? If they are valid only for groups and communities that accept them, are they "merely" communal rights but not "human" rights? Only if one insists that the adjective "human" here can only refer to the individual's species-being. That could be a theological approach, for example where humans are understood to be sacred. For social constructionism, however, the adjective "human" refers to the potentially universal

---

[10] So the following claim records contingent experience rather than some kind of necessity or inevitability: "Before radical evil, both secular humanism and ancient belief have been either utterly helpless victims or enthusiastic accomplices" (Ignatieff 2001:86).

embrace of the human rights idea, currently a contingent work in progress. If socially constructed human rights one day attain universal embrace, they become, contingently and without necessity, a particularism shared by all persons, hence universally valid solely as a matter of empirical description of a historical event. And that which becomes everywhere shared is, at that point, no longer ethnocentric or particularistic or relative.[11]

How might this approach function in practice? Take, for example,

> Islamic figures [who] have questioned the universal writ of Western human rights norms. They have pointed out that the Western separation of church and state, secular and religious authority, is alien to the jurisprudence and political thought of the Islamic tradition. The freedoms articulated in the *Universal Declaration* make no sense within the theocratic bias of Islamic political thought. The right to marry and found a family, to freely chose one's partner, is a direct challenge to the authorities in Islamic society that enforce the family choice of spouse, polygamy, and the keeping of women in purdah. In Islamic eyes, universalizing rights discourse implies a sovereign and discrete individual, which is blasphemous from the perspective of the Holy Koran. (Ignatieff 2001:60)

In this context, human rights as political not theological might focus on the cultural construction of patriarchy or the systematic subordination of women to men, so often a major impediment to human rights. Human rights as political could oppose this cultural construction to a very different cultural construction: universal access to education. The patriarchal effect of Islamic belief at the societal level might be limited by such access. After all, recent research identifies a strong link between patriarchal values and religious faith in general: whether dealing with Christianity, Judaism, or Islam (to speak of just the Abrahamic

---

[11] What is universally embraced does not then become necessary or eternal in a social constructionist approach, and as distinguished from theological approaches. To be sure, the international system envisaged by the victors of World War II is unlikely to be the final word in human history. Correspondingly, there will never be a final *Universal Declaration of Human Rights* but only particular declarations, each eventually "stuck" historically in the particular circumstances of its articulation. Better, from a social-constructionist standpoint, would be ever-renewed declarations for an ever-changing world. Human rights are an idea embedded in a particular period of human history and may well be superseded one day by newer, better, and more effective ideas. In this sense, human rights are never above politics; they are not "higher principles" against which contending "lower principles" might be judged (as some religions claim to do), and they are not a means to cloture, resolution, and conclusion in the fractious fray of competing moral claims and visions in everyday life.

creeds), scholars report a positive correlation between patriarchy and religiosity.[12]

Consider patriarchy within Islamic contexts. One might ask: Does Islam bias people toward patriarchy in ways so general that the bias remains even after accounting for other key distinctions, such as sex, age, education, and religiosity? Further, what determines patriarchal values more strongly: living in an Islamic society or simply adhering to Islam regardless of social environment? Research suggests that being a Muslim always contributes to stronger patriarchal values and that it does so irrespective of how strongly Islam dominates a society.[13] It suggests that Muslims are not more patriarchal simply because they are more religious or less educated but because they are Muslim. It shows that Muslims are not more patriarchal simply because most of them are found in dominantly Islamic societies; they are more patriarchal than non-Muslims even in dominantly non-Islamic societies. In short, research suggests that Muslims are more patriarchal than non-Muslims in all societies (Fetzer and Soper 2005; Buijs and Rath 2002).

Second, the patriarchal effect of Muslim denomination appears to be mediated by a person's level of educational achievement. Studies reveal that, in general, more educated persons tend to be more tolerant and egalitarian than persons with less education, and that higher levels of tolerance and an egalitarian outlook generally correspond with lower levels of patriarchal values (Inglehart and Norris 2003a). Patriarchal values decline with rising levels of formal education. Higher levels of educational achievement decrease individual patriarchal orientation similarly across dominantly Islamic and non-Islamic societies alike.

---

[12] Burn and Busso (2005); Paxton and Hughes (2007); Peek, Lowe, and Williams (1991). This view is hardly uncontested. Moghadam (2003) views patriarchal values as extrinsic to Islam and other religions. Ross (2008) ties the pronounced patriarchal features of Islamic societies to their per-capita oil and gas rent (which reduces the number of women in the workforce, and hence also their political influence).

[13] Using the World Values Survey, Welzel and Alexander (2009) examined the patriarchal values of about 105,000 respondents from some sixty-five countries. They looked for patriarchal tendencies in the socially transmitted interpretations of Islam, leaving aside whether such tendencies are favored by Islamic scriptures such as the Qur'an. The survey identifies culturally supported patriarchy in various domains, including labor market participation ("When jobs are scarce, should men have more access than women to jobs?"), education ("Is a university education more important for a man than a woman?"), political leadership ("Do men generally make better political leaders than women?"), and lifestyle choice ("Would you approve or disapprove of a woman who wants to have a child as a single parent but without a stable relationship with a man?").

Third, sex has an antipatriarchal effect: women are consistently and significantly less patriarchal than their male reference group in Islamic and non-Islamic societies as well as among Muslims and non-Muslims.[14] The gender gap in patriarchal values tends to increase with higher levels of educational achievement (Welzel and Alexander 2009). Fourth, persons from younger generations drive a growing social emphasis on sexual equality. Correspondingly, membership in a younger cohort generally correlates to diminished patriarchal values (Inglehart and Norris 2003a).

These findings offer cultural clues to changing the cultural phenomenon of patriarchal orientation, above all by a focus on formal education, indeed a focus on the education of Muslim women and girls in particular (whether Muslim or not, women and girls are more susceptible to education's antipatriarchal effect than are males) (Blaydes and Linzer 2006). The education of these women and girls (and the quantity and quality of that education) might generate opportunities for oppositional cleavage to develop within the community and to challenge, and sometimes even reduce, theologically based patriarchy. For example, an economy that stresses and rewards formal knowledge can develop and mobilize the intellectual potential of both sexes and thereby contribute to sex-egalitarian structures.[15]

Socially Constructed Human Rights as a Politics of Agency

In some theological approaches, believers do not so much hold a particular faith as they themselves are held by it. To be held by a belief that humans are sacred, in particular, will not of itself prevent inhumane behavior, of course. Indeed, inhumanity can be inflicted precisely in the name of a higher sacredness or for some sacred purpose or because one knows oneself to be commanded by God or to be in possession of infallible higher truths. History shows as much. But instead of being held by norms, one might consciously and self-reflexively hold them. Here the individual is no passive receiver of human rights messages; he or she engages human rights as a form of politics, where to be integrated into a human rights

[14] One finding (noted on p. 28 above) of the positive correlation between patriarchy and religiosity may be related to another: the World Values Survey found that among Muslims, men are more religious than women (Sullins 2006).

[15] Strong democracy is one sex-egalitarian structure. Inglehart and Norris (2003b) as well as Fish (2002) suggest that, among many other factors, patriarchy in Islamic societies discourages the development of democracy.

order is to freely recognize its moral authority. "Freely recognize" marks the actor's autonomy in the sense of self-determination. To be sure, communal identity cannot by itself legitimate just any practice as consistent with human rights. Some aspects of some group identities violate human rights (as I suggested in the example from some Islamic communities).

Further, within any community or polity there needs to be a place to which an oppressed minority might turn for protection. This is a core goal of *universal* human rights: to protect minorities from violation in communities that have not accepted them. If the minority believes it has rights, but the majority believes otherwise, the minority is in danger. I see three interrelated ways to respond to such common situations. As political not theological, human rights as "agential" respond (a) to the absence of agency in politics by fiat (b) as a moral language that (c) facilitates groups and communities giving rights to themselves. Let us examine each in turn.

(a) One nonagential approach to human rights is politics by fiat in the manner, say, of international instruments such as the *Universal Declaration*. Such instruments generally do not show how it is that human rights exist, whether as historically contingent cultural artifacts or as transcendent truths; such instruments merely *declare*, that is, assume, that human rights are valid, indeed valid universally. To be sure, the UN drafting committee found that its respondents (from a variety of intellectual, spiritual, and political backgrounds but not including those of indigenous or Islamic peoples in particular) all pointed to the notion of the "dignity of the human person" in their respective traditions (UNESCO 1949). The respondents constituted a numerically tiny elite that did not represent, but somehow presumed to represent, the world's peoples.[16] What kind of representation can a group hardly representative of the world's peoples provide? In part, none, because it sought to solve the problem of representation by the nonrepresentative means of careful strategy with respect to the foundation of the putatively universally valid rights it proclaimed. For example, it drafted a secular document not because the drafters were secularists but because the plethora of the world's competing religious traditions precluded an agreement on any declaration that did not bracket questions about possible theological grounds for human rights. There is no "God" in the preamble because there could be no agreement

---

[16] In Maritain's (1949:10) account, the Declaration attempts not the "affirmation of one and the same conception of the world, of man and of knowledge, but the . . . affirmation of a single body of beliefs for guidance in action."

on which divinity is the real one or whether faith or atheism is right and true. The committee assumed, plausibly, that the peoples of the world would not be able to agree, but it never asked them, anyway.

Ari Kohen offers a variation on this approach by regarding the *Universal Declaration* as "represent[ing] a political consensus of overlapping ideas from cultures and communities around the world" (Kohen 2007:134). The "process by which it was drafted and the deliberations surrounding the subsequent human rights instruments represent the best possible proof of the universal applicability of the rights that they espouse" (ibid.). Speaking of the men and women who drafted and ratified the document in 1948, he asserts that "everyone was able to agree upon and endorse a common foundation: the *dignity* of the human person" (Kohen 2007:12). But this secular argument from consensus is defeated by the absence of input, or consultation, with the billions of persons in whose names the self-selected elites spoke and acted.

International human rights instruments *proclaim* the individual's "dignity" as bald assertion and as political fiat, eschewing the need for discursive arguments (the addressees of such proclamations are not regarded as participants in a dialogue). Rights by fiat may be meaningless anyway inasmuch as the status of a country as a member of the UN, or as a signatory of human rights documents, hardly predicts whether it actually recognizes its citizens as bearers of human rights.[17]

The drafting committee's effort to address the issue of representation by nonrepresentative strategy is problematic in another regard: rights by fiat cannot be rights somehow neutral vis-à-vis the countless ways in which any conception of rights must make at least some substantive presuppositions. The *Universal Declaration* makes any number of presuppositions. For one thing, it is culturally particular in various ways. It privileges the individual over the family as society's primary unit; rights over duties as the basis of interpersonal relationships; legalism over reconciliation, repentance, or education as the basis for dealing with deviance; and secularism over religion as the modus vivendi of public life. The *Universal Declaration* also presupposes human rights primarily as individual

---

[17] "Although the ratings of human rights practices of countries that have ratified international human rights treaties are generally better than those of countries that have not, noncompliance with treaty obligations appears to be common." Further, "treaty ratification is not infrequently associated with worse human rights ratings than otherwise expected." Hathaway (2002:1940) found "not a single treaty for which ratification seems to be reliably associated with better human rights practices and several for which it appears to be associated with worse practices."

rights, as distinguished from group rights, whether economic, social, or cultural. (To be sure, the committee secondarily endorsed covenants on economic, social and cultural rights to be ratified together with the *Universal Declaration*, over objections of many, particularly Western, states.)

My argument does not deny certain significant achievements by this politics by fiat, including the International Criminal Court (ICC), which allows citizens to bring instances of human rights abuse to a legal forum, and efforts at transitional justice to deal with violations of human rights by governmental officials in Liberia, Cambodia, Sierra Leone, Rwanda, Chile, and even Australia and Canada. Further significant achievements of politics by fiat include the African Human Rights Charter; adoption of human rights language in new constitutions from the Czech Republic to South Africa; and the proliferation of human rights instruments since 1948 addressing heretofore marginalized groups. Finally, I note that various targeted groups throughout the world may reference the idea of human rights when they feel endangered. Here one might argue that the proliferation of rights-talk among people in communities underrepresented, or not represented at all, suggests that the UN drafting committee presciently intuited some of the rights-relevant hopes and preferences of billions of people despite the committee's inability to poll them.

But these achievements, welcome as they are, do not mitigate the problematic fact that the world's population was not consulted on the drafting of the *Universal Declaration*. Nor do these achievements suggest that the vast majority of the world's peoples now agrees that its drafting was a positive thing for them. They indicate, rather, that particular instances of politics by fiat have provided a variety of groups and individuals with a moral language to challenge the authority of those who might well have prevented them from ever making their voices heard. And to be sure, community-constructed rights will never be free of all of the problems of unequal distributions of power. After all, politics is always a matter of contestation, disagreement, strategizing, and power plays. But to the extent that these nonideal factors may stem more from the actions of the local participants (as addressees of the rights they themselves author) and less from the actions of nonparticipants (such as far-off elites), socially constructed norms come closest to the ideal of positive law: as the *self-determination* of a political or other community and as self-determination by individuals.

(b) As political not theological, human rights are a kind of moral language with a capacity to help protect individuals from oppression, abuse, and violence, whether by the state, religion, the family, or tradition.

As political, this moral language does not prescribe particular cultural practices; it prescribes the right to speak about and criticize particular cultural practices. It is a worldly language with no need of otherworldly dimensions or qualities. Invented, contingent, not without alternatives (individuals can be defended by other "languages" as well), it is hardly an ultimate trump over all other moral approaches. But sometimes it may allow speakers to defend themselves against possible oppression. And sometimes it can affect how we treat others and how they treat us: "To belong to a society in which the language of honor is dominant and the language of human rights has no place is to be a certain sort of person. It is to live a moral life that revolves around knowing one's position in the hierarchical social order of an extended family, executing the role-specific duties appropriate to that position" (Stout 1988:71). As a moral language, human rights sometimes might empower those who speak it and those who hear it, especially those without any local right to speak or to be heard. This would be the case where this moral language persuades potential speakers to reject those social institutions and mores that deny such rights. The inspiration for socially constructing human rights this way might lie outside the local culture, although not always or necessarily, of course; no culture is monolithic, and no individual is entirely a creature of his or her culture.

(c) Hence a central task of the human rights project is to create local conditions in which groups and individuals at the bottom of social hierarchies, and oppressed minorities and socially marginalized groups, might deploy human rights as a moral language to win for themselves the human rights they want. That is the task I advocate in this chapter: that *we* choose human rights, that they do not choose us, as distinguished from a theological approach in which persons are held by beliefs rather than holding beliefs. In this social constructionist approach, people have human rights if, as a group or community, they collectively choose to embrace them. Human rights as a moral language constitute a political relationship among moral beings who give themselves their own morality. That language may generate a social solidarity among persons *as bearers of human rights.* Solidarity may often be significant to efforts toward overcoming some social, political, and cultural differences (in part, possibilities for solidarity are limited by such differences). But the fact that different communities under different circumstances may well differ from each other in the moralities they give themselves does not preclude one particular morality – human rights – from eventually becoming universal, in the sense of being gradually embraced by more and more of these communities. The human rights project is a project of different cultures eventually freely giving themselves the same or similar human rights commitments.

The distinctively political nature of a social constructionist conception emphasizes human agency. Consider, by analogy, the politics of self-granted rights in a context that in part appealed to human rights. When Thomas Jefferson writes in the Declaration of Independence that certain rights are "inalienable," he is not, in fact, finally discovering what has always already been the case. Rather, he and his addressees decide, of their own volition, that they enjoy such rights as an emerging American political community constituted first by the Declaration (1776) and subsequently (and differently) by the federal Constitution (1787). The American polity and the rights it grants to its members are contingent, beginning in the 1770s and extending a decade or more, before which such rights were not available to the individual to embrace – because there was no community to recognize any such embrace. That is, the rights to which the Declaration appeals could find recognition only within the polity to which the Declaration aspired; Jefferson's text asserts rights redeemable only once the corresponding polity had been constructed. Until then, a member could not observe in fellow communal members the same embrace, for the community in which such an embrace became possible still lay in the future. The text famously speaks of natural rights as rights received from a "Creator." But in practice, and contrary to the document's wording and self-understanding, those rights were socially constructed.

The argument from social construction suggests how the Declaration of Independence can be coherent with respect to the need for any right to be recognized if it is to be a right in any practically meaningful sense, namely as conferring entitlements and immunities on all members of a political community and enforceable against family, state, and religious institutions (an idea that will challenge some aspects of some traditional cultures yet without rejecting them in toto). The same argument holds for human rights. Grounded politically not theologically, human rights are hardly the work of cultural consensus. In principle, areas of agreement as to which rights are *human* rights, and how they are best interpreted and applied in concrete cases – including instances where one human right conflicts with another – can always be enlarged and deepened, of course. That contingent possibility points up the fact that the politics of human rights has never been a work of consensus. How human rights are best construed remains an open question. From a Western perspective, for example, they might be understood in terms of Richard Rorty (1989), as solidarity created not found, or in terms of John Rawls (1999a), as based on an overlapping consensus, or in terms of Jürgen Habermas (1999), as legitimated by procedurally achieved agreement among affected persons.[18] But it remains that there are no consensually held interpretations of human rights or even approaches to interpretation within the West or within any one civilization or culture, let alone for the world entire.

But that lack of agreement does not condemn us to moral parochialism. Even under circumstances of abiding disagreement, what groups and communities give themselves, when they give themselves human rights, cannot simply ratify local beliefs and preferences. I earlier argued that a social constructionist approach takes an objectivating stance toward history and tradition more easily than a theological approach. From an objectivating stance, what groups and communities give themselves needs to be more normatively "thin" than "thick," for a "relatively thin conception of the good" may be "the most that people can secure rational agreement on" (Stout 1988:225).[19] If human rights are ever to "command universal assent," then likely because they are backed "only as a decidedly 'thin' theory of what is right" (Ignatieff 2001:56).[20] For the human rights idea will "travel better if separated from some of its underlying justifications," and certainly if separated from thick justifications (Taylor 1999:126). If, by contrast, human rights were pursued as something normatively thick – in terms, say, of theological foundationalism – they

---

[18] Whereby Rawls sees prospects for an intersubjective method of consensually justifying belief in human rights more widely than does Habermas, who links this method to necessarily democratic procedures. Rawls suggests that at least some nondemocratic forms of political self-determination might also generate at least some human rights for their members. For his part, Habermas (2003a:109), unlike Rawls or Rorty, sees an abiding role for theological approaches with respect to the generation of normative meaning: "only if the secular side, too, remains sensitive to the force of articulation inherent in religious languages will the search for reasons that aim at universal acceptability not lead to an unfair exclusion of religions from the public sphere, nor sever secular society from important resources of meaning." The problems and prospects of mixed strategies may well be promising in a practical sense but are beyond the scope of this chapter. The assertion that mixed strategies are a viable option would not detract from my argument that, under all circumstances, political reasons for human rights have better prospects than theological ones for finding universal acceptability. Still, a mixed political/theological strategy would be better than a purely theological one.

[19] For a developed account of "thick norms" and "thin norms" and how they relate, see Gregg (2003b).

[20] Even then, a global human rights consciousness does not require exactly the same beliefs. If it did, it would never be possible.

then would run up against other normative thicknesses that would discourage their free embrace within local cultures. If constructed as normatively thin, however, human rights can be something mundane rather than auratic: not spellbinding but rather binding by local cultural conviction and preference. In other words, political not theological.

The next chapter pursues this political vision but now addressed to that other ancient yet still influential version of an otherworldly approach: metaphysics.

2

Human Rights

Political Not Metaphysical

In common usage, validity might be predicated of claims, possessions, or justifications – but not of rights. I challenge this usage even as I build on it. When I speak of the possible validity of human rights, I refer to human rights as *claims* that justify how humans *should* be treated. To make a human rights claim is to regard that claim as valid, as a claim to validity, as a validity claim. In this sense, human rights are widely regarded as universally valid a priori, as we saw in Chapter 1 with respect to theologically based conceptions. There I asked: How are valid human rights possible – independent of historical contingency and the perspectival qualities and contextual dependencies of human understanding, experience, and belief? In this chapter I ask the same question – How can human rights be valid? – but now with regard to metaphysics.[1] The project of metaphysics began in earnest with Plato: through contemplation, it is the project to uncover true being, deeper truths, higher laws beneath, behind, above, or within the contingency, contextual embeddedness, and mere perspectivalism of our everyday phenomenological world.[2] Metaphors such as "deeper" and "higher" point to essences, eternal and unchanging, that mark "true being."

---

[1] Like theology, metaphysics encompasses a very wide variety of understandings, approaches, and traditions.

[2] Max Weber describes (appropriately enough in a lecture on politics) the Socratic invention of the metaphysical concept "by which one could put the logical screws upon somebody so that he could not come out without admitting either that he knew nothing or that this and nothing else was truth, the *eternal* truth that never would vanish.... [F]rom this it seemed to follow that if one only found the right concept of the beautiful, the good, or, for instance, of bravery, of the soul – or whatever – that then one could also grasp its true being" (Weber 1958:141).

The tendency to prefer an unchanging, infinite universe in endless time is reflected in the metaphysical assertions of eternal, unchanging fundamentals or essences of things or ideas or values. The fact that, until the twentieth century, no one (not even Einstein) could even *imagine* that the universe is expanding may reflect the widespread and tenacious tendency to metaphysical thinking. Contemporary cosmology, which is naturalistic rather than metaphysical, teaches that space and time are finite (even if they are without edges or borders) and that everything in the universe, like the universe itself, is changing constantly. From this naturalist standpoint, nothing is eternal and nothing is unchanging. The cultural spheres of law, morality, and ethics (spheres relevant to human rights) are, of course, unlikely to be a realm of absolutes in an otherwise non-absolute universe.

In the scientific and technological age of Western modernity, meta-physics has less purchase in complex modern societies than at any time since the modern era began roughly five centuries ago.[3] It has less pur-chase as a source of legislation, as a basis for social integration or com-munal behavior, or as a guide for civic creeds and public philosophies. But it still informs some contemporary worldviews, including several prominent approaches to human rights. I argue that one signature of Western modernity – the conviction that, through enlightened political agency, we humans *can* pull ourselves up morally by our own normative bootstraps – is lost, rejected, or betrayed wherever the possibilities and features of human rights are rendered metaphysically. I argue that meta-physics is a treacherous route to human rights and that a nonmetaphysi-cal alternative is both possible and plausible. That alternative is *political*[4] in the sense of "socially constructed," that is, not inherent in "human nature" but generated by (some) humans toward including (some or all) humans in political community. My argument proceeds in four steps: (1) in place of a *metaphysics of personhood* I offer a naturalist alternative; (2) in place of a *metaphysics of dignity* I propose dignity as political achieve-ment; (3) in place of a *metaphysics of identity* I argue for social integration through difference. (4) I then limn the proposal's potential as a political vision.

---

[3] Religion, another ancient way of thinking, continues to exercise an influence on political communities across the globe today that, even if diminished from earlier ages, remains exceedingly powerful in many parts of the world.

[4] Baynes (2009), following Rawls (1993), uses "political" in a related sense.

A Naturalist Alternative to the Metaphysics of Personhood

To ask after the "human" of human rights is to inquire about rights-bearing personhood. I propose a nonmetaphysical, naturalistic account.[5] By *naturalism* I mean the claim that the natural world contains no information about normative systems.[6] Normative systems, including human rights, can only be social constructions. We can construct moral systems in part by drawing on a moral capacity we possess as *biological* beings (as I argue in terms of recent research in evolutionary anthropology). By *naturalism* I also mean that the moral status of a bearer of human rights (or the moral worth of a creature capable of bearing human rights) is neither metaphysical nor natural but rather an artifact of human culture. By *culture* I mean (for example) a legal or legislative or other communal decision that an embryo is a person and not property (or, alternatively, is indeed property and not a person).[7]

A naturalist approach can tie human rights to moral agency without investing moral agency with some kind of metaphysical status. For example, human rights could be regarded as inalienable only by means of legal postulate, that is, by means of the moral agency involved in creating legislation or interpreting laws.[8] Rights so constructed would not only protect individuals from untimely death or unnecessary misery but also facilitate their moral agency, in two respects. First, "inalienable rights ensure that abridgments will not be neutralized by the cooperation of the rights-holder or the connivance of others" (Meyers 1985:7). Second, entitlement entails a duty of exercising the entitled right because a rights-holder "cannot cease to be entitled to the good an inalienable

---

[5] In Chapter 5 I address a feature of human behavior relevant to a naturalist account but which I bracket in this chapter (to reduce the level of analytic complexity): non-rational and irrational behavior.

[6] And not only because "our information about the world comes only through impacts on our sensory receptors" (Quine 1992:19).

[7] *Davis v. Davis*, 842 S.W.2d 588 (Tenn. 1992). A woman sued her ex-husband to obtain "custody" of frozen pre-embryos to donate to childless couples. A court of appeals found that pre-embryos are not "persons" but did not hold that they are "property." It identified a right to be free of state interference in reproductive choices and held that the ex-husband has a constitutional right not to beget a child.

[8] "Inalienable" in the seventeenth and eighteenth centuries meant that the individual rights-holder could not transfer these rights to another; today it often means that others cannot take away such rights or declare them to be forfeited. The older view adopts the perspective of the rights-respecter; the contemporary one, the perspective of the rights-holder.

right confers" on him or her (Meyers 1985:8). Moral agency of this sort integrates the individual into the intersubjectively shared norms of a linguistic community. It secures norms within the private and public contexts of a shared way of life, for human beings in general but equally for a specific individual, unique and "morally nonexchangeable" (Habermas 2003a:35). To be sure, relations of mutual recognition are kinds of intersubjective agreements, formal or informal, that rely on social institutions and frameworks for enforcing preferred behavior, as ways of acting and as ways of being treated by others. Moral agency relies on social institutions to enforce ways of "acting toward some subject for it to be capable of having legal rights" (Darby 2009:101).

Further, a naturalist approach can tie inalienable human rights to nonmetaphysical capabilities whose realization would bring dignity and respect to the individual. By *capabilities* I mean what Martha Nussbaum calls the "most important functions of the human being, in terms of which human life is defined" (Nussbaum 1992:214). In her account, one set of capabilities includes mortality, the body, a capacity for pleasure and pain, and cognitive capabilities (perceiving, imagining, and thinking).[9] These are basic features of any possible human way of life, anywhere, at any time. Another set concerns the individual's capacity to function on the basis of good health, nourishment, shelter, mobility, intellectual freedom, and community: phenomena that legislation and public planning *should* provide to citizens.[10]

A naturalist approach resonates with a social constructionist approach, as we see for example in the work of Michael Tomasello.[11] He describes aspects of "universal human nature" – biologically understood – that, I would show, resonates with a socially constructed vision of human rights. The possibility of human rights relies on the organization of political community as well as on the psychological disposition of the individual, insofar as that disposition motivates the individual's political and moral behavior. In other words, the practice of human rights relies on social structure (as I show in Chapters 6, 7, and 9) as well as on personality

---

[9] As well as early infant development, practical reason, affiliation with others, relatedness to other species and nature, play, and separateness (Nussbaum 1992:216–220).

[10] Nussbaum constructs the set of relevant capabilities as singular even though conceptions of flourishing likely are plural in any community and are hardly singular across communities and ways of life. Still, she acknowledges that different cultures place different weights on various capabilities and interpret them differently.

[11] His research focuses on processes of social cognition, social learning, and communication or language in human children and great apes.

structure (Chapters 4 and 5). Each reinforces the other at those points where human culture (which is particular) and human biology (which is "universal" within the species) "meet." Tomasello provides one human rights-relevant example: altruism emerges "naturally" in very young children (altruism, then, is not imparted initially or entirely by culture). Altruism is based, at least in part, on the young child's initially indiscriminate helpfulness toward others. Such helpfulness is an "outward expression of children's natural inclination to sympathize with others in strife" (Tomasello 2009:13).[12]

To be sure, the path is very long from natural dispositions to institutionalized, norm-guided social roles. But humans might traverse it through socialization into a uniquely human feeling of species-wide identity, a "sense of shared intentionality" that creates mutual expectations and even rights and obligations (Tomasello 2009:57–58). Although a peculiarly anthropological sense of "we" guarantees neither the eventual emergence of the human rights idea in any particular culture, nor a consensually held conception of human rights across different cultures, it does suggest a potentially universal basis in terms of which cultural agreement on human rights might one day be crafted. This sense of "we" might begin with the natural altruism and mutualism of the very young child and encourage, develop, and socially reinforce these traits through socialization and education and other political and cultural institutions. It could also encourage those aspects of local culture that already facilitate such traits along historical, cultural, and ethical dimensions. In these ways, among others, a naturalist approach and a social constructionist approach reinforce one another.

---

[12] Naturalism and social constructionism come together in other ways as well. Tomasello observes that infants "understand imperatives in a cooperative fashion" (Tomasello 2009:19). These features encourage collaboration that, over time, could affect complex social norms and institutions. The "process primarily responsible for human cooperation in the larger sense of humans' tendency and ability to live and operate together in institution-based cultural groups" is not principally altruism but rather mutualistic collaboration, the process by which "my altruism toward you ... actually helps me as well, as you doing your job helps us toward our common goal" (Tomasello 2009:52–53). Perhaps mutualistic activities provided a protected environment for the initial steps in the evolution of altruistic motives. Perhaps individuals extended their helpful attitudes outside this early environment through reciprocity, reputation, punishment, as well as social norms and institutions: "Internalized social norms, with accompanying guilt and shame, ensure that coordination with the group's expectations need not involve any overt behavior," where norms "provide the background of trust in which agent-neutral roles and shared cooperative activities with joint goals and joint attention enable social institutions" (Tomasello 2009:95–96).

Naturalism implies that human beings are entitled to human rights only if human beings so entitle themselves. The ascription of human rights to persons is itself cultural behavior, an act of imagination, of invention – and of politics. Key to any politics of human rights is how we understand "human being" with respect to the capacity for bearing human rights. A naturalist definition entails that nonbiological entities such as corporations or nation-states cannot bear human rights because they lack a capacity to grant themselves rights (if considered as corporate entities rather than as the humans who populate them). That entailment is uncontroversial. But a naturalist definition readily generates controversy when it distinguishes – as it must – among various *biological* categories with respect to their status vis-à-vis human beings capable of granting and bearing human rights. For example, one might argue that human tissue is "human" even though it is not itself a human being. At a level of greater biological complexity, the embryo is also tissue yet might be thought to have more purchase than a skin graft on the (definitionally problematic) category of "human." After all, the embryo is genetically programmed to develop into what – at some point of development and certainly by the point of birth – is unmistakably a human being. Of an embryo we can ask: Is it itself "human" in the sense of a capacity for granting and bearing human rights? Is it instead something that is not yet "human" but could, in time, *become* "human"? Or are "potential humans" ultimately *always already* "human" in the sense of possessing a rights-bearing capacity? And how do we appropriately evaluate "potential" with respect to certain groups of unmistakably biological humans who nonetheless, and for various reasons, might be thought to lack the potential to grant and bear human rights, whether permanently (brain-dead persons), sometimes (persons with multiple personality disorder), or only temporarily (infants, say, whose future socialization can be anticipated now)?[13]

The naturalist answers: something (whether tissue or infant, embryo or brain-dead person) possesses a human rights–bearing capacity only if socially constructed to do so.[14] As rational agents with physical bodies, minds, continuity of consciousness, and a capacity for moral agency, humans *can* construct social norms (such as human rights) for themselves. Note that a naturalist standpoint hardly entails ascribing human

[13] I return to some of these questions in Chapter 8.
[14] So corporations and nation-states might well possess human rights *if* so construed. Still, considered as corporate entities rather than as collections of human beings, they cannot so construe themselves; unlike humans, they are not themselves agents.

rights to a creature simply because it is biologically "human." Rather, it is culturally "human" *because* we ascribe human rights to it. But how, exactly, is ascription in this sense to be understood? How does it operate? In the following sections I analyze these questions in terms of two common answers: because human beings possess some kind of "dignity"; because human beings are morally equal with each other.

Not Metaphysics of Dignity but Dignity as Political Achievement

In what sense might all persons be *equal* in their possession of human rights? As foils to my position on equality, consider several alternatives.[15]

Theological approaches, which I address in Chapter 1, include notions of humans equal in their relationship to divine or supreme beings. The *Book of Genesis* depicts humans as "created in the image of God" (*Genesis* 1:27): each person equally a reflection of the divine and, on that basis, equally possessed of qualities that today (but not at the time of the book's composition or during most of the millennia since then) might be thought to ground human rights. A religion that regards the shedding of human blood to be an offense against God (*Genesis* 9:6), for example, would regard anyone's blood in that way, if that religion were to be self-consistent. The Biblical text, in any case, here makes no distinction among different persons or groups.[16]

Another ancient approach argues for moral equality by means of natural law. In Sophocles' great play, Antigone confronts domestic positive law (King Creon's edict that enemies of the state shall be denied burial) with her "natural" obligation, experienced as conscience, to give her brother a suitable burial. In the modern era, the sixteenth-century Dominican friar Bartolomé de Las Casas criticizes, from the standpoint of Christian natural law, the Spanish conquistadores' brutal treatment of Amerindians.

In these examples we have the metaphysics[17] of otherworldly boundaries that might be used to ground human rights in terms of a "natural"

---

[15] Here I would re-think human rights not by drawing on unusual ideas but rather by drawing on well-known ideas in a novel way.

[16] A different theological approach invokes the same trope: all humans as equal in their relationship to a divine or supreme being, in this case as members of a new class or group constituted by choice: "There is neither Jew nor Greek, there is neither bond nor free, there is neither male nor female: for ye are all one in Christ Jesus" (*Galatians* 3:28). A contemporary thinker might consider such equality among group members to provide members (if not nonmembers) equal rights.

[17] And in some cases, metaphysics with theological assumptions.

order vulnerable to transgression and sacrilege. Kant offers a modern alternative: a secular metaphysics of human dignity as such. According to Kant, the human being (like every rational being) exists as an "end in itself, *not merely as a means* to be used by this or that will at its discretion; instead he must in all his actions, whether directed to himself or also to other rational beings, always be regarded *at the same time as an end*" (Kant 1998:38).[18]

In this way, Kant uncouples the metaphysics of human dignity from theology. A further step, one that Kant does not take, would be to uncouple human dignity from metaphysics. I take this step in terms of a wholly naturalistic conception of the human being.[19] It regards the universe, which humans can observe and understand in terms of natural causes and effects, as characterized exclusively by natural forces (such as mass and energy) and without inherent purpose or meaning. Such naturalism is as old as the pre-Socratic philosopher Thales. Subsequently it found support among some late medieval scholastics (including Jean Buridan and Nicole Oresme). In the modern age, Galileo and Voltaire, among many others, championed it.

But unlike anyone from Thales to Voltaire and beyond, I extend this conception to an account of human rights by regarding human nature as it is biologically understood. Such an understanding allows for cultural constructions with normative dimensions, such as rights, politics, and social institutions. Social institutions range from political communities, property rights, and legal tender to customs, mores, friendship, and marriage. My account allows for human rights solely as cultural constructions.[20] The notion of naturalistic human rights has antecedents extending from Hegel (who sees individual freedom developing through natural and historical processes) and Émile Durkheim (who urges modern society to create human rights in response to the moral anomie of urban, industrial civilization) to Talcott Parsons (according to whom modern society responds to various pressures by tending toward the universal inclusion of all members and rights attendant upon such inclusion).

---

[18] A practical imperative follows for Kant: "So act that you use humanity, whether in your own person or in the person of any other, always at the same time as an end, never merely as a means" (Kant 1998:38).

[19] Chapter 8 takes this conception in a biological direction.

[20] Naturalism allows for embracing the idea of universal human rights, or for a universal embrace of the human rights idea, as Chapters 3 through 9 show in various ways.

Unique to my naturalistic approach is how I go beyond Kant to uncouple human dignity from metaphysics. Consider the following notion of individual rights. It cannot be trumped by the preferences, designs, or goals of a political community's majority groups. Such rights have no metaphysical character.[21] Their plausibility depends on the answers to two questions: (a) Why are collective goals sometimes insufficient justification for denying desired legal capacities, or for imposing unwanted legal obligations? (b) Why might a particular this-worldly quality of human beings – the capacity to do justice – entail equal concern and respect for all members of the community?

(a) From a naturalist perspective, collective goals by themselves are insufficient to justify denying rights or imposing obligations. Only goals compatible with human dignity provide sufficient grounds. From a naturalist perspective, the normative substance of human dignity is not something possessed; rather, it is an intersubjective relation of mutual respect and egalitarian affiliation. Affiliation of this sort does not subordinate the individual to the group (with respect to the individual's legal capacities and obligations). Rather, it operates in terms of relational symmetry: to each person it grants opportunities to lead an autonomous life. And to each it offers conditions for interaction with others on an equal basis.

This approach allows political community to accord each person's life a specific weight all its own. Community could do so by *constructing* individuals as possessing intrinsic value – rather than by appealing to some metaphysically intrinsic value. Members of a political community might embrace this notion of dignity, but not in the objectivating language of empiricism or in the passionate language of religious faith. They might embrace it in terms of what Georg Simmel calls a "web of affiliations." Such a web is not some collective goal; after all, an

> overlapping of group-affiliations cannot occur if the social groups involved are too far apart with regard to their purpose and in terms of the demands they make upon the individual. And a group which wants its members to become absorbed unconditionally in its activities must regard it as incompatible with this principle if an individual is differentiated from other members by virtue of his simultaneous affiliation with another group. (Simmel 1964:146)

A web of affiliation is a kind of social circle marked by interaction in a general sense (a "formal" circumference) as well as by common values

---

[21] Dworkin (1977:xi) argues along these lines, if only tentatively.

and dispositions to associate in certain ways (a substantive "density"). It reflects current forms of socialization, and it reflects social controls that influence individual behavior. Any given web is distinct from any other web in its display of particular cultural patterns and programming. Different webs may also differ with respect to forms of interaction.[22]

(b) In the idea of human rights, the traditional notion that some persons possess dignity[23] becomes the post-traditional idea that all persons possess it. Dignity, traditionally constructed as status bound, is then regarded as status free. As something situated in a linguistically structured way of life, as something that takes shape in the political, social, and legal categories of recognition in local community (and potentially across communities), dignity as a basis for human rights need not invoke some metaphysical human nature that endows people with a moral ontology that entails human rights. Then the path to human rights no longer traces back to some putative "essence" of man. Instead it traces back to persons who construct human rights for themselves (and who recognize the human rights of others who have constructed such rights for themselves). The social construction of the individual's dignity is equal with that of every other individual.[24] The "human" of "human rights" is then understood biologically not metaphysically, in ways I develop in later pages.

Not Metaphysics of Identity but Social Integration Through Difference

I turn to the work of Johannes Morsink for a contemporary example of a metaphysical approach to human rights. Morsink contends that people have always already possessed human rights, indeed as something ontologically given. They are given on the basis of "human dignity," and such dignity is inherent to the individual. But Morsink cannot redeem the core presuppositions of his account: that human rights are (a) universally valid a priori, (b) discoverable simply through intuition, and (c) available as a transcendental form of acultural knowledge that provides practical, moral standards to guide human behavior. Morsink's is a metaphysics

---

[22] See Levine (1999:1111–1112).

[23] In medieval philosophy, for example, the term *dignity* was "mostly used in the plural, thus indicating the different dignities of people in accordance with their different ranks, order, and estates in a feudal society" (Bielefeldt 2000:95).

[24] Human rights would not be inalienable on metaphysical grounds but could be constructed as inalienable by legal postulate, say in legislation or judicial interpretation.

of identity along several dimensions. It claims that "our" consciences are identical, perhaps as individual expressions of the "conscience of humanity." "Identity" then functions as a means of social integration, at least with respect to moral behavior. To claim that our consciences have a capacity for outrage because we possess human rights (and not the other way around) is to assert the normative integration of *all* persons. The claim is this: we are (or we can be) integrated morally because we are, metaphysically, identical with each other in the sense of our innate knowledge of human rights and their morally necessary and culturally neutral determination of our social behavior.

(a) The metaphysics of identity has three dimensions. First, it is an ontology: "people everywhere and at all times have rights that are not man-made, but inherent in the human person from the moment of birth" (Morsink 2009:17). "Not man-made" means *metaphysical* in this sense: by virtue of their humanity alone rather than, say, by political means. The most common political means to rights today are institutional: rights as the procedurally achieved results of legislatures or as the product of judicial interpretations of the laws. Second, the metaphysics of identity is an epistemology: "people everywhere have known all along (especially in situations of gross abuse and violation) about inherently existing human rights"; humans know "especially" under conditions where human rights are violated (Morsink 2009:59).[25] Third, the metaphysics of identity is a politics: it asserts a direct, causal, motivational link between very particular and highly abstract cognition on the one hand and, on the other, equally particular and highly principled behavior (in the sense of the Socratic conviction that "to know the good is to do the good"). The claim here is that human rights norms are an "essential component of the fight against conditions of oppression and suppression around the globe" (Morsink 2009:3). Morsink argues that a very particular kind of

---

[25] Elsewhere Morsink argues for human rights knowledge of a very different sort, as certain knowledge gained contingently: "we learn what rights are from the wrongs we encounter" (Morsink 2009:58), including the "experience of radical evil with its attendant discovery of human rights" (Morsink 2009:59). For some persons, then, universal knowledge is acquired at Time = 0; for others, at T > 0 ("our *discovery* [alone or in groups] of human rights") or even at T + T′ > 0 (the "later *justification* of this belief to others after we have made our discovery"; Morsink 2009:58). Of course, someone who never encountered wrongs or radical evil (however unlikely, to be sure) would never know what Morsink elsewhere claims to be *innate* knowledge: that of human rights. But even someone who has encountered wrongs and evils may not "learn what rights are"; he or she may learn instead to perpetrate wrongs and evils. Brutalizing experience turns some victims into brutalizers.

validity – universal validity a priori – facilitates the development of forces of rebellion against powers and institutions that violate human rights. Other forms of validity (such as contingent validity a posteriori) lack this politically motivating force.

(b) For the metaphysics of identity, human rights are discovered not made. In our knowledge of human rights, we merely discover (or rediscover), completely or partially, what we already know. We do so through contemplation alone. Contemplation is tied to intuition and to sentiments understood as carriers of objective moral knowledge: "our moral sentiments *do* help us discover truths and do yield knowledge of the world" (Morsink 2009:103). Through sentiments, "people discover" the "metaphysical universality of human rights" (Morsink 2009:59). They discover it by contemplating the "kinds of creatures that human beings are, namely, ones with inherent moral rights" (Morsink 2009:103). What's more, conscience triggers contemplation: our consciences have a capacity for outrage *because* we possess human rights – not the other way around. Hence our moral intuitions, like our putatively innate knowledge of human rights, are not tentative, subjective hunches but forms of objective knowledge that we do not acquire but always already possess.

(c) In this account, the moral knowledge of human rights, derived from intuition, is "transcendental" or acultural. Moral knowledge is valid independent of culture and human artifact; it is not shaped by the cultural milieu into which the knowing individual has been socialized. Moral knowledge of this sort warrants moral judgment, sanctioning the "kind of cross-cultural judgments" made by the United Nations committee that drafted the *Universal Declaration of Human Rights* (Morsink 2009:101–102).[26]

None of these claims can be sustained.

Ad (a) Perhaps recourse to metaphysics is motivated by an anxiety that the possibility of moral behavior requires some kind of moral objectivism. In fact, moral relativism is quite adequate as a basis for beliefs that have the power to motivate moral behavior (and that can do so across cultural, historical, and economic boundaries). Various features of everyday life, for everyone, everywhere, offer strong reasons for human rights. Think of the individual's lifelong dependence on other people for care and recognition. Consider the permanent vulnerability of the body to illness and other harms. Reflect on the constant accessibility of the mind to psychological assault, or the enduring susceptibility of one's self-regard

---

[26] Chapter 1 critiques this understanding of the drafting committee's work.

and self-respect to reputational injuries. Consider someone's defenselessness against the violent consequences of a breakdown in the network of relations of mutual recognition, or of a breakdown in the normative regulation of interpersonal relations. In each of these examples, most people likely would concede that their vulnerabilities mirror those of other human beings. If so, they might well be open to the idea that if it is morally wrong to violate one person in any of these vulnerabilities, then it is wrong to so violate any person. This train of thought is hardly guaranteed, to be sure. But it is hardly implausible – and it requires no treacherous metaphysics of human identity.

Ad (b) A metaphysical epistemology – as in the claim that human rights are discovered not made – has no resources to adequately address any number of questions it raises. In the course of a human lifetime, when exactly does the individual intuit or retrieve this "innate knowledge"? When does one become conscious of what one supposedly always already knows? Perhaps at the point of conception? But the fertilized egg has no consciousness. Maybe as an infant? But infants do not display the kind of moral maturity incarnated in the idea of human rights. With puberty? Few teenagers are sources of profound moral insight.

Ad (c) Empirical observation does not support a view of human rights as transcendental; there is no empirical evidence for acultural norms. All norms can be traced to particular cultures (and, often enough, to multiple particular cultures). Norms are culturally embedded in several ways. Above all, no social, political, or legal norm is neutral with respect to worldview. Not for that reason alone, no norm is freely embraced by all members of all cultural communities. Perhaps no norm can even be described without prejudging what one describes.

Moreover, *Homo sapiens sapiens* evolved about two hundred thousand years ago.[27] At what point in history did such creatures possess transcendental knowledge? Or if humans always already know transcendentally, then at what point in the anthropological record do they become "humans" in the sense of knowing in transcendental ways? And why are there no traces of such knowledge for more than one hundred ninety thousand years, and then only sparsely in most of the last ten thousand?[28]

---

[27] To limit ourselves to just one type of human; *Homo neanderthalensis* and *Homo erectus*, for example, are much older, and scientists today count about twenty kinds of hominids over the millennia.

[28] Further, Morsink cannot redeem his metaphysical claims to objective, timeless, and absolutely binding norms. Consider his assertion that "when our moral intuitions are operating normally they bring us into contact with this objective . . . realm of universal values,"

My alternative to the metaphysics of identity draws on Georg Simmel (1858–1918), whom I introduced earlier. It builds on the claim I make throughout this chapter for socially constructed human rights with a capacity to become universally valid, and to become so contingently. My alternative employs a politics of social integration of a very particular sort. I mean *integration* in terms of a density of contact that Simmel calls "affiliation": integration at intersecting points on the network or web of the individual's social relations.[29] In this account, the individual is no discrete, unconnected, self-supporting being. But neither is community monolithic, all-encompassing, or all-embracing. Rather, "society arises from the individual" and the individual "arises out of association" (Simmel 1964:163). On the one hand, a web of group affiliations is an emergent social structure, "an ellipsis of social circles in which individuals create and maintain some long-lasting and many temporary and contingent ties" (Pescosolido and Rubin 2000:70). On the other hand, a web comes from individuals interacting "on the basis of certain drives and for the sake of certain purposes," oriented on distinct norms or driven by particular values (Levine 1991:1104).[30]

where "objective" means existing externally to our own intuitions or moral perceptions of it (Morsink 2009:104). He discovers "normality" in putatively acultural objective values, as in the proposition that moral intuitions can operate "normally" or "abnormally." "Normal" as a standard refers to "bring[ing] us into contact with...our own intuitions or moral perceptions of...universal values." One wonders: how exactly do we establish such contact? What is the nature of such contact? How do we know when we have established it? And given that different persons and different epochs have intuited universal values in some ways distinct from those intuited by other persons, including persons in other eras, how might anyone adjudicate among competing universalistic intuitions in a way plausible to all participants (or otherwise affected persons)? Questions about "our moral intuitions operating normally" become all the more acute where Morsink suggests that the "dictum that ignorance of the law is no excuse translates into a call to obey one's indwelling conscience of humanity" (Morsink 2009:100). His argument rests on undefended metaphysical premises about reasons why "ignorance of the law" might be indefensible. For example, "Article 5 of the [Universal] Declaration [of Human Rights] ('No one shall be subjected to torture or to cruel, inhuman or degrading treatment or punishment') supposes that there are indeed clear cases of torture and other forms of inhuman treatment in violation of this universal taboo" – unless, of course, the person making this determination has had his or her "normal conscience blocked or overridden by external or internal deformities" (Morsink 2009:111–112). Everything rides on the definition of "normal." Morsink's metaphysical standpoint understands itself as offering nonperspectival definitions. Yet its understanding of moral standards can only be embedded culturally, and can only be culturally particular.

[29] One alternative to the idea of multiple affiliations would be that of an individual's complete commitment to a very few institutions; another would be his or her very weak commitment to most institutions.

[30] Simmel understands that social structures, such as affiliations of the individual with various social groups, are constituted by the norms those structures embody; he understands

Even non-normative webs of affiliations can integrate members morally. They can do so despite differences among members. In particular, they can integrate members into a human rights community at the levels of both (a) individual and (b) community.

(a) To understand what Simmel means by affiliation, consider his example of a child. The child is passively connected to his or her family or caretakers. In time, and through choices, he or she comes to self-consciously affect and determine some of those associations. This may involve breaking some of those connections, such as the narrow boundaries of his or her childhood (and later, of his or her adult life so far). Significant for my alternative to a metaphysics of identity is that these affiliations are heterogeneous. That is, each is composed of distinct individuals who may never be deeply similar to each other. In fact, increased heterogeneity fosters increased individuation: the child becomes increasingly individuated as he or she increasingly associates with others, and associates with increasing numbers of others, including distant others. Individuation involves the child gradually moving from natural or biological relationships (to his or her mother, for example) to more social ones, such as to his or her colleagues at work. With time, he or she moves more and more from "externally" determined associations – the family, culture, the language into which he or she was born, and other of his or her original group affiliations – to associations that he or she may choose, such as profession, spouse, religious faith, and political orientation. These are groups of persons who are "'related' to him or her by virtue of an actual similarity of talents, inclinations, activities, and so on. The association of persons because of external coexistence is more and more superseded by association in accordance with internal relationships" (Simmel 1964:128).

In some cases, the terms of those associations may be extremely broad. They might extend, for example, from socioeconomic status to mother

that human affiliations are norm guided (Simmel 1896). Peter Blau (1964:278–279), who classifies affiliations in terms of their primary functions, associates each type with particular values. Some affiliations are oriented toward social integration (e.g., in family, in kinship, or in religious community) and perpetuate values and social solidarity; other affiliations are oriented toward preserving communal organizations for production and distribution (e.g., educational institutions or the economic system); and yet other affiliations focus on the deployment and coordination of resources (e.g., political activity). Simmel understands that value-laden or value-oriented affiliations, "by creating multiple pulls among the individual's values, norms, and sanctions," where "multiple groups pull the individual in different directions" (Pescosolido and Rubin 2000:57), can also generate social problems: "external and internal conflicts arise through the multiplicity of group-affiliations, which threaten the individual with psychological tensions or even a schizophrenic break" (Simmel 1964:141).

tongue to profession. Each affiliation is a point at which the individual "intersects" with others. *Intersection* refers to some degree of shared identity. Our individual identity is determined at least in part by our group affiliations, that is, by the particular constellation of associations peculiar to each of us.[31]

Toward each of the associations of which we are members, we tend to behave more or less in terms of our affiliation, in three respects. First, the individual "finds a community for each of his inclinations and strivings which makes it easier to satisfy them" (Simmel 1964:162) and the "same person can occupy positions of different rank in the various groups to which he belongs" (Simmel 1964:151). Second, we can always assume very different perspectives on each of our various affiliations, or different attitudes toward them. Third, our individuality is generated through the combination of affiliations that is specific to each of us: the "specific qualities of the individual are preserved through the combination of groups which can be a different combination in each case" (Simmel 1964:163). This particular combination generates, expresses, and preserves our uniqueness. And the more affiliations one has, the more individuated one is. In other words, each of us is a unique cultural composite of intersections of various social networks. This composite constitutes the uniqueness of our personality; the greater the number of one's affiliations, the greater one's uniqueness: "To belong to any one of these groups leaves the individual considerable leeway. But the larger the number of groups to which an individual belongs, the more improbable is it that other persons will exhibit the same combination of group-affiliations, that these particular groups will 'intersect' once again" in a second individual (Simmel 1964:140).

The individuation of a person achieves a certain balance precisely through its breadth. A person can be self-dependent yet, at the same time, connected widely rather than in the narrow, parochial ways of ascriptive characteristics. Complex modern societies offer greater possibilities than do traditional societies for affiliation along dimensions of, say, occupation, political orientation, or socioeconomic class rather than race, ethnicity, or sex.

In this interpretation of the idea of a web of affiliations I see potential for generating a shared human rights consciousness that requires no

---

[31] "Each thing has a part in as many ideas as it has manifold attributes, and it achieves thereby its individual determination. There is an analogous relationship between the individual and the groups with which he is affiliated" (Simmel 1964:140).

metaphysics of identity. Here the relevant feature is the way that members of the same affiliation may affect or influence each other. That influence extends to the ways in which one or the other affiliation may have formed the individual, so that one affiliation may influence another via the individual who is a member of both: "as the individual becomes affiliated with social groups in accordance with the diversity of his drives and interests, he thereby expresses and returns what he has 'received' though he does so consciously and on a higher level" (Simmel 1964:141). As the increasingly individuated individual becomes affiliated with each additional group, he or she possibly brings to the new affiliation some aspects of some of his or her other affiliations.

A human rights consciousness requires, of course, a particular concern for other human beings. The metaphysics of identity presumes that such a concern always already exists. But from the standpoint of a web of affiliations, one sees how greater individuation may render the individual less one-sided and better able to place him- or herself in the shoes of others. Simmel suggests that it is the "highly discriminating person of catholic training and activities who tends to have cosmopolitan reactions and convictions; one-sided people perceive what is human only in terms of their own limited horizon, since they are lacking in empathy for people different from themselves and are unable to experience vicariously what is common to all men" (Simmel 1964:179).

I would extend Simmel's use of empathy to the idea of a human rights consciousness. Such a consciousness requires empathy toward others, despite all differences between the actor and his or her addressee. Empathy then shades into a tolerance of some types of differences among human communities, cultures, and individuals. The individual in his or her web of affiliations need not be threatened, in his or her identity or moral capacity, by those differences, or at least not by all of them (some he or she might reject precisely on human rights grounds). On the contrary, he or she might well be enriched by some of them, and if so, then precisely through his or her affinity with them.

Of particular interest to the advancement of the human rights idea are those affiliations in which the individual finds him- or herself at the intersection of two groups that stand in some tension with one another. An individual may even be "affiliated with two groups which regard each other as opponents" (Simmel 1964:157). The individual might then function as a kind of bridge from one group to another. In principle, sometimes an individual might function as a kind of transmitter of human rights ideas (present in one of his or her affiliations) to a

group (another of his or her affiliations) that is not committed to human
rights.

One type of affiliation that might advance the idea of human rights
would be a form of solidarity in which the pain, distress, or anxiety (or
contentment, satisfaction, or joy) of one member is felt by other members
of the group. Here a kind of "human rights personality" might be developed and encouraged: a personality capable of granting human rights
to (or recognizing human rights in) others without needing to invoke
some human rights–generating metaphysical "dignity" of the other (an
approach I develop in Chapter 4).[32] Solidarity via affiliation might take
the form of genuine concern for the human rights–related welfare of
at least some of the other affiliates, and in at least some affiliations. But
even solidarity along these lines does not presuppose, and hardly entails,
some unrealistic level of agreement and harmony within the group. After
all, any of an individual's affiliations is characterized by both interconnection and "separateness." That is, any of an individual's affiliations
is characterized by identity and difference; the individual shares some
things with the affiliated group but hardly everything. An employer, for
example, is affiliated with all other employers, and not only in a formal
sense. He or she likely shares more than a few interests with other affiliates, that is, with his or her fellow employers. Yet as an employer, he or she
is also in competition with some of his or her fellow employers. Thus the
employer's affiliation with other employers is sometimes marked by bitter competition with precisely those persons to whom he or she is bound
by an interest – say, in legislation that impacts one's particular business
as well as the general business climate.[33] In this way, a web-of-affiliations

---

[32] At least by analogy to what Simmel discusses in terms of "honor": "The extent to which
associations [based on interest] also form a tightly-knit group may be gauged on the basis
of whether and to what extent such a group would feel that his honor was diminished
whenever any member suffered an insult or a deprivation of his honor. In this sense the
association possesses a collective sense of honor, whose changes are reflected in the sense
of honor of each member" (Simmel 1964:163).

[33] Simmel describes this relationship as an "innerlicher Gegensatz" (1989:243), an internal
contradiction or tension:

A typical example of multiple group-affiliations within a single group is the competition among persons who show their solidarity in other respects. On the one hand the
merchant joins other merchants in a group which has a great number of common
interests: legislation on issues of economic policy, the social prestige of business,
representation of business-interests, joint action as over against the general public
in order to maintain certain prices, and many others. All of these concern the world
of commerce as such and make it appear to others as a unified group. On the other
hand, each merchant is in competition with many others. To enter this occupation

approach allows for tensions *internal* to group affiliations. Presumably persons affiliated along the lines of a human rights consciousness would also experience various internal tensions, including understandings of human rights (primarily as individual rights rather than group rights, say, or more as political rights than economic rights).

(b) This nonmetaphysical approach has a distinctively cognitive quality: an affiliation is in part a mental act, an act of consciousness. The individual's identity, as well as his or her integration into the community, are also acts of consciousness. Humans, despite their differences, are always connected through such acts. And in a sea of difference, some acts of consciousness may uncover points of sharedness among individuals. Marx makes this point with his notion of class consciousness. For the wage-earning class, the particular kind of work each member does is irrelevant; what matters is the fact that one has nothing to sell but one's capacity for labor. For those who own the means of production, which particular means is irrelevant; what matters is that one purchases labor power rather than sells it. Individual members of each class are defined in part by their shared, class-specific relationship to capital. But unlike Marx, Simmel does not reduce the social actor to his or her membership in a socioeconomic group. When, for example, he speaks of a "unitary social consciousness" among members of the wage-earning class, he intends much more than what Marx means by "class-consciousness." He is picking out one particular, socioeconomic affiliation from the plethora of an individual's multiple affiliations; he is focusing on one consciousness, but only as one among many simultaneous consciousnesses. None takes complete precedence over others.[34]

Cognizance of affiliation is particularly relevant to the generation of solidarity along the lines of human rights. Affiliation does not require any particular identity among members except along dimensions of that

---

creates for him at one and the same time association and isolation, equalization and particularization. He pursues his interest by means of the most bitter competition with those with whom he must often unite closely for the sake of common interests (Simmel 1964:155).

[34] "The *solidarity of wage labor* exemplifies a group-formation based on a pervasive social awareness. This social consciousness is especially interesting because it presupposes a high degree of abstraction over and above the particularities of individuals and of groups. No matter what the job of the individual worker may be, whether he makes cannons or toys, the very fact that he is working for wages makes him join the group of those who are paid in the same way. The workers' identical relation to capital constitutes the decisive factor, i.e. wage labor is in a similar condition in the most diversified activities" (Simmel 1964:172).

particular affiliation. Along other dimensions, in persons' other affiliations, each member of a group is likely to be quite different from every
other member. Webs affiliate persons who are very different from each
other; they affiliate through *difference* not identity, and such differences
do not preclude or undermine group identity or solidarity. One such
group could be a human rights community, a community of persons with
a shared human rights consciousness. Such a group is still possible as
an affiliation among persons significantly different from each other in
several ways. On the one hand, "As the person becomes affiliated with a
social group, he surrenders himself to it. A synthesis of such subjective
affiliations creates a group in an objective sense." On the other hand, the
person also "regains his individuality, because his pattern of participation is unique; hence the fact of multiple group-participation creates in
turn a new subjective element" (Simmel 1964:141). Because the member never ceases being a distinct individual, and as a distinct individual
can still work together with other individuals by "impersonal means for
impersonal ends" (Giddens 1990:20), he or she is constantly moving
between identity and difference.

Whereas the metaphysics of identity denies deep and abiding differences among fellow advocates of human rights, my alternative builds
those differences into its account of a human rights community. For
example, some affiliations may motivate the seeking out of other, "com-
pensating" affiliations because the individual "feels and acts *with* others
but also *against* others" (Simmel 1964:155).[35] Some affiliations may offer
alternatives to current communal and personal identities. Of particular
interest are alternatives that include human rights–oriented beliefs and
behavior, especially where they stand in opposition to the individual's
social environment or group-wide history.[36] Here we have the critical
capacity of a web of affiliations. For even if the individual, standing at the
"point at which many groups 'intersect'" (Simmel 1964:141), is circumscribed in his or her moral personality, her or she is circumscribed only
in part. In part, he or she might challenge some social arrangements,

---

[35] For example, an "individual's need for a clearer articulation and for a more unambiguous development of his personality forces him to select certain groups. And from their
combination he gains his maximum of individuality – the one group offering him opportunities for socialization, the other opportunities for competition. Thus, the members of
a group in which keen competition prevails will gladly seek out such other groups as are
lacking in competition as much as possible" (Simmel 1964:156).

[36] Some empirical research (unrelated to human rights topics) supports this idea that
"Network structures offer alternatives for community identity as well as personal identity"
(Pescosolido and Rubin 2000:54).

reconstitute others, or even craft new ones for any number of reasons or motivations – including an embrace of the human rights idea.

Two Kinds of Political Potential

The political potential of my approach lies in its local purchase. That purchase, normative localism, provides an alternative to the widespread embrace of normative universalism – for example, as it finds expression in the claim that "human rights point to a universal community in which alone they can be realized" (Moltmann 1977:135). The human rights idea may indeed point to some kind of universal community. But if so, then it does not point to universal community as a necessary condition for the embrace and practice of human rights. At most it points to universal community as a logical implication of the idea of human rights. Perhaps that implication can be pursued only asymptotically, as a regulative idea, an orienting goal, and one never to be reached. Or perhaps a universal community could be constructed;[37] such a construction would be no easy task, to be sure, but it is not logically or empirically impossible. In any case, I argue for the possibility of human rights realizable locally, even if in only some locales and only some of the time. As a practical matter, human rights under limited conditions may be the currently best possible outcome for human rights advocacy. The web-of-affiliations model, in its capacity to generate increasing interconnectedness, is one means to approaching the long-term goal of a universal community, whether asymptotically or otherwise. It is a realistic means to a realistic goal, and therein lies its political potential. A realistic means requires no collective identity as a condition for an embrace of human rights. It requires no metaphysics to generate whatever kind and degree of identity may be needed. Nor does it construe the putative moral identity of all persons as the foundation for norms universally valid a priori. The web-of-affiliations model seeks to show that differences among people need

---

[37] A similar point can be made against Morsink's critique of a social constructionist approach to human rights: "Constructivists . . . can plausibly argue that before the modern era of radical egalitarianism, the rights individuals had were based on their particular locations in the social and political hierarchies of the societies in which they lived. . . . [A]s they see it, each age is free to construct its own theory of justice to match the moral intuitions of its own time and place. Some of these old constructions are better than others, but none have a claim to priority, for there are no moral intuitions or arguments that cut across ages and cultures" (Morsink 2009:145). But a priority could be socially constructed, in the same sense that a universal community could be constructed – without metaphysics.

not preclude or undermine the kind of affiliations that might plausibly encourage an embrace of human rights. Consider Simmel's example from

> where the moral life is tied to religion. For the individual his religion is as a rule the only religion; another religion is out of the question for him. He bases his moral convictions upon the special precepts of his religion. Subsequently, experience may convince him that the moral persuasion of other individuals is as genuine and as valuable as his own, but that it has been derived from completely different religious ideas. Only in rare cases is he likely to conclude that morality is connected only with the religious mood in general, i.e., with what is common to all religions. He is more likely to draw a more far-reaching conclusion, namely that morality has nothing to do with religion at all. On this basis he will arrive at the view that morality is autonomous and he will not associate morality with the residual concept of the generally religious, which would be equally justified on logical grounds (1964:187).

Affiliations of the sort Simmel imagines might be affiliations of social solidarity, including solidarity with distant others. The work of solidarity would then be a permanent task, one to be undertaken anew each day.[38] Solidarity as daily political activity: with this idea I offer a distinct alternative to the metaphysical notion of a pregiven collective identity ("the inherent dignity of man," say, or "inherent rights by virtue of one's humanity alone"). Here we have identity stripped of metaphysics because it is identity that is mundane, quotidian, and participatory. Here we have human rights as artifacts, not human rights delivered by metaphysical givens. In principle, these artifacts can be constructed by anyone, anywhere, at any time; and they can be shared, transferred, copied – by anyone, any group, any culture.

Human rights are possible as part of the everyday fabric of an ordinary individual's everyday life along two dimensions of the individual's political and social life. (a) One dimension: his or her membership in political community as it concerns his or her status as someone who may claim human rights, and may do so on the basis of individual human dignity. (b) A second dimension: everyday interactions among individuals that

---

[38] This is a conception very different from a purely domestic situation of solidarity: political community would again and again generate anew its collective identity in the famous sense of Ernst Renan (1882): as a "plébiscite de tous les jours," a "daily plebiscite." Identity is then a political artifact, carried by its continual reassertion by the members of community – or otherwise lost.

reinforce mutual recognition among persons who mutually accord each other dignity. I develop both dimensions and use recent work by Jürgen Habermas as a foil.

(a) Habermas imagines human dignity as a kind of "portal" through which the "egalitarian and universalistic substance of morality is imported into law." And he regards human dignity as the "conceptual hinge that connects the *morality* of equal respect for everyone with positive *law* and democratic lawmaking in such a way that their interplay could give rise to a political order founded upon human rights" (Habermas 2010:469). The idea that the "*moral promise* of equal respect for everybody" needs to be "cashed out in *legal currency*" is compelling (Habermas 2010:470). After all, moral claims such as human rights are ineffective until they assume the form of "enforceable subjective rights that grant specific liberties and claims" that are "*specified* from case to case in adjudication" and "enforced in cases of violation" (Habermas 2010:470). But I find Habermas's next step unpersuasive. He argues that the concrete terms in which such moral claims *would* be spelled out, *can* be spelled out only through "democratic legislation," such that human rights can only "become political reality in the robust shape of effective civil rights" (Habermas 2010:470). This view renders human rights co-original with democracy. It regards human rights as rights enacted through a democratic procedure in the manner of civil rights legislation in the liberal constitutional state.

To be sure, to the extent that most citizens of democratic states enjoy robust civil rights, they are likely to enjoy any number of human rights as well – if human rights are understood in terms of what is often called the "first wave": as individual *civil and political* rights as distinguished from second-wave *group* rights or third-wave *economic* rights. But democracies constitute only a small minority of the world's nation-states. Habermas's approach to human rights does nothing for the majority of the world's populations. The recognition of each citizen by all other citizens "as subjects of equal actionable rights" might be accomplished if each person recognized all others as possessing human dignity (Habermas 2010:472). But the possibility of human rights finding ever wider recognition – and, ultimately, global embrace – requires the generation of a "morality of equal respect for everyone" – even, indeed especially, in nondemocratic political orders (Habermas 2010:472).

Although a democratic order is more likely than any other to treat members as subjects of equal actionable rights, it is not the only order capable of so treating its members.[39] The web-of-affiliations approach is workable in at least some nondemocratic orders. For in most cases, webs of affiliation are not predicated on political relationships. As for those webs that are so predicated, they need not be predicated on specifically *democratic* relationships. Social solidarity, here understood in the narrow sense of recognizing others' human rights (including the self-assigned human rights I promote in Chapter 4), is possible in many different forms, and not only in democratic ones.

(b) Improbable as it seems, an "internalized, rationally justified morality anchored in the individual conscience" *can* be united with the "coercive, positive, enacted law" that "serves rulers and elites and governments that are not democratic" (Habermas 2010:470). What's more, it can be established outside the framework of the constitutional state. Consider human rights in terms of the nonmetaphysical notion of human dignity I developed above.[40] Habermas argues that human dignity, as a modern *legal* concept, is "associated with the status that citizens assume in the *self-created* political order" (Habermas 2010:473). My counterargument: human dignity can be associated with the status that individuals assume in the collectively generated web of interactions. Human dignity can be so associated in many respects, to varying degrees, and quite beyond the political order. With Habermas I agree that, "As addressees, citizens can come to enjoy the rights that protect their human dignity," but I differ with his further claim that citizens can enjoy such rights "only by first uniting as authors of the democratic undertaking of establishing and maintaining a political order based on human rights" (Habermas 2010:473). I disagree with the restriction Habermas intends by the term *only*; this chapter would suggest that citizens may come to enjoy such rights *also* through a web of everyday interactions. Some of these interactions could potentially develop the mutual respect for dignity from which a free embrace of human rights for others might follow. This approach may not be possible in all of the world's political communities, but it is possible in more than just the democracies.

In short, a metaphysically conceived human dignity cannot ground human rights as an ontological feature of persons. If human rights are

---

[39] Habermas calls for extending "collective political identities beyond the borders of nation-states" toward a "multilevel global system of a constitutionalized world society" (Habermas 2010:475, n. 21). But this approach does nothing to counter the problem posed by the nondemocratic nature of most polities.

[40] In the second of my four steps, where in place of a *metaphysics of dignity* I propose dignity *as political achievement*.

social constructions, then we can have no transcendental knowledge of them. So we overtax the finite constitution of human rights if we demand to know them metaphysically. A human rights community does not require the metaphysical identity of its members with each other because human rights are possible as political, and as constructed, on a naturalist footing.

From these first two chapters of critique I now move to developing an alternative in Chapter 3. That alternative is this-worldly and political: locally valid human rights.

3

Generating Universal Human Rights
out of Local Norms

In the preceding chapters I identified and analyzed a number of problems with the widespread conception of human rights as universally valid a priori. Part of the problem, I argued, has to do with exactly *how* authors attempt to ground the most ambitious form of moral authority imaginable. Chapter 1 identified problems inherent to theological efforts; Chapter 2, those intrinsic to metaphysical endeavors. Despite their many differences, theological and metaphysical approaches both invoke otherworldly sources. In this chapter I turn to my alternative. Entirely thisworldly, it grounds human rights in their own addressees. Relevant norms are then valid because they are authored by their addressees. Eventually universally valid human rights would be the product of any number of communities across the globe each of which generated, for itself, human rights norms that would be locally valid initially. Later, in Part III, I show how locally valid human rights might be advanced in ways that would bring them ever nearer to universal validity, a validity not a priori but one achieved by ordinary men and women first of all in their communities.

Theological and metaphysical approaches might counter that my alternative cannot render human rights universally valid but valid only idiosyncratically and parochially, as rights that cannot rise to the level of *human* rights. Nonuniversal norms cannot do the work of human rights, metaphysical and theological theorists might argue. Curiously, such critics would find unexpected support from a viewpoint neither theological nor metaphysical: in anthropology. This is not to say that anthropology seeks norms universally valid a priori; it doesn't. Rather, anthropology, or at least prominent strands within it, argues that local norms are unlikely to have any extralocal purchase and certainly no universal purchase – short of their coercive imposition in an act of "cultural imperialism," that is, one belief system's coercive imposition on another.

Anthropologists are peculiarly sensitive to issues of cultural difference. They call attention to practices, most often in non-Western communities, regarded as unjust by many observers. Even if unintentionally, some anthropological studies implicitly invite criticism by outsiders intent on protecting those whom they view as victims. By "presenting the offensive practice in its full cultural context," the anthropologist may reveal its "latent functions in addition to its manifest or stated functions" and so "provide valuable information about how to control or prevent the practice" (Salmon 1997:61). To be sure, anthropologists are subject to professional codes of conduct. To their human research subjects they are obliged to declare sponsorship, research objectives and methods, and the degree of confidentiality available; to material cultures they can offer preservation and protection. As individuals, anthropologists may feel bound not only by the institutionalized norms of their profession but also by personal convictions that reject everything from misuse of their subjects to the legacies of colonial exploitation.

As a system of beliefs, social science, and anthropology in particular, makes claims that it regards as generally valid. The discipline of social science is a cultural construction that would make generally valid claims about other cultural constructions. For culture is a human artifact, a provenance always particular: artifacts are the work of particular groups at particular times in particular places. And so it is that many cultural expressions are plausible only locally; most are relative in their claims to validity. Cultural relativism entails moral relativism. Moral relativism, though empirically plausible, is often politically and socially problematic with respect to the rights and obligations of groups and individuals. Like all social sciences, the discipline of anthropology wrestles with relativism when it confronts the Janus-faced quality of cultural norms. In their regard for others' beliefs, practices, traditions, and material culture as inherently interesting and valuable, anthropologists promote respect for many of them. Yet they are hardly morally indifferent to all they observe in culture and community and sometimes are repulsed by what they discover. This Janus-faced quality found striking expression sixty years ago when what the United Nations claimed as universal human rights collided with what the American Anthropological Association interpreted as cultural imperialism. As the UN drafted its *Universal Declaration of Human Rights* in 1947, the AAA – a professional organization dedicated to the study of profound and enduring cultural difference – disputed the notion of rights valid across all cultural boundaries. It sought to discourage the drafting committee accordingly: "How can the proposed *Declaration* be applicable to all human beings and not be a statement of rights conceived only in terms of values prevalent in the countries of Western Europe and America?" After all, "what is held to be a human right in one society may be regarded as anti-social by another people, or by the same people in a different period of their history."[1]

The discouragement rests on two assumptions and one entailment. The assumptions: that any rights claim is necessarily a cultural claim and that cultural "validity" can only be local because no single cultural system is universally embraced.[2] The entailment: that unless human rights are somehow acultural, some rights claims will conflict with some aspects of the respective self-understandings of some cultures beyond the ones making those claims. If all rights are cultural constructs, then no right is culture free. Or so the AAA argued in 1947. Fifty years on, it changed its position. It now claims that every person, regardless of native culture or local community, does indeed possess universal rights simply as a human, quite regardless of differences among humans' cultures so intriguingly significant as to justify a discipline of cultural anthropology.[3] Yet the AAA's statement provides no reasons as to how it is that all persons possess human rights regardless of culture. Nor does it explain why its arguments from 1947 are mistaken. It cannot tell anthropologists "whether their responsibility ends with describing the practice and placing it in a cultural context, whether they are obligated to protect the practice from outside interference, or whether they should help to end the practice" (Salmon 1997:56–57). It cannot say whether "they have a further responsibility to protect, or at least not interfere with, this culturally sanctioned practice." It does not know whether "they must also consider their responsibility to cooperate with members of their own culture who are trying to end the practice on the grounds that human rights are being violated" (Salmon 1997:57). The AAA simply sought to dissolve by declaration what remains a philosophical and legal puzzle, but also a political problem, at least for human rights advocates.

The philosophical puzzle confronts social scientific and humanistic explanations in their quest to defend nonidiosyncratic claims: If there are no value-free spheres, just how valid can even the most rigorously

---

[1] AAA (1947:539, 542).

[2] By *valid* I mean that which, within a culture, marks an idea, belief, or practice in ways that members recognize and, to varying degrees, identify with.

[3] AAA (1999).

vetted social-scientific knowledge be? And if a morally neutral or value-free understanding of human behavior is impossible, what can we really know about ourselves as cultural beings? The same puzzle arises for legal practice and jurisprudence: in the quest for legal justice, given the necessity to interpret legal rules and other norms and because interpretation is perspectival in its possible validity, is justice possible only as something relatively valid? If so, how should we behave with respect to adjudication in cases in which one right conflicts with another?

The political problem follows from the assertion that human rights can only be a particular, culturally specific vision of the individual's moral worth. The problem also follows from the assertion that human rights can only be a particular determination of the moral parameters limiting how the political community may or may not treat the individual.[4] The problem is that the very idea of human rights, as commonly understood, implies a claim to *universal* validity. How does a community realize the potential for universal validity of a cultural construct that is valid only locally? Not by coercion, to be sure: the human rights idea would be contradicted by the coercive imposition of human rights. What then? I respond to these puzzles and problems with three claims: (1) locally valid human rights are possible as "normatively thin" claims; (2) they have critical potential; and (3) they can promote a community's self-representation, thereby allowing for diversity in ways that human rights as cultural imperialism cannot.

Particularisms: Thick and Thin

The idea of "human" rights invokes a claim to universal validity. But how can something universally valid be a matter of perspective and interpretation – which, as cultural artifacts, is all that human rights can be? The answer, I argue, rests on a notion of universal validity that is not a priori but rather contingent, an initially local validity that can become consensual over time. A locally valid norm can move toward consensus insofar as it moves from "thickness" to "thinness."[5] Both thick and thin norms can be codified and implemented through a legal system; both offer reference points for advocating some particular behaviors and beliefs

---

[4] In a world of nation-states populated by citizens, what is specific to "human rights" in distinction to "rights of the citizen" is that the former, even as culturally particular for those who embrace them, apply to the individual whether citizen, visitor, refugee, or stateless person.

[5] For a general theory of thick and thin norms, see Gregg (2003b).

as well as for decrying others. But whereas thin norms are widely generalizable, thick norms are not. If generalized to others, thick norms would violate identities, communities, and ways of life in their integrity and self-understanding. Violation is just what "cultural imperialism" refers to: one belief system's coercive imposition on another.

With this distinction in mind, let us return to the dispute a half century ago between the UN committee and the AAA, a dispute in the form of a "vicious circle of human rights." On the one hand, coercion offers itself as a means toward realizing the claim to universal validity, a claim raised by conventional conceptions of human rights. After all, if human rights are not valid for all humans, they are hardly "human" rights if by *human* one means "humankind" or "humanity." And if the idea of human rights is either rejected by many communities or understood by many in ways that are mistaken, force might seem a necessary, if unfortunate, means toward realizing the spread of human rights. On the other hand, as social constructions, human rights can be valid only locally, at least to begin with. To treat them as universally valid a priori is to pursue the human rights project in a way that undermines it: coercively. To treat human rights as thick norms is to treat them as a compulsive means to an end that abjures all compulsion.

I would break this impasse by attempting universal validity as something embraced universally but *only contingently*. Norms of *eventual* universal validity can be derived from particular cultural ideas and practices that initially are valid only locally. From normatively thick local norms I would derive a version of normatively thin human rights. Human rights so construed are generalizable beyond local origins, yet without coercion. They begin as a matter of local norms whose validity can still be more than local without being immediately universal.[6] Human rights are then neither discovered nor revealed; they can be socially constructed in ways that abstract from deep cultural particularism even as they themselves are culturally particular.[7] To be unable to escape particularism completely does not condemn us to its deepest forms. Nor does it preclude us from moving toward consensual agreement on this or that particular set of norms.

---

[6] The claim that human rights involve aspects of cultural imperialism (see, e.g., Bell 1996; Ghai 1994; Kennedy 2004; Mutua 1996; Rajagopal 2003) is not new; my proposal for human rights as a normatively thin construction is new.

[7] Shue (1980:178, n. 13) formulates what might be thought a normatively thin human rights culture as "basic human rights." He posits universal rights to security, subsistence, and liberty as rights without which no others are possible. This conception is normatively thin in the sense that it specifies the conditions (namely the three primary rights) for the plethora of secondary rights that might constitute a particular human rights regime. But it cannot specify those secondary rights themselves.

I show that normatively thin human rights can be generated out of thick local norms: thin can be derived from thick, that is, locally valid thick norms (whether civil, political, economic, social, or cultural) can become thin, or at least thinner.[8] This thick-to-thin process is not likely to be linear. It is likely to be an interplay of goals immediately realizable and goals that remain aspirational, that is, realizable only progressively. Probably it would be an interplay of nonjusticiable claims that orient and direct political and social trends, on the one hand, and claims that *are* justiciable, on the other. Human rights so derived can motivate people insofar as people are more likely to embrace human rights because they are rooted in *local* cultural and political understandings.

Before attempting this derivation, I offer three clarifications. First, cultures and political communities are not homogeneous entities; all cultures and all communities are marked by internal tensions, disagreements, and contradictions. To reduce the complexity of my analysis, I treat culture and community without regard to this aspect. Second, normative thickness is not specific to any particular culture: thick norms are found in all cultures.[9] There is, for example, nothing peculiarly Western or non-Western about them. Third, by "human rights" I mean more than the liberal individual rights championed prominently in the American and French revolutions. The Declarations of 1776 and 1789 each generated a notion of human rights as civil and political rights of the individual.[10] These rights are now often called the "first wave"

[8] Mine is not the only approach persuaded that human rights come about through some kind of process. But it does not argue that to become a human right, a norm is first "idealized," then conceptualized and/or positivized, and finally "realized" or institutionalized (Drzewicki 1995:172; Eide 1999:602–604; Donnelly 2003:§6.4), or that norms undergo a "process of more precise specification, starting with a broad, fairly abstract concept or ideal – for example, fair trial or social insurance – moving to more detailed conceptions, and finally acquiring precise institutional form (including, but not necessarily limited to, 'positivization' understood as justiciability)" (Donnelly 2007:49).

[9] Even if human rights are, as some maintain, a peculiarly Western artifact, precisely Western human rights activists have for years been fighting for the right, say, of the unrepresented to represent themselves (via elections, freedom of speech, and so forth). The imperialism charge against human rights is usually leveled by non-Western governmental elites championing every political community's right to be free of foreign aggression, domination, and occupation but also of unwanted, nonindigenous political beliefs, values, and practices.

[10] Civil and political rights find expression in the *Declaration of Independence* (1776), *la Déclaration des droits de l'homme et du citoyen* (1789), and in some of the amendments to the U.S. Constitution (particularly the Bill or Rights and the Fourteenth Amendment of 1868). These rights create a sphere of individual autonomy vis-à-vis the state: the right to private property but also to individual life, liberty, and, by implication, bodily integrity;

or "first generation" in the history of systematic human rights thinking. They are followed by the so-called second generation of ideas animating various socialist and labor movements in the last decades of the nineteenth century and the first decades of the twentieth.[11] A "third wave" conception followed from decolonization after World War II: notions of collective rights such as a community's right to socioeconomic development, a right to a safe environment (free from malaria or violence, say), or a "people's" right to political and cultural self-determination.[12] The first generation is not the only one promoted by the West. The United States recognizes the first and some of the second; the European Union (EU), the first and more of the second. But no state today wholly recognizes the third, and none recognizes all three as equally genuine human rights. Further, none treats social, cultural, and economic rights as immediately enforceable domestic law, although some regard them as aspirations or norms to guide public policy. Such nonrecognition hinders the realization of human rights

and freedom of belief and expression, of correspondence, assembly, and movement; and freedom from arbitrary detention and arrest. Together these various rights entail a far-reaching general right of legal equality of all citizens with respect to race, ethnicity, sex, language, religion, and national origin. In 1948, the UN General Assembly proclaimed a *Universal Declaration of Human Rights* in thirty articles. The first twenty-three guarantee many of the civil and political rights of the great eighteenth-century revolutions: equality; nondiscrimination; life, liberty, and security; no enslavement; no torture or degrading treatment; recognition as a person before the law; equality before the law; remedy by a competent tribunal; no arbitrary arrest or exile; fair and public hearing; innocent until proven guilty; privacy in the family, home, and correspondence; free movement; asylum from persecution; a nationality and freedom to change it; marriage and family; private property; freedom of belief and religion; opinion and information; peaceful assembly and association; political participation and free elections.

[11] I mean social and economic rights, including those to employment, shelter, food, and various forms of welfare (unemployment insurance, medical care, and education, for example). Five articles of the *Universal Declaration* speak to such rights: social security; desirable work and trade union membership; rest and leisure from work; an adequate standard of living; education. Whereas the "first wave" would free the individual from public tyranny (such as oppression by the state), the "second" would protect the individual from private tyranny and in particular from the vicissitudes of the market economy.

[12] The *Universal Declaration* includes two such rights: a right to participation in the cultural life of a community and the obligation to communal duties as essential to the individual's free and full development. Other international instruments declare additional group rights, including the self-determination of peoples (the UN Charter, 1945; the International Covenant on Civil and Political Rights, 1976; the International Covenant on Economic, Social and Cultural Rights, 1976); the legitimacy of anticolonial struggles (Declaration on the Granting of Independence to Colonial Countries and Peoples, 1960); and freedom from genocide (Convention on the Prevention and Punishment of the Crime of Genocide, 1949).

inasmuch as civil, political, economic, social, and cultural rights are likely to be interdependent. They may even be indivisible. The idea of human rights is multidimensional, after all. A right to fundamental equality with all other human beings, for example, involves freedom from oppression along multiple dimensions: political, economic, cultural, and so forth.[13] Again, for reasons of complexity reduction, I will not belabor this point.

How can human rights be a cultural particularism? A cultural particularism of only relative validity is normatively thick in that its validity is only local. It might find wider embrace the more normatively thin it can become. It might find universal embrace if it can become particularly thin. In the case of human rights, such an embrace would be a contingent construction by a plurality of political communities each with its own local norms. Thin local norms could be congruent in a number of ways. Some local norms might develop, as they were "thinned out," into human rights norms; some might be reinterpreted in ways normatively thin; some might be revealed, from a normatively thin standpoint, as always having been human rights norms.

If human rights are regarded as one normative particularism, then the task of the human rights project is to generate agreement on human rights in widely different cultural and political contexts in which the advocated rights are attuned to local distinctions, peculiarities, and preferences. That is, the cultural particularism of human rights needs to be attuned to the cultural particularisms of the target community. *To be attuned to* means pursuing normative thinness as a particularism that is (a) cultural and (b) nonparochial. My goal is to construct human rights in just this sense.

(a) Thin norms are themselves cultural particularisms, of course, but they travel better than thick norms, which are also particularisms. But not all particularisms are equally "particular." Although thin norms can be abstracted from thick ones, thick ones can hardly be based on thin ones. Note the clear directionality here: thin might be supported by thick, but thick cannot bind support for thin. Indeed, some thin norms

---

[13] The multidimensional politics of a moral human existence corresponds to the multidimensionality of human rights epistemology in a sense captured by Merton (1973:129): "We no longer ask whether it is the Insider or the Outsider who has monopolistic or privileged access to social knowledge; instead, we begin to consider their distinctive and interactive roles in the process of seeking truth." On the one hand, the observer's or outsider's perspective is not privileged over that of the participant or insider. On the other, one does not need to "be Caesar to understand Caesar" (according to Georg Simmel and Max Weber; see Runciman 1978:66).

may be abstracted from thick ones, but they cannot move irretrievably far from thick norms. Further, some thin norms allow for some thick norms. Proceduralism is one such thin norm: it presupposes participants' freedom and equality and an environment relatively free of systematic exclusion, fear, violence, and subordination that might undermine participation. It is morally minimalist, even amoral, because it entails no particular outcome. An organization like Amnesty International offers a different example of moral minimalism. It appeals to a repressive regime for the release of particular political prisoners without demanding that the regime accept the organization's comprehensive worldview. Strategic success is possible precisely on the basis of such moral minimalism.

Many a thick norm might be developed into some thinner alternative, however. For example, a norm that recognizes, in terms of freedom of belief and practice, religion X but no other faiths has, in recognizing the freedom of conscience for one religion, the potential to recognize that freedom for all religions: to move from recognizing the conscience of *one* religious community to recognizing the idea of *any* community's freedom of conscience. Similarly, a norm that recognizes all men, but not women, equally as humans has the potential, in its recognition of the very idea of equality, to recognize *both* equally as humans.

In this sense, inside most any particular culture is potential for a human rights consciousness – if the human rights idea can itself be understood as a cultural particularism, but one that is normatively thin, and if many a thick norm can be developed into thinner alternatives. Particular cultures have specific customs, histories, and memories as well as very particular conceptions of the social good. The idea of "humanity" (the idea of all human individuals taken together) is not specific in this sense. It is also normatively thin: after all, even as each person is always already embedded in particularist norms, each is simultaneously part of humanity. The notion of humanity is a cultural artifact, but one normatively thinner – hence more inclusive – than the cultural artifact of, say, Western literature, Islamic jurisprudence, or Confucian philosophy.

At the same time, members of the one are always members of the other; each member of the human species participates in these or those particular thick cultures even as there is no global thick culture. A thick culture of human rights might be spread by voluntary embrace, but this seems exceedingly unlikely inasmuch as it would require a far-reaching homogenization of the world's cultures and communities. Even advocates of normatively thin human rights are likely to reject reducing geographical regions and their inhabitants to a monolithic or internally undifferentiated culture, religion, or mentality. Homogenization is less likely to further human rights than to destroy them inasmuch as persons denied various forms of identity, including cultural identity, are thereby denied the capacity to bear rights. I develop this argument in later pages where I advocate a human right of self-representation and cultural self-determination.

(b) Human rights culture, even as normatively thin, remains a cultural particularism. But cultural particularism as such need not defeat cosmopolitan goals. Even cultural understandings that are distinct from one another in their particularity are not immune from one another's perspectives and criticism. As Edward Said suggests, the "answer to Orientalism is not Occidentalism. No former 'Oriental' will be comforted . . . to study new 'Orientals' – or 'Occidentals' – of his own making" (Said 1994:328). A "former Oriental" can forbear subjecting others (including the subjectors) to what he or she has been subjected to. That is, even if all possible standpoints are ethnocentric to some extent, those that can become less so might eventually develop into nonparochial particularisms.

Not possible is some transcendental meta-viewpoint allowing for a completely nonethnocentric comparison of two or more different viewpoints. Such a vantage is not necessary, however, *if* particularism can be nonparochial – and standpoints not deeply ethnocentric *can* be nonparochial. Such a standpoint will not be *universally* valid, but it need not be; it is enough that it can be *more-than-locally* valid, valid as normatively thin human rights culture. Perhaps no culture is without some elements compatible with human rights in the sense of the idea of reciprocity as central to justice. And perhaps no culture is without some elements compatible with human rights in the sense of all cultures' sensitivity to human suffering. Further, no culture renders its members wholly insensitive to emotional and physical abuse perpetrated against others: victims of human rights abuses "generally resent what is done to them" and "would rarely concede that, because such behavior is common in their country, their tormentors are acting quite properly" (Scanlon 1979:88).

As I earlier claimed, not all particularisms are equally "particular." Even as a particularism, the human rights idea can rise above parochialism because, unlike nationalism, capitalism, or democracy – to name three of the most powerful phenomena of modernity, each of somewhat particular cultural origin – it is not au fond a response to particular contingencies of particular historical epochs.

How can normative thinness be more than parochial yet less than universal? The particular cultural origins of human rights and their cultural embeddedness need not preclude their eventually gaining a status of more-than-local validity, even universal validity (again, as an empirically observable, historically contingent development rather than something a priori). The thick-to-thin process is open-ended and implies no extremes. That is, some culturally particular norms can become less thick and more thin, or they can become less parochial and more cosmopolitan. And the possibility of their becoming so does not presuppose some apex of "absolute thinness," "complete cosmopolitanism," or a climax otherwise entirely free of particularism (such end points are notions of doubtful coherence, anyway). A dynamic work in progress has no fixed and perfect end point; it is always pragmatic, never Platonic. This process is open-ended in the sense of the "reiterative activity" of architects who, according to Michael Walzer, do not aim at designing buildings so "right" as to render all future architecture unnecessary: "Rightness is relative to the architectural occasion: the needs that the building is intended to serve, the materials at hand, the reigning aesthetic idealism" (Walzer 1994:52). Each architect may attempt the "right" building but not the same "right" building or not a building "right" in the way that other buildings might be "right." Each inevitably falls short (perhaps each in its own way), and each building "immediately becomes an object of critical reflection and debate – models for the future that are imitated or revised or rejected. Indeed, they are imitated *and* revised *and* rejected, in endlessly reiterated architectural efforts with endlessly differentiated results" (Walzer 1994:52).

Pretensions to a thick-to-thin process more open-ended than this would only hide or deny cultural particularism.[14] And as hidden and denied, particularism can function in ways hegemonic and imperialistic. It can assert the speaker's moral superiority and thereby legitimize the speaker's aggression toward the addressee. By contrast, the thick-to-thin process doesn't deny human rights' constitutive imbrications with culture – which is to say, it doesn't deny the moral relativism of human rights. And yet the moral sky does not fall on the moral relativist. On the contrary, relativism allows for human rights, constructed as culturally particular, as more than locally valid. Relativism need not, as James Nickel says it must, deny the "possibility of trans-cultural moral criticism that appeals to international

---

[14] Cheah and Robbins (1998) chart developments toward a "new cosmopolitanism" they take to be less vulnerable to my critique; I remain unpersuaded.

human rights to create a shared standard of argument" (Nickel 1987:71). (I address the critical potential of locally valid human rights below, under the rubric "critical capacity of local norms.") Relativism *can* create shared standards. It can do so because it can be open to cultural consensus as long as that consensus is achieved by the participants themselves. For instance, given a high degree of overlap and hybridization among various cultures, some cultural claims might well be "universal" in the sense of describing cultural phenomena very widely embraced – the validity of natural scientific claims, for example, at least as a body of information taught in local schools and employed by local engineers and physicians.

How can human rights, as a cultural particularism, be expandable in their validity yet without coercion? As I reconceive it, the project for human rights aims not, as often thought, to establish a relationship between the normative universalism of human rights and the normative particularism of a given political community. If human rights are one particularism among others, then human rights advocacy promotes one particularism over others. It champions an increasingly generalizable particularism (human rights) over particularisms not easily generalized for any number of reasons (think of cultural particularisms such as traditions of female genital mutilation or child labor or prostitution legitimized by filial duty toward impoverished parents, examples I explore in Chapter 7).

If it is to advance the cause of human rights, a relationship between two particularisms cannot be compelled. Forced implementation negates the normative foundation of the very human rights culture it would found. The logic of this claim can be made clear in counterargument. Kant offers an indirect one. (The argument is "indirect" because he is speaking with respect to political community rather than human rights, but the structure of his argument can be applied to human rights without violating the integrity of that structure.) Kant sees no self-contradiction in the coercive generation of a noncoercive polity. Because a constitution, as the distributive unity of the "will of all," by itself cannot preserve peace, Kant posits a need for the collective unity of all. This unity is not state based but global; it is a kind of generalized civil society: "Before so difficult a problem can be solved, *all men together* (i.e. the collective unity of the combined will) must desire to attain this goal; only then can *civil society* exist as a single whole. Since an additional unifying cause *must therefore overrule the differences in the particular wishes* of all individuals before a common will can arise, and since no single individual can create" the unifying cause, the "only conceivable way of executing the original idea in practice, and hence of inaugurating a state of right, is *by force*. On its coercive authority, public right will subsequently be based" (Kant 1997:117; emphases added). I would reformulate this passage in terms of my concern with human rights, but within the logic of Kant's argument: A coerced unity at the highest nonlocal level is the precondition for a plurality of local communities that, although still differing from each other, can all be human rights communities. That is, the idea of human rights can be a local norm in every one of these different communities only if that idea is established – by force, if necessary – prior to or as a condition of an allowable local community.

By Kantian logic, then, a forcible approach would be needed for human rights conceived as thick norms to be imposed in place of other thick norms. This is just what *normatively thick* human rights entail: rights uniform across diverse communities because they will have imported their own culture into each of these communities. By contrast, my proposal for human rights conceived as *thin norms* allows that different communities can each realize an embrace of human rights as a kind of "open culture." As open culture, human rights can assume many of a variety of particular forms, depending on their specific venue and the particular political culture in which they are enforced.[15] In short, normatively thin human rights do not require coercive promotion. They entail prodding, perhaps, but not involuntary enforcement or imposition, even in a world of politics, power, and social stratification.[16]

Critical Capacity of Local Norms

This capacity for critique is central to the argument for human rights as social constructions initially valid only locally. The possibility of critique means that the putative incommensurability of different cultures – as the AAA claimed in 1947, challenging the UN's conception of universal human rights – need not entail an uncritical tolerance of just about

[15] They cannot, of course, assume all forms. To be coherent, a pluralistic approach, including cultural relativism, must have limits even as people may disagree as to where to draw them. The Taliban's systematic discrimination against women would not be compatible with any plausible form of human rights because it effectively excludes half of humanity from membership in the very "humanity" to which the idea of human rights presumably is addressed.

[16] Put differently, an imperialist and an anti-imperialist would affirm diametrically opposite positions. From a normatively thin standpoint, the anti-imperialist would reject the coercive enforcement of human rights, not their coercion-free promotion.

anything. For example, it needn't entail the impossibility of intersubjective meaning.[17] Cross-community and transcultural communication is intersubjective. To be sure, the notion of locally valid human rights does entail the *partial* subjectivism of a culture's own horizons, or the *partial* parochialism of a culture's beliefs, or the *partial* provincialism of a culture's claims.[18] The point, however, is that relativism, subjectivism, and parochialism need not defeat the project for human rights any more than the project is defeated by the contingency, cultural embeddedness, or contextual specificity of any given culture or any given political community. Relativism and parochialism allow for local consciousness of some independence, critique, even opposition. They allow it through a self-correcting normative perspective. In later pages I elaborate these features as aspects of an "objectivating stance" toward other communities or cultures.

The relativism of locally valid human rights does not preclude the possibility of creating shared standards of argument and judgment; it does not preclude plausible criticism across political communities or cultures. This possibility rests on the capacity of locally valid human rights for what I call "indigenous critique." By *indigenous* I refer to a normative standpoint internal to a community or culture. If norms are always already culturally embedded, then this or that norm is always already vulnerable to violation, internally or externally. A culturally *internal* violation damages rights recognized by the violating culture itself; a culturally *external* one injures rights not recognized by the violating culture. In terms of culture, something internal is likely something indigenous. Hence an internal violation is likely a violation of the indigenous. Correspondingly, an internal critique is a critique of something indigenous to the community or culture in question.

If construed in normatively thin ways, human rights norms can generate a normatively thin standard by which to evaluate indigenous practices, as I now show in terms of an objectivating stance. The same standard would allow a human rights standpoint to identify violative practices as culturally internal. Such an imminent critique would seek to advance human rights locally (not universally), and could do so without

---

[17] A point that Ricoeur (1969) made long ago.
[18] For human rights to be more than a parochial culture without being cosmopolitan is akin to Parekh's (2000:113) notion of a political liberalism capacious enough to comfortably include nonliberal elements. Turn this argument over and one finds on the obverse the promise of Rawls's notion of a decent hierarchical society: a nonliberal society that can be tolerant nonetheless.

coercion or imperialism. In so doing, it would deploy human rights as local standards rather than universal ones.

A rights claim can trump local understandings by a warrant itself normatively thin. For example, publics might hold each other accountable for observing commonly accepted rule formulations. Human rights publics across the globe might establish interconnections through partially shared political understandings, moral orientations, perhaps even ways of life if they discover that in some ways they are similar to some other communities in some beliefs and some practices. To avoid coercion and imperialism, members of each community might not hold members of *all* other communities accountable, but only those members who share the same normatively thin conception of human rights. They might do so even as they denounce communities they find wanting on the grounds that no one should be denied human rights because of an accident of birth into an illiberal, intolerant culture, polity, or religion.

And if, under conditions of normative relativism, a political community is capable of *internal* critique, it is capable also of reasonably criticizing *other* political communities. It is possible as one particularism taking an objectivating stance toward another. That is, any culture has a capacity to reflect on itself, to assume a hypothetical stance toward itself. Its members can take this stance toward their culture's traditions, understandings, and preoccupations. To be sure, a culture cannot jump over its own shadow: its hypothetical stance toward itself will still be internal; it will still describe itself in its own vocabulary. But if one cultural particularism can assume an objectivating critical attitude toward itself, then it can assume such an attitude toward other cultural particularisms. In short, a normatively thin human rights culture does not preclude an objectivating stance of one political community toward others.

How can an objectivating attitude facilitate a critical capacity? When a human being responds to another person, he or she can do so only because he or she has learned, through the lifelong process of being socialized into communal life, to respond to a "generalized social other." According to George Herbert Mead, the "individual experiences himself as such, not directly but only indirectly, from the particular standpoints of other individual members of the same social group or from the generalized standpoint of the social group as a whole to which he belongs" (Mead 1967:138).

The generalized aspect of the generalized other is its universal quality: it refers to all human others as such. Humans regularly think in terms of universals: the idea of a human being as such, for example, or of a right as such (notions that come together in the concept of "human rights"). Intersubjectivity in the form of discourse depends on our capacity to share such universals as commonly understood meanings. "To share" entails each participant taking the attitudes of others toward him- or herself, then "crystallizing all these particular attitudes into a single attitude or standpoint which may be called that of the 'generalized other'" (Mead 1967:90). Each of us can be affected by the attitude of any particular person because each of us has learned to be affected by "persons as such," by the generalized other. Each of us can generate in others our own attitude in part because that other person has similarly learned through socialization to take the attitude of the generalized other. One has the same reaction, or would behave the same way, as most any other person in similar circumstances. The institution of private property, for example, rests on the mutual recognition of property rights; such recognition is a matter of every member of the community taking the attitude of all others.

Social cooperation requires a shared set of habits of response. For example, under various circumstances, all members of a community likely react the same way to the individual – say, a thief: theft is the same phenomenon whether committed by *this* person or *that* one. But the individual's shared set of habits does not extinguish individualism: the "way in which individuals act under specific circumstances gives rise to all of the individual differences which characterize the different persons" (Mead 1967:198).

The individual's socialization inculcates patterns of belief and behavior promoted by the socializing community and culture. Some of the patterns are universally shared, such as recognizing other people as human beings rather than as animals morally or intellectually inferior. Different individuals share similar patterns of expected behavior and anticipated experience. Patterns within the individual more or less reflect patterns within human interaction in general. The isomorphic quality of that refection allows for wide differences and variations among individuals and for distinctive individuality: different persons are affected by different aspects of the pattern or are affected in different ways by the same aspects. After all, each approaches the pattern from a unique viewpoint "within the whole process of organized social behavior which exhibits this pattern" (Mead 1967:202).

Here we have a kind of perspectivalism at the level of knowledge. Mead identifies a relativism also at the level of the individual's "normative constitution." That is, individuals have social values that attach to them in

ways peculiar to them, even as those values are social not private phenomena. Any yet no one is simply or necessarily bound by the values, and in
principle anyone can criticize them, reject them, or entertain alternative
values. We can do so "only insofar as we can call out in ourselves the
response of the community; we only have ideas insofar as we are able
to take the attitude of the community and then respond to it" (Mead
1967:180). The individual assumes in him- or herself the attitude of one
or the other group, responds to that attitude, and alters that attitude in
the way he or she responds to it. In this way, the individual's attitude
affect his or her social environment.

This reciprocity is the foundation for an objectivating stance that possesses critical potential. Self-consciousness inheres in the individual's
ability to take the attitude of others, indeed of others who themselves
have the same ability, such that responses within a community are patterned in the sense of raising common expectations in each individual of other persons – expectations that are justified if they are often
enough met. The individual views him- or herself from the perspective of this or that person, and these perspectives together endow him
or her with a certain social self. To see oneself in this way is to be
aware of one's differences from others. Consciousness of differences
between the individual's viewpoint, circumstances, or behavior and those
of another individual raises questions of comparison, such as: Which is
more preferable and by what criteria? Depending on how such questions
are answered, the individual may find points to criticize either in his
or her case or in that of others (or in both). From criticism, change
sometimes follows. One imagines an alternative to the status quo of
one's community by engaging one's own opinion and criticizing those of
others.

Here Mead offers a way of seeing how one socially constructed particularism, such as one culture or community, can assume an objectivating
stance toward another: by taking the attitude of the other and thereby
relativizing one's own attitude. This is to move from moral maximalism
to a goal-oriented moral minimalism whereby "no particular maximum
is the sole source of the moral minimum, let alone of all the other maxi-
mums" (Walzer 1994:13). This standpoint is normatively thin. To assume
a moral minimum is to begin from a deep particularism and to move in
the direction of a norm that is less particular and more generalizable. It
is to work within a tradition even while reaching beyond it through self-
interpretation, indeed through a kind of immanent critique. It is to call
into question the local and the indigenous; it is to expose tensions and

contradictions internal to a thick perspective yet without abandoning the local, the thick, the particular.

A political community can work *in its own way* toward a culture more oriented toward human rights, and toward human rights more thin than thick. Although thick norms remain at the center of all cultures and political communities, in each case the "growing" of local human rights ideas, attitudes, and orientations can lead to the spread of a normatively thin human rights culture. Such a culture would not constitute a cosmopolitan language but rather a state-based one of "networking mutually intelligible and translatable native languages of emancipation" into each other (Sousa Santos 2002:227). Human rights could then spread internally, community by community, perhaps even state by state. To be sure, "native languages of emancipation" will not all conceive of emancipation in the same way. They may overlap to some extent, however, inasmuch as the putative civil and political rights of the individual are related inextricably to putative social and economic rights as well as to putative cultural rights.

Such a learning process might contribute to rendering human rights more and more the everyday language of an increasing number of political communities, despite all their diversity, across the globe. It might contribute to a community's own political goals. Worst-case scenario: a community might regard human rights as a very distant goal. Best-case scenario: a community that develops some of its thicker norms into thinner norms may discover, like Moliere's *Bourgeois Gentilhomme*, that it has been speaking "prose" (human rights language) all along. Or it may persuade itself that reaching the point of speaking and acting on human rights language is not too distant from what the community at any given time finds culturally acceptable.

Anti-Imperialism by Means of Local Self-Representation

"Human rights imperialism" can be thought of as either Orientalizing or Occidentalizing. By *Orientalizing* I mean an asymmetrical relationship in which the representing culture assigns and the represented culture merely resigns. It resigns itself to being more or less marginalized by the representing culture. The coherence of such representation depends on the representing culture; likely it provides the most powerful, perhaps the only, version available to its judges. Representation in this sense simply ignores, dismisses, or represses the self-understanding of the represented culture. A normatively thick human rights approach might Occidentalize political liberalism, just as it might Orientalize the illiberal Other. A normatively thin human rights understanding would not Orientalize Western civilization and its notion of human rights as an ideological fiction. Nor would it Occidentalize non-Western civilizations and their respective notions of human rights. It would not dismiss human rights goals – such as habeas corpus, education for women, freedom from torture, or prohibition of slavery – as merely one more imperialism.

Orientalization and Occidentalization are forms of representation. Each misrepresents in the sense of "cultural imperialism": one belief system's coercive imposition of its own thick norms on another, usually disguised as a moral particularism pretending to universal validity. In this sense, human rights construed in normatively thick ways then "represent" other cultures as incapable of representing themselves: they Orientalize them. So construed, human rights implicitly represent themselves as morally entitled, even compelled, to advocate this particular human rights perspective throughout the world, sometimes by coercion if need be, that is, regardless of local preference and understanding.

To be sure, advocacy is not inherently imperialistic, but coercive advocacy can be imperialistic. Human rights advocacy is of that kind if understood to imply its own moral duty, even prerogative, to reform and manage political communities with different moral orders – precisely because those communities do not satisfy the standards, do not meet the cultural preferences, of the representing culture (in this case, the culture of human rights as thick norms). Human rights of this sort cast other understandings, perhaps even the communities that hold them, as morally needy, sometimes to the point of "needing" intervention by a thick human rights culture.

Representation of this sort is a power relationship. It not only distinguishes the speaker's world from that of the addressee, it also creates a "directionality," a one-way discourse *from* the representing party *to* the one represented.[19] Human rights then certify the speaker's moral superiority: cultural preferences for human rights are morally superior to all competing cultural predelictions. Representation assumes a

---

[19] "One way" means a monologue, not a dialogue. A monologue precludes, for example, deploying the "resources of the Islamic tradition and question[ing] many of the liberal political categories and principles," rejecting "liberal conceptions of individual autonomy, human rights, and individual freedom" for an Islam interpreted as opposed to such conceptions (Mahmood 2004:75). I say (controversially to some Muslims): "*An* Islam," that is, a particular version among all the versions that make up "Islam." From this perspective, no one version may be taken to preclude all alternative versions.

patronizing stance toward that which is being represented, like an outsider telling locals what their moral worth is. Marx captures this sense of
locals who cannot represent themselves (*cannot* in the sense of "are incapable of"); they can only be represented by others (Marx 1975:307).[20]
Because the "aggrieved" or "benighted" cannot represent themselves, a
thick human rights culture must speak for them. Human rights of this
sort manipulate targeted communities or cultures already in the way it
represents them.

Representation contains within itself the potential for force in the
sense of unilateral intervention. A putatively universally valid cultural
claim may sometimes justify unilateral intervention into the cultural
understandings and practices of particular communities. Such a claim
would have the target community transform itself or would itself transform it to be more compatible with human rights conceived as thick
norms.

The core, then, of human rights imperialism is the coercive (mis)re-
presentation of the target community or culture. It is an outsider telling
the locals who they are and how they must change to suit the standards
of – whom else? – the outsider. It constructs the represented as incapable
of self-representation, like a puppet, without capacity for understanding
grand moral imperatives such as human rights.[21] Represented as incapable of representing itself, a political or cultural community can develop
a sense of its identity only negatively. Its moral worth is assigned by the
representer: thickly construed human rights that reject and condemn
other cultural communities and render mainly negative verdicts on the
represented. If the only standpoint that counts is that of the representer, then the represented cultural and political communities can hardly
count on a favorable verdict from a representer who self-appointedly sits
in judgment on them.[22]

---

[20] "Sie können sich nicht vertreten, sie müssen vertreten werden."

[21] A people so represented might be thought analogous to individuals diagnosed as mentally
ill: both lack the moral capacity to be members of the community (of citizens or of
nations) and hence might be thought to warrant paternalism (see Campbell 1986:144–
145). One wonders: If moral lack is defined in terms of norms not shared by the person
(or society or culture) being judged, may socially conditioned standards of "normality"
then justly be imposed on the person (society, culture) who does not regard his or her
condition as undesirable? The criteria for paternalistic nonvoluntary treatment might
be narrowed. In human rights terms, one might advocate unilateral intervention to stop
grave violations of residents' human rights but not to reengineer a particular culture and
society.

[22] For example, a dominant culture *marginalizes* a weaker one by claiming to understand
the subject culture in a way superior to that culture's self-understanding (see, e.g., AAA

By contrast, human rights thinly construed can be compatible with the principle of a political community's self-determination. For localism not universalism means normative relativism not normative universalism. Relativism has a (not unlimited) capacity for respecting the autonomy of political and cultural communities. Respect for autonomy is respect for diversity, though in one sense and not another. It is not respect for diversity in cases where human rights would be violated. As a matter of self-coherence, the idea of human rights must reject its own violation, hence also any moral conceptions incompatible with human rights. The proselytization of religion X in a community where religion Y is widely practiced, or an institutional requirement that pupils learn language Z rather than their mother tongue, would diminish diversity likely without benefit to the targeted community. By contrast, diversity is served by deploying, say, Western medicine to cure diseases outside the West because doing so preserves lives and thereby local culture and ways of life. Respect for autonomy *is* respect for diversity even when the reduction of diversity is the *insider's* goal: when the local community freely welcomes non-native institutions, beliefs, or practices. In this case outsiders cannot object to the local community's self-generated loss of diversity.[23]

What resources might facilitate human rights as locally valid social constructions? John Rawls articulates a common understanding of human rights: they "do not depend on any particular comprehensive religious doctrine or philosophical doctrine of human nature." Rather, he says, they are culturally neutral. What's more, they are universal as the "necessary conditions of any system of social cooperation" (Rawls 1999b:68). By contrast, I've argued that the human rights idea is a particular cultural preference. At any given time it distinguishes "us" from "them." It does so in the sense of "we human rights partisans" as distinguished from "those partisans of human rights differently conceived," "those who conceive of human rights as universally valid," "those with different cultural preferences," or "those who simply reject the human rights idea."

But the human rights idea does not distinguish liberal from non-liberal communities. Rawls agrees on this point, if only in part: he argues for "preserving significant room for the idea of a people's self-determination," a claim that doesn't distinguish between different kinds of communities deserving or possessing a right to self-determination

---

1947:540). And a dominant culture *manages* a weaker one by asserting that the subject culture cannot know what is in its best interests.

[23] Sometimes the preservation of diversity is the outsider's goal, not the insider's.

(Rawls 1999b:61). Yet he implicitly construes political liberalism in terms of universal validity: "Liberal peoples must try to encourage decent peoples and not frustrate their vitality by coercively insisting that all societies be liberal" (Rawls 1999b:62). Even as Rawls makes clear that human rights do not require a liberal organization of society, liberal peoples are the tutors here; liberal society is here the standard against which other societies are measured in what might be called their "present capacity for human rights."

A normatively thin approach differently configures the relationship between the liberal West and nonliberal parts of the world.[24] The problem of human rights is Western when the actors are Western; the problem is non-Western when the actors are non-Western. For "them" to become more like "us" would be for them to *embrace human rights as thin norms*.[25] But to do so, they would not have to *become like us culturally in some deep sense*: to embrace human rights, people need not adopt liberal democracy, Enlightenment reason, or Western modernity. They might constitute nonliberal human rights communities instead. The liberal West might expose them to a normatively thin human rights culture and to cultural cues encouraging the adoption of human rights norms – but on grounds local, not universal or otherwise nonindigenous (from which point their normative force might one day extend to, and bind, more and most and even all communities). Some forms of local change, change that would aid the local human rights project, are not always themselves

---

[24] The notion of cultural superiority is not peculiarly Western. Human rights conceived as a Western cultural particularism is Western because it emphasizes, say, individual autonomy over group rights, or it favors political liberalism over other conceptions of political community. After all, although major non-Western cultures claim cultural superiority for themselves (Chinese, Indian, and Islamic, among others), they expressly do not do so on the basis of political liberalism. Human rights proponents from all cultures criticize some Western governmental and business behaviors as human rights violating. The grounds of such criticism do not presuppose liberal democratic culture. And some social theorists, harking back to the *L'Anneé Sociologique* during Émile Durkheim's editorship in the first two decades of the twentieth century, interpret the need for universal norms of human decency (i.e., human rights) to be a critical response to Western civilization with its liberal capitalist economics.

[25] Sometimes "compliance with [some] human rights norms may require not a change of practices but merely an expansion of existing practices" (Nickel 1987:78). Or a society whose religious beliefs mandate respect for the individual, tolerance for persons of other beliefs, or equal justice for all provides plausible bases for enhancing a normatively thin conception of human rights. Hollenbach (1982) suggests as much in the case of Islam. Consider as well nongovernmental organizations (NGOs), some of which have international memberships from different sociopolitical "cultures" in the sense of those advocating equality for women, or equality for homosexuals, or environmentalism.

deeply cultural: a regime's callousness to the populace's welfare, on the negative side or, on the positive, procedures for political bargaining and compromise that do not require the participants' allegiance in ways that might compromise participants' identity and self-respect. *That* would be human rights advocacy without cultural imperialism.

The question is: How do we get there? I begin to answer this question in the following two chapters. They explore two seemingly unlikely but, in fact, quite promising resources for constructing this-worldly human rights whose advocacy would be quite free of any form of outside or inside coercion: first, the cultural and political dynamics of a "human rights–capable" personality, and then the neuropsychological dynamics of human rights–supportive emotions.

THIS-WORLDLY RESOURCES FOR HUMAN RIGHTS AS SOCIAL CONSTRUCTION

4

Cultural Resources

Individuals as Authors of Human Rights

Chapters 1 and 2 rejected traditional otherworldly foundations for human rights, specifically various theological and metaphysical understandings of human rights as universally valid a priori. Chapter 3 developed an alternative approach: human rights as initially valid only locally – valid only where locally embraced, and embraced because authored by their addressees. So conceived, human rights are this-worldly even as they retain a capacity for eventual, contingent, universal validity. This and the next chapter, which together form Part II, develop two practical resources – one cultural, one biological – for generating this-worldly human rights from local norms. This chapter develops the first of these resources: human personality as a product of socialization and capable of granting itself human rights. Such an approach can only be welcome given that we have no evidence that human rights exist independently of human imagination and social constructions, which is to say: no evidence that humans are endowed with pre-political, universally valid rights a priori. Why anyone might hope for such evidence is obvious: it might endow the human rights idea with moral objectivity and universal validity. At the same time, it would relieve humans of the burden of moral invention. (And what might weigh more heavily than providing for the moral welfare of all others?) Most efforts to provide such evidence claim a theological or metaphysical origin. They have never worked. This is still an issue because those efforts are again and again renewed instead of abandoned. But if, as I propose, human rights are regarded as cultural artifacts – socially constructed, contingently valid – then they appear as preferences of distinct human cultures at particular times in history.[1]

---

[1] A social constructionist approach challenges a number of contemporary authors. For example, an otherworldly notion of "sacredness" forms the core of Perry's (2007) recent

87

To view them this way accords with viewing humans themselves as "cultural products" – insofar as they bear rights. To be "human," says Hannah Arendt, is to be "political" in the sense of consciously having responsibilities to one's community. Hence a person outside that community (the refugee or stateless person, for example) is not "political" but merely a "human being in general," subsisting in the existentially diminished condition of no political status or legal rights. The "loss of human rights... coincides with the instant when a person becomes a human being in general – without a profession, without a citizenship, without an opinion, without a deed by which to identify and specify himself" (Arendt 1994:302). Men without political community are "only men" in the sense that Giorgio Agamben (2005) describes as "la nuda vita" and Jacques Rancière (2004:298) as the "rights of those who are only human beings, who have no more property left than the property of being human." But once in possession of those particular cultural constructs that are rights, the individual can be a good deal more than his or her merely biological self.

Arendt is right to regard a communal life of shared responsibilities as the main venue for human rights: if available at all, then they are available *only in political community* (or rather, in certain types of political community). Only there can cultural constructs protect the individual's *physical* well-being, including a right to the satisfaction of basic needs with respect to food, shelter, and basic medical care and a right not to be killed or to be subjected to gratuitous pain. Only in political community can cultural constructs protect the individual's *psychological* well-being through personal liberties of speech, association, and conscience.[2] But Arendt is mistaken in rendering human rights as (a) derivable solely from the state and (b) separate from nonpublic or private life.

(a) On the one hand, human rights may be profoundly related to the state and its legislative and legal systems, which can introduce human rights into a community's daily life and there enforce them. The state can

---

contribution to a long-standing debate about whether human rights require a specifically theological foundation (a debate robust already in the work of John Locke [1632–1704] or John Finnis [born 1940]). Human rights for Perry follow from an inherent and inalienable "sacredness of human beings." It grounds the moral capacity of all human beings, their moral equality with each other and their moral obligation to one another, including the obligation of human rights. Similar arguments have been advanced by other contemporary authors, including Murphy (1988), Gaita (1991), and Hampton (1998), all of whom I discuss in Chapter 1.

[2] Beyond such basic rights might be a right to education, free choice of employment, and equal pay for equal work, among other possibilities.

mobilize relevant resources and allocate support to a network of human rights bearers. And human rights are best defended within a system of states and in the interstices of such systems, often at the temporary intersection of particular social movements and as a response not only local but sometimes international.

On the other hand, consider Edmund Burke (1999) who, at the end of the eighteenth century, rejects revolutionary France's *Déclaration des droits de l'homme et du citoyen* (1789), asking rhetorically: "Do we ground such respect for universal human rights in nature, in history, or in human rationality?" None of these, he answers, for the abstract "rights of man" are no rights at all: only *citizens* have rights – and they have them only by virtue of membership in a particular political community. In our own time, Arendt reformulates Burke's claim: vis-à-vis the concrete situation of European refugees following the First and Second World Wars, abstract "human rights" are as nothing.

But if, like Arendt, we presuppose that only the state in particular can author rights – that the only real rights are those given to (at least some) members of the political community by virtue of their belonging to it – then we render human rights entirely a gift of the state. We then ignore social movements quite beyond the state that sometimes have been able to move this or that state to recognize certain rights (as I show). And in many cases, laws alone cannot bring about change, for example at the level of family life: "Ethnographic evidence generally from around Africa shows that the key predictor of the custom of female cutting is ethnicity or cultural group affiliation" (Quataert 2009:174). Here, ethnicity or group affiliation may not be accessible to legal norms that would change unwanted behaviors; legal norms may leave entire areas of human interaction unexamined or may not provide members with protection from unwanted practices.

Finally, the state does not enjoy a moral monopoly of speaking authoritatively on behalf of its citizens (likely it never has). Thus the administration of George W. Bush hardly spoke for all or most American citizens in its defense of using torture to extract information from suspected terrorists, even as the torturers operated under the government's full protection.

(b) In rigid fashion, Arendt also separates the political from the social; she separates the life of public discourse and public action from private, personal "life entrapped in its 'idiocy'" (Rancière 2004:299). Human rights then appear not as Burke views them – as naïve, unworldly utopianism – but rather as peculiarly apolitical. The plight of refugees, then, is "not that they are not equal before the law, but that no law exists for them; not that they are oppressed, but that nobody wants to oppress them" (Arendt 1994:295–296). To invoke a term made famous by Carl Schmitt, what Arendt describes is a "state of exception," or what Rancière (2004:299) sees as "beyond any account in terms of conflict and repression, or law and violence." In this way Arendt depoliticizes one of the most striking phenomena of politics, particularly in the long twentieth century: large numbers of political refugees. To be in a condition "beyond oppression" is to be in a condition *beyond* politics, in Arendt's sense. Yet refugees – among so many other groups who are products of politics and problems for politics – hardly find themselves beyond politics in every sense.

Arendt comes to her notion of an apolitical space by separating the political sphere from the wholly personal sphere, what she calls the "dark background of mere givenness" (Arendt 1994:301). Her public-private dualism contrasts *zoe*, or human life solely in a biological sense, and *bios*, human life as social construction or cultural creation – including *bios politikos*, the culture of political speech and political practice. By claiming that modern democracy contaminates the integrity of *bios* with *zoe* and thus depoliticizes the political sphere, Arendt walls it off conceptually from refugees and the circumstances that generate them.[3] Yet refugees certainly experience political power and political repression even as Arendt would depoliticize them by displacing them to an extra-mundane, quasi-sacred sphere that she imagines as politics in some ideal sense.

But to displace human rights beyond politics is to evacuate their protest potential. That is, to conceive of politics as noble words and patrician deeds is to undermine critical, oppositional, emancipatory politics, for it is to reduce the rights of the rightless to the rights of the members of legal community. It is to reduce the rights of man to the rights of the citizen. If human rights are possible only as political behavior, culture, or claims, then the rightless gain nothing from human rights conceived as somehow beyond politics.

One can, of course, agree that human rights are meaningful only within political community yet reject Burke's and Arendt's reduction of human rights to civil rights. One can retain Arendt's insight without succumbing to the depoliticizing consequence of her approach. And one can do this by re-thinking human rights in two respects.

---

[3] Compare Rancière (2004:299–300).

The first respect is the proposition I began with: rights possible only in political community can only be socially constructed, and their normative foundation can only be contingent. But what exactly does it mean to say that human rights claims are embedded in this or that particular culture and political community? It means that, if they are not to be co-opted or defanged by that community, they must be political in a sense agonistic, critical, oppositional. This is one sense of politics as active not passive (I describe a further sense below): human rights as nothing but their practical, effective consequences for individual men and women. For I focus on causal efficacy not epistemic validity, on human rights as a belief system in which belief is not so much truth guided as behavior guiding.[4] I view them not only as political but also as peculiarly pragmatist. The pragmatist point is this: if nonempirical rationales for human rights are unpersuasive or ineffective (as metaphysical and theological approaches are), then we should consider empirical rationales. To that end, I propose assertive selfhood as a practical origin of rights falling in with empirical rationales through local political practice.[5]

I reconceive human rights in a second sense as well: to be political *within community*, human rights can be "self-authored" or "self-granted." In this sense, too, they would be active not passive: human rights as authored by their addressees. (1) I propose human rights as generated and recognized through a personality structure of "assertive selfhood." (2) I identify three features of self-authorship: emergent through collective political action, as a critical stance, and borne by nonidiosyncratic norms. (3) I show that human rights, so conceived, require a field of

[4] A pragmatic notion of human rights is merely one more species of belief with its own foundation, of course. The notion of belief as primarily action guiding derives from Charles Sanders Peirce (1986:21). He asserts, for example, that "Conviction determines us to act in a particular way." From John Dewey (1981:128) comes the search for valid propositions as an attempt at practical problem solving: "this is the meaning of truth: processes of change so directed that they achieve an intended consummation." Equally pragmatic is the spirit of Marx's (1976:372) eleventh thesis on Feuerbach, the claim that philosophers have always only interpreted the world in various ways but that what matters is to improve it. The pragmatist understanding is distinct from Marx's in that it dispenses with the self that Marx elsewhere construes metaphysically. Resonant with pragmatism is Marx's emphasis on human agency.

[5] If a foundationalism universally valid a priori adds nothing to the project for human rights, why not discard it? Support for discarding comes from Hannah Arendt even as she explicitly rejects the pragmatism I promote in her name (as I argue in later pages): "I am rather certain that I am neither a liberal nor a positivist nor a pragmatist" (Arendt 1953:80). Here I draw insights from Arendt that I consider pragmatist rather than postmodern; elsewhere (Gregg 1998) I distinguish pragmatism from postmodernism.

recognition as a social structure supportive of claims to assertive self-hood. I suggest that the capacity to self-grant depends critically on the participant's personality structure as well as on the structure of some of the social institutions he or she inhabits. Whereas personality structure concerns the *internal* or psychological disposition of the individual insofar as it motivates his or her political behavior, social structure concerns the *external or formal and material arrangements* of political community. And like any political vision, (4) the project for self-granted human rights has distinct limits, above all with respect to the many inequalities among potential self-authors.

Assertive Selfhood

I propose self-assignment as an act of moral autonomy in a sense analogous to Martin Luther King's (1967:43) when he wrote that the African American "will only be truly free when he reaches down to the inner depths of his own being and signs with the pen and ink of assertive selfhood his own emancipation proclamation." To be sure, the capacity for assertive selfhood will not "reside" in the individual independently of his social environment. That is, the term *truly free* cannot realistically mean (to invoke King's context) "free within a society still deeply racist." Still, the capacity for assertive selfhood might contribute to overcoming some aspects of institutionalized racism. To do so, it requires a society that, in at least some of its parts (such as culture and institutions), rejects racism and offers rejecters some degree of support. In the case of human rights, self-assertion requires a social environment to some extent supportive of self-authored human rights, particularly in aspects of tradition, practices, and institutions otherwise unsupportive. Dorothy Roberts gives an American example: although a "sober assessment of racism's intransigence counsels against a naïve faith in the moral power of the Constitution alone to bring about racial equality" in America, "it need not defeat Blacks' instrumental fidelity to the Constitution as part of a social movement for equal citizenship. Blacks' constitutional fidelity is not the faith that the Constitution will end racism. The constitutional allegiance of Black leaders such as Douglass, Du Bois, and King was grounded in their participation in the social struggle for citizenship rights. They could hold fast to a vision of an ideal Constitution despite their awareness of constitutional evil because of their commitment to a liberation movement" (Roberts 1998:232). In a different context, Rosa Parks in 1955 affirmed the rights she did not have as an inhabitant of Alabama, which banned black passengers from riding in the front of public buses. She did so by taking a seat in the front of the bus and remaining there in the face of hostile urgings to move.

From a pragmatist standpoint, human rights that are socially constructed and contingently valid "exist" only if enforced. Enforcement over time is a matter of *local* recognition as well as broad embrace implying some degree of institutional support. But the need for enforcement doesn't mean that the main guarantors of human rights can only be great powers possessed of significant economic and military might, or international organizations backed by coalitions of such powers. That conclusion would only reinforce the strikingly unequal distribution of power among states, among regions, and among economies in the world today.[6] From the status quo standpoint, human rights for the powerless can only be gratuitous grants from the powerful. Such grants render the mighty all the more powerful, and they render individuals merely passive recipients of rights. Human rights gained through "philanthropy" deprive their recipients of autonomy and equality. This misguided approach even allows for paternalistic intervention in John Stuart Mill's (1984:118) imperialist sense: "nations which are still barbarous have not got beyond the period during which it is likely to be for their benefit that they should be conquered and held in subjection by foreigners." Rights that depend on others for their existence and exercise are rights of persons morally, legally, and politically dependent. In fact, outside intervention on any grounds – whether authoritarian or liberal democratic – might *protect* rights temporarily but could hardly fully institutionalize or otherwise adequately *establish* them. Human rights that become effective through unilateral military intervention cannot be sustained on that basis; a fundamental presupposition of self-granted human rights is that "no one can be liberated or emancipated by others, from 'above'" (Balibar 1994:213). Self-granted human rights are a form of self-help. They constitute self-help only if their addressees do not passively benefit from others' doings – whether by courts, states, the UN, NGOs or other humanitarian organizations.

Given a supportive social structure, what kind of personality structure might be capable of self-assigning human rights? I propose socializing individuals in the belief that they, together with other members of their

---

[6] It might only reinforce powerful, liberal democratic states and their organs as the main enforcer and guarantor of rights, which is problematic for so much of the nonliberal but human rights–capable world.

group or social movement, belong within a certain category. By virtue of self-granting, they belong within a category of human rights bearers from which they are currently excluded because of the social, political, or cultural environment as presently configured.

From the perspective of that social and political environment, the individual who accords him- or herself human rights appears to be "in excess" of that environment insofar as it does not recognize this self-grant. Yet the participant need not succumb to that perspective. He or she need not regard him- or herself as some kind of "supernumerary."[7] He or she might self-regard as someone denied recognition of the human rights he or she grants him- or herself. Correspondingly, "democracy" cannot be reduced to the institutional environment but might be composed of persons with no special qualification for political selfhood "except the [paradoxical] fact of having no qualification" (Rancière 2004:305). Otherwise "democracy" is marked by that Arendtian depoliticization that renders individuals the supplicants of the state's rights-bestowing magnanimity. By contrast, democracy in the sense of democratized access to human rights is not something to be determined by tiny, elite cultures of experts. Nor is it merely the outcome of bargaining among unequal interest groups. It is the repeated action of generating an individual's recognition as a member of a public sphere, a member *not* in the sense of an outsider being "brought in" but rather as someone who authors him- or herself into membership. Here *membership* refers to a human rights community; *democratic politics* refers to the act of granting human rights to oneself and recognizing others who do the same.

Only if they can meaningfully enact their own qualification as rights bestowers can individuals oppressed by their state (or community or culture or religion or family) plausibly refer to human rights as the normative foundation of their criticism. These rights become theirs only when they oppose the denial of such rights.

Features of Self-Authorship

A capacity for self-authorship would have three features. First, the self-granting individual would view him- or herself not as a predefined carrier of rights but rather as a subject who emerges through collective political action, such as a social movement. The individual would author the very

---

[7] That is, a person "in excess" of the usual, proper, or prescribed membership or qualification for membership in political community and communal rights.

human rights addressed to him or her and grant him- or herself a right to be acknowledged as bearing human rights regardless of contingent factors that might be used to distinguish between "insiders" and "outsiders," "rights-bearers" and "nonbearers." Such factors might be legal status, immigrant status, economic status, or the community's needs for social security. As a form of "framing," socialization might foster a certain way of looking at the world. The individual would frame him- or herself as an author of his or her own human rights. To be sure, perception and framing are always embedded biographically, politically, and historically. The way we perceive ourselves and our environment is influenced to various extents by that environment, even in ways of thinking and perceiving. Thus persons discriminated against might react by regarding themselves as inferior; persons accorded respect might respond with a healthy self-regard.

Second, critical ways of perceiving oneself and one's environment might encourage self-granting behavior. "Critical" means someone or some group without rights intervening in the status quo, challenging the community that excludes them from rights. Critical ways might be facilitated by a "broad" socialization more likely to promote characteristics of independence, individualism, and self-expression – more likely, that is, than narrow socialization with its traits of obedience and conformity to current cultural standards (Arnett 1995:617–618). A broad socialization might facilitate a capacity to unsettle some authorities by linking political legitimacy not to norms prior to politics (as in norms grounded theologically or metaphysically) but to what I develop (on pages 96–99) as "democratized access" to the interpretation of guiding elements of local culture. I refer to a culturally authentic socialization into a personal conviction of a self-granted right to interpret one's local culture. Interpretation can be core to challenging the status quo where the status quo opposes or hinders the recognition and defense of human rights, however construed locally. Sally Engle Merry (2006) provides one example of the complexity of local understandings by victims in cases of battered women in Hong Kong, where victims (wives battered by their husbands) mediated their understanding of injustice with beliefs in traditional kinship obligations (namely, the subordination of women to men, and wives to husbands, in Confucianism).[8] The point is that local groups offering

---

[8] Here "human rights movements do not require the adoption of a human rights consciousness by individuals at the grass roots," and "commitment to rights" need not be "deep or long lasting" and may include "quite different levels of commitment to rights"

mutual aid and self-help to women with problems personal, familial, or communal might effectively reinterpret traditional understandings of kinship obligations in ways that could further human rights.

A personality structure capable of undertaking critical reinterpretations of local culture, in this way facilitating the self-authoring of human rights, would likely include a psychological capacity to challenge authority. Granting oneself human rights will surely challenge the political and cultural environment to some extent in all cases, and more in some than others – in nonliberal communities (as I show) but also in liberal ones (as in the examples drawn from the American Civil Rights Movement on pages 92–93).

But simply challenging that environment is not the ultimate goal; recognition of the asserted rights is. To be effective, any self-authored right depends on *recognition within its social environment*. That environment includes institutional enforcement of rights locally regarded as socially binding *because*, among other things, *they are locally recognized*. The task of the project for self-authored human rights is to achieve recognition even in local environments hostile to them, and to do so *from within* the local culture.

Indigenous interpretation of *indigenous* culture means human rights authorship *locally* plausible, plausible in terms of elements of the surrounding culture. Perhaps all cultures, if not all political communities, harbor some indigenous potential for broader forms of socialization supportive of authorial or interpretive empowerment that – if deployed accordingly – might advance the idea of individuals assigning themselves human rights. In Islam, for example, precedence exists for a democratized right to interpretation: "Modern reformers in the twentieth century began to reinterpret key traditional Islamic concepts and institutions – rulers' consultation (*shura*) with those ruled, consensus (*ijma*) of the community, reinterpretation (*ijtihad*), and legal principles such as the public welfare (*maslaha*) – to develop Islamic forms of parliamentary governance, representative elections, and religious reform" (Esposito 2004:96). Note that the author refers to Muslims in predominantly Muslim societies; by contrast with Muslims assimilated into predominantly non-Muslim societies, they are indigenous. Here we observe an

---

(Merry 2006:215). Movements here need to frame human rights in "images, symbols, narratives, and religious or secular language that resonate with the local community. When a group of batterers is taught not to hit in Hong Kong, this is presented as part of Confucian ideas of marriage" (Merry 2006:220). I address framing human rights at length in Chapter 7.

intermeshing personality and social structure that could support indigenous cultural interpretation toward self-authored human rights.

One means to local recognition is cultural interpretation. Assertive
selfhood is possible only where there is a *democratized right to interpret the
major cultural sources of one's community*. And it is possible only when that
right allows interpretations unwelcome to the authorities, or repugnant
to vested interests, or in opposition to dominant understandings. Human
rights via assertive selfhood are possible "beyond any particular formulation which has been given of them" (Lefort 1986:258). They are possible
as a vehicle not "for what we know justice to be" but rather "for criticizing
the pretenses of justice as it is" (Kennedy 2004:353).

I do not underestimate the practical difficulties of realizing this
approach: confronting cultural or political differences within any community will generate significant tension. Cultural and religious traditions
often are invoked precisely to exempt specific customs and practices from
criticism, local and foreign. But family codes, cultural practices, religious traditions, and domestic laws that govern and restrict many aspects
of individuals' lives would not be off-limits to challenge by self-granted
human rights.

To be sure, some aspects of all cultures, of all social systems, of all polities discourage the indigenous critical cultural interpretation I advocate
as necessary for self-authored human rights. A human rights–based critique of, say, the status, roles, and experiences of women can easily and
quickly generate very deep resentment on the part of the addressees –
if they regard status, roles, and experiences as based in and expressive
of communal, religious, cultural, or ethnic identity. The critique – and
with it, human rights – then appear to threaten the community's very
integrity.

But democratization of participation in the interpretation of one's
own culture need not require a liberal democratic polity. And human
rights advocacy (promotion that eschews unilateral imposition from
without) should not expect or demand that all communities become
liberal democratic before pursuing local human rights. Jack Donnelly
is representative of this unpromising approach where he argues that
the

> International Bill of Human Rights rests on an implicit model of a lib-
> eral democratic (or social democratic) welfare state. The legitimate state,
> as envisioned by internationally recognized human rights norms, is demo-
> cratic. Political authority arises from the sovereignty of the people. It is
> liberal. The state is seen as an institution to establish the conditions for the

effective realization of the rights of its citizens. It is a welfare state: recognized economic and social rights extend well beyond the libertarian right to property. And all three elements are rooted in the overriding and irreducible moral equality of all members of society and the political equality and autonomy of all citizens (Donnelly 1999:68).

The idea of human rights is otiose if it makes sense only where it is already most plausible locally, for then it would not even offer an instructive contrast with other polities: within the liberal democratic state. Donnelly's approach offers nothing to the possibility of human rights in communities where they are most needed: there, where they are least plausible locally. If "democratic politics is the only secure foundation for rights" (Ingram 2008:414), then the outlook for human rights can only be bleak, given the enduringly undemocratic landscape of so much of the world. But the observance of human rights itself neither requires nor presupposes the liberal democratic state. Within some nonliberal Islamic societies, for example, the "debate about the virtues of democracy is not simply a debate between Islam and Western liberalisms, but a debate within Islam itself" (Esposito 2004:76). In that spirit, my alternative urges that potentially anyone can acquire such value commitments – even in social, cultural, and political environments that in many ways do not resonate with such commitments. This potential might sometimes be realized by "democratized access" to local interpretation and thus to human rights–friendly reinterpretations ultimately secured through understandings and practices of at least some communal members. Provocative interpretations need ultimately to become a permanent feature of any community in which human rights are to establish a foothold.

Socialization toward a capacity for self-granted human rights is possible in at least some nonliberal political communities (and likely in all liberal ones). Democratized access to local cultural interpretation is possible even within a polity not itself democratic. Consider two examples. John Rawls speaks of a "decent hierarchical society." Such a society has no "aggressive aims" and recognizes that "it must gain its legitimate ends through diplomacy and trade and other ways of peace" (Rawls 1999b:64). Further, it secures human rights, has a legal system that imposes on its members "*bona fide* moral duties and obligations (distinct from human rights)," and is served by judges reasonably persuaded that the "law is indeed guided by a common good idea of justice" (Rawls 1999b:65–66). It also has a "decent consultation hierarchy" that mediates between the government and various corporate groups. Finally, it allows for dissent from governmental policy. Malaysia[9] and Singapore[10] might be examples of states that could plausibly become decent hierarchical societies. To this taxonomy David Miller adds neopatrimonial regimes with patron-client relations between politicians and supporters. Here, "political leaders are representative insofar as they meet their obligations to their clients, as understood within the culture of the country in question. In receiving the benefits – jobs, money, public works, etc. – client groups give their tacit consent to the regime" (Miller 2007:246). Various African countries provide examples of rule by elites with popular acquiescence where the populace has little or no control.[11]

A social structure supportive of self-granted human rights falls easily within the parameters of liberal democratic regimes. One example is the American Civil Rights movement, which I referenced in regard to King's notion of assertive selfhood. That movement in some ways looks back to earlier antislavery movements and, in other ways, contains lessons for contemporary movements for equal rights for gays and lesbians.

Third, self-authorship is possible and meaningful only in political community, that is, as something intersubjective rather than subjective and idiosyncratic. Self-authorship then refers to individuals within groups that claim and assert human rights for themselves. Self-authored human rights are conceivable as products of social movements rather than of individuals by themselves; in social movements, the individual human rights author could stand in reciprocal relation with others. Reciprocity is key here: to grant oneself human rights is always also to recognize others in their self-granting activity inasmuch as self-regarding rights necessarily implicate other-regarding duties. I use "reciprocity" in George Herbert Mead's sense of the conformity facilitating "generalized other," by which he means the attitude of the whole community but which I would reconfigure as the attitude of possibly only part of the

[9] Malaysia practices arbitrary and preventive detention and abuses migrants, refugees, and asylum seekers.

[10] Singapore's legal framework perpetuates an authoritarian state tightly controlled by the ruling People's Action Party, which has won all elections since 1959 and is often represented by as many of eighty-two of the eighty-four parliamentarians with full voting rights. Singapore law authorizes censorship of content and distribution of print material and films, severe limits on public processions and assemblies, and prolonged detention of suspects without trial. Its penal code mandates caning along with imprisonment for some thirty offenses, including drug and security offenses. Singapore is believed to have one of the world's highest per capita execution rates, although statistics are not made public. Most sentences involve some twenty drug-related offenses for which execution is mandatory.

[11] See Chabal (2002).

community, of subsets of the community such as critical social movements: the "individual experiences himself... from the particular standpoints of other individual members of the same social group, or from
the generalized standpoint of the social group as a whole to which he
belongs" (Mead 1967:138). For "it is in this form that the social process or community enters as a determining factor into the individual's
thinking" (Mead 1967:155), to some extent giving him "his principles,
the acknowledged attitudes of all members of the community" – or, I
would argue, members of even marginalized subgroups – "toward what
are the values of that community" (Mead 1967:162) or group and to
some extent toward dependable mutual expectations of behavior within
groups or communities.[12]

Socialization is also key here. Communal members may reasonably
expect fellow members often enough to observe many norms into which
they were socialized even as the meanings and applications of some
norms are contested within the group or community. For a core goal of
any socialization is to *reproduce social standards*, thereby generating group
expectations of individual compliance and, consequently, a dependable
degree of reciprocity within the community. Socialization into a capacity
for self-authorship would be socialization into more than the free advocacy of some of the norms to which one has been exposed. Although
such advocacy need not be uncritical, it remains that most people are
more likely to embrace than reject many of the norms into which they
have been socialized. This may hold even for subgroups, including oppositional subgroups, of the larger community. Further, such reciprocity
may be only partial; it may hold for some persons more than others;
it may sometimes fail and is never unconditionally guaranteed. Even
then it remains the single most effective means of encouraging certain
beliefs and behaviors (which could be friendly toward human rights)
and discouraging others (which might be hostile to human rights). The
following section develops this point.

Field of Recognition

The effectiveness of an individual group member's self-granting depends
on other persons recognizing those self-authored human rights. Recognition of this sort has three requirements: (a) it must extend from the

---

[12] This conception need not assume complete consistency or comprehensiveness.

public to the private spheres of life; (b) it cannot be idiosyncratic; and (c) it must be local.

(a) The nationalist elites and religious authorities in postcolonial regimes pursued nation building while opposing women's movements critical of the patriarchal family and its protection in laws of personal status. Decades later, a globalized social movement pushed for recognizing "gender-specific vulnerabilities of women and ... of violence directed at women in many different cultural and political contexts" (Quataert 2009:140).[13] The movement sought to incorporate these often non-public phenomena into the human rights discourse, analogizing domestic violence (not heretofore regarded as a human rights violation) and torture (already regarded as such). Rhonda Copelon (1994:121–123) argues that domestic abuse displays criteria of terror as defined by the UN Torture Convention: whether as a matter of battering, vengeance, or enforcing family honor, it is coercion that intentionally inflicts "severe physical and mental pain and suffering." Kenneth Roth (1994:327–329) suggests that domestic violence – and one might add other "private sphere" phenomena, including child marriage, rape, the defiling of children, or polygamy, especially in the context of AIDS – should be regarded as a human rights matter even if it displays no political motive. Or one might argue that domestic violence is properly understood as political in the sense of social control that aims at the systematic subjugation of women *because* they are women.

(b) To function as a right quite beyond a mere assertion of power, human rights self-assignment cannot be purely subjective. Without recognition by at least some social group, one cannot effectively grant oneself rights; indeed, without such recognition, it makes little sense to say that one even has a right to grant oneself rights. Single or isolated acts of self-assertion – if they remain single or isolated – cannot ground rights. Many authors regard the state as the main or even sole venue for such recognition. According to Frank Michelman (1996:203), whether one has rights "depends on receipt of a special sort of social recognition and acceptance – that is, of one's juridical status within some particular concrete political community. [Arendt's] notion of a right to have rights arises out of modern-statist conditions and is equivalent to the moral claim of a refugee or other stateless person to citizenship, or at least juridical personhood, within the social confines of some law-dispensing state."

---

[13] See Thompson (2000:260).

But one's juridical status within the law-dispensing state is hardly the only possible route to recognition of self-granted human rights. If it were, self-authored human rights could have no purchase in most if not all states today. In many cases, recognition is more likely to be granted by fellow activists within a social movement, indeed as an element of belonging to that movement. (American slaves who rejected their status had more in common with abolitionists than with the general population.) Group recognition of someone's self-authored human rights renders them nonidiosyncratic. Nonidiosyncrasy is a desideratum internal to the idea of human rights. For some human rights will conflict with others inasmuch as different rights may well derive from different normative systems, for example – in the case of female genital cutting – an individual's right to bodily integrity in distinction from his or her community's right to the preservation of its cultural integrity. A right to cultural integrity might, in some cases, promote female genital cutting whereas a right to bodily integrity disallows it. Conflict between some human rights would only be exacerbated if they were based wholly on individual self assertion.

The desideratum is no less acute for social movements championing their claims to this or that human right. To be sure, all human rights–oriented social movements are idiosyncratic. Each takes place in unique contexts under unique conditions; they cannot be explained all in the same terms. Moreover, the precepts of different moral systems yield few points of convergence. But the practical success of, say, Amnesty International in defending political prisoners across the world depends on constellations of small groups (based in religious or educational institutions or in neighborhood organizations) spreading out, weblike, with each systematically "adopting" one prisoner from each of three contexts: the communist bloc, the anticolonial movements, and Western countries such as the repressive dictatorships (in the 1960s) of Spain, Greece, and Portugal.

As an example of nonidiosyncratic approaches by social movements claiming human rights, consider the engagement on behalf of Eastern European dissidents following the Helsinki Accords of 1975. Information about dissidents began to circulate, despite the government's monopoly on media, as of 1968 with the clandestine *Chronicle of Current Events*. The authors defended their challenge by appeal to Article 19 of the *Universal Declaration*, which guarantees "freedom of opinion and expression." The group granted itself the right "to receive and impart information and ideas through any media and regardless of frontiers" (Quataert 2009:85). It demanded that the authorities follow the Helsinki Accords to which the

Soviet Union was a signatory, and it claimed rights specified in the Soviet constitution yet never actually provided. In these ways, among others, social groups argued against the traditional claim that state sovereignty gives jurisdiction entirely to the state. And with various forms of pressure, from resolutions to investigations, social groups actively intervened.

(c) I argued earlier that self-granted human rights need to find *local* recognition if the assignation is to be more than merely idiosyncratic or private and hence ineffective because it is powerless in its utter isolation from any field of possible acknowledgment. Local recognition of the individual's self-assigned human rights requires a space shared by recognizers and recognized alike. It wants a field of public, communal acknowledgment of the rights work of individual "authors." I develop that argument in several points.

First, recognition would occur *not before* self-assignment but rather *as a condition* of the individual's being able to self-assign (simultaneous with self-assignment or immediately following). Second, it would require some degree of correspondence between various social structures and the individual's personality structure, where *correspondence* means "mutually reinforcing." Correspondence might be facilitated by kinds of socialization that generated shared and expressed values that found support in particular institutions. For example, members of a political community might agree on the merits of some social institutions – the media, legal system, and civil service, say – because they agree on norms embodied in such institutions. Behind the norm of a public's putative right to know is the institution of a free press; behind the norm of proceduralism stands the institution of an independent judiciary; behind the norm of citizens as discrete but equal subjects of bureaucratic administration one finds the institution of an apolitical civil service. In each case, personality and social structure correspond to a meaningful extent. One value (inculcated by socialization) that might stand behind a communal institution of self-granted human rights would be what I've proposed as "assertive selfhood."

Developing local recognition of self-authored human rights would be one of the greatest tasks of the human rights project as I reconceive it. Consider an example of failure along this dimension: movements for social-economic rights, especially for a "right to development" in the context of anticolonial movements.[14] Precisely a lack of local recognition

---

[14] No NGO movement has ever championed this right, at least no movement comparable to movements advocating other rights.

was one factor in the strange path of at least one strand of human rights discourse for some colonized peoples. This was a path from initial irrelevance, then (at its height) to emancipatory potential against foreign colonial powers, and finally to a reversal: it offered a subversive challenge – now indigenous – to postcolonial regimes. Having failed to develop local recognition of locally claimed human rights, this elite strand of human rights discourse never led to effective social movements of protest or reform.

The emancipatory hopes of many colonized peoples after World War I were focused largely on self-determination. The Atlantic Charter of 1941 held out the promise not of human rights but of self-determination, racial equality, and development.[15] Here human rights talk was a by-product of what would become a postwar international security regime; it possessed what was at best merely rhetorical value (taken very seriously by colonized peoples but not at all by Prime Minister Churchill and only strategically by President Roosevelt). The real concern on all sides was the idea of self-determination, which at the time meant opposition to the West, many decolonized states, supported by communist states, championed it. In short, the anticolonial movement was never a human rights movement.[16] Not surprisingly, the UN's *Universal Declaration of Human Rights* did not include a right to self-determination. In the mid-1950s, African and Asian countries attempted to strengthen demands for self-determination and racial equality by redefining each as a human right. But in subsequent years these newly independent countries emphasized principles of non-intervention, territorial integrity, and economic development – but not human rights for their own populations.[17] The UN began in 1946 with fifty-one member states, twelve from colonized areas of the world (four from Africa, three from Asia, five from the Middle East). Between 1955 and 1960, about fifty newly independent African and Asian countries joined the UN, gaining a majority of votes. Their majority status allowed them to define the subjugation of peoples to foreign domination as a human rights violation by proposing self-determination as a human right and by attacking racial discrimination as a human rights abuse.

And yet human rights discourse, deployed by indigenous actors locally, now threatened to undermine the newly won power of some African and

---

[15] Ibhawoh (2007:141–172); Esedebe (1994:112–125).
[16] Simpson (2001:300).
[17] Murray (2004:271–279).

Asian leaders, who responded by denying ethnic or other groups the very right to self-determination that they had employed in their respective anticolonial struggles.[18] They also rejected, as illegitimate Western influence, the very international labor norms that they themselves had championed before independence.[19] At the same time, these states used human rights rhetoric as a political strategy to unmask the injustices of the postcolonial world order and to champion a "right to development" and its codification within the UN.[20] In the early 1970s, this rhetoric framed the industrialized countries as morally responsible for Third World underdevelopment and as morally obligated to offer restitution for the colonial past.[21] It attempted to deflect Western charges of Third World human rights violations perpetrated not only by the state but also in cultural practices, particularly those affecting the treatment of women and children.

Parts of the Third World either rejected this particular version of human rights or constructed their own, local tradition of human rights, then argued for that tradition's legitimate place in international affairs. As it became clear that such rhetoric remained without effect, African and Asian countries tried to apply the human rights idea to legitimate their economic agenda – yet without specifying any human right to aid domestically.[22] The effort to catch the West with its own moral language had failed; in many ways, locally constructed human rights language failed as well because it never became locally established.

Limits of the Project for Self-Granted Human Rights

The project for self-authored human rights is inherently unlikely and, for the foreseeable future, will remain difficult to realize. But it is not impossible. The end of slavery, equal rights for women, and the widespread prohibition of child labor became possible in the recent past despite what, for most of history, must have appeared to be their utter unlikelihood.

Still, the project confronts a number of serious problems. Above all, the notion of self-granting implies the equality of people's capability to

---

[18] See, e.g., Parkinson (2007:103–132).
[19] Maul (2007).
[20] Eckel (2009:479).
[21] M'Baye (1972/1973:534).
[22] Eckel (2009:481).

self-grant. But all persons will never be equal in this respect, for two reasons, among others: (a) not all persons are able to acquire the capacity for self-assertion, and (b) nonegalitarian starting conditions often result in nonegalitarian lives.

(a) Not all persons can be socialized into a capacity for self-granting. Thus children (at least temporarily) as well as the mentally deficient will have little or no prospect of becoming the moral agents that self-authoring human rights addressees become.[23] Hence the mere humanity of all persons, or simply their species membership, hardly suffices as equal grounds for all persons to become self-granters. Whether someone is dependent or autonomous (in the sense of being able to grant him- or herself human rights) is not a matter of his or her status or nature as a human being (his or her "humanity"). It is a matter of human *behavior* and *culture* and other social constructions that inform and influence that behavior. Hence the appeal, so common in theories of human rights, to notions of the individual's "humanity" or "human dignity," is quite unpromising.

My alternative (adumbrated above, under the rubric "features of self-authorship") is socialization into assertive selfhood. The problem for my approach is how to secure assertive selfhood for those persons lacking it.[24] Such persons are no less vulnerable than morally capable persons to the depredations against which human rights would protect. Their individual lack of potential to develop assertive selfhood does not justify downgrading their goals for realizing human rights for themselves. Along the lines of what might be called the "logic of reciprocity" inherent to the notion of self-assigned human rights, insofar as a group or community cannot bring all persons with disabilities or otherwise incapable of assertive selfhood up to the same threshold of a capacity for self-granting, that group or community fails to realize the full potential of self-authored human rights.

(b) By means of socialization, some persons may come to regard as egalitarian a "right" to interpret their own culture. This idea resonates with Arendt's view of equality as something socially constructed: "We are not born equal, we become equal as members of a group on the strength of our decisions to guarantee ourselves mutually equal rights" (Arendt

---

[23] Nor would the unborn.
[24] To be sure, "moral agency is not a single uniform property – different persons exhibit it in different ways" (Meyers 1985:115).

1994:301). The claim that "we" decide to give ourselves rights, and that "we" do so mutually, is a claim to self-authoring or self-assigning.

Thomas Jefferson's 1776 Declaration of Independence, the French revolutionaries' 1789 *Déclaration des droits de l'homme et du citoyen*, and the UN's 1948 *Universal Declaration of Human Rights* do not themselves render their addressees equal with respect to critical interpretation of their own culture. Thus equality (the *Universal Declaration* in Art. 7 proclaims that "all are equal before the law") as well as the principle of equal pay for equal work (Art. 23) are easily confounded by any number of local inequalities, such as those based on a person's sex, race, socioeconomic status, level of education, or meaningful access to any number of social institutions, including the media, politics, and the economy.

The individual who authors his or her own right to critical cultural interpretation does not thereby simply render him- or herself equal to all other interpreters in this respect. The claimed human right, if understood as social construction, requires a kind of political and cultural performance to lend practical force to that claim. But just how can an individual's performance entail rights, human rights in particular? If he or she performs as a member of a social movement, *performance* then refers to the group's range of politicking. Politicking itself might instantiate the demanded rights *at least within the group itself*. Yet the goal does not end with the movement itself, of course, but requires outcomes quite beyond the group, for example recognition throughout the political community, ideally and ultimately including state recognition.

Are there characteristics of such performance, true across different movements, that might be specified in advance and made available to movements in formation? In addition to this general question, a very particular question poses itself: likely, in any given social movement, not every member *can* so perform. Consider someone without the capacity for language or with other impairments. Might guardians of some kind grant such persons the human rights they cannot grant themselves? How so? Indeed, what forms of guardianship might be adequate – if any? And just what vehicles of expression might be arranged for them? And what if the person suffered from a type of "mental deprivation . . . so acute that . . . the life there is simply not a human life at all, but a different form of life," such as someone in a "persistent vegetative condition, or an anencephalic child" (Nussbaum 2006:187)? Here no guardian could facilitate such an individual's performance through some expressive vehicle. The individual could only be an addressee but never an author. Inequality of this sort in the "distribution" of the capacity to assertive selfhood would seem to be ineradicable.

Further, even nondeprived human beings may be unequal in the capacity to perform the act of self-granting because, within any given society, the basic "capabilities" for realizing self-ownership are likely maldistributed.[25] Different concentrations of "liberties, rights, incomes, wealth, resources, primary goods, utilities, capabilities" (Sen 1992:88) may lead to substantive inequalities of "incomes, utilities, well-being, and positive freedoms to do this or be that" (Sen 1992:21). Some of these inequalities may derive from the wider socioeconomic and geopolitical context. Be that as it may, such inequalities make it difficult, if not impossible, for indigenous groups of self-authoring individuals to form. This problem cannot be solved by declarations of formal equality.

And then there's the maldistribution of the will to assertive selfhood. Not all persons in principle capable of granting themselves human rights may actually do so. Some might not do so because they were not socialized into assertive selfhood. That incapacity might result from inequalities in the social environment. It might result from health- or environment-related factors (thus chronic poor health could inhibit the development of assertive selfhood, as could a perpetually unsafe environment). It might follow from the individual's lack of voice, influence, or power within the community. It might be occasioned by certain social norms and political institutions. For example, a lack of political liberty and civil rights might render individuals susceptible to economic insecurity and major disasters in ways that discourage the development of assertive selfhood. In some cases it might even be a matter of choice to forego assertive selfhood.

At the outset of this chapter I cited Rancière's formulation of human rights as the "rights of those who are only human beings, who have no more property left than the property of being human" (Rancière 2004:298). *Property* refers to a characteristic. But it might well be read as "possessions" if one thinks of human rights as inhering in a person's

---

[25] By "capabilities" I refer to Amartya Sen's "capability approach" (and to Nussbaum's, which is similar). It offers one conception of the individual overcoming barriers to his or her assertive selfhood. That approach "builds on a general concern with freedoms to achieve (including the capabilities to function)" (Sen 1992:129). Relevant functions may "vary from the most elementary ones, such as being well-nourished, avoiding escapable morbidity and premature mortality, etc., to quite complex and sophisticated achievements, such as having self-respect, being capable of taking part in the life of the community, and so on" (Sen 1992:5).

having legal property in him- or herself. A prominent philosophical tradition, extending from John Locke (1690) to contemporary libertarians such as Robert Nozick (1974), argues as much.[26] If all those who grant themselves human rights are *formally* equal, then their de facto inequality must have other sources, such as "inequalities of incomes, utilities, well-being, and positive freedoms to do this or be that" (Sen 1992:21). Inequality then flows from different concentrations of "liberties, rights, incomes, wealth, resources, primary goods, utilities, capabilities" (Sen 1992:88).

C. B. Macpherson analyzes this egalitarian approach as the "possessive-individualism" of a liberal market society in which the individual's "humanity" is his or her proprietorship of his or her person. Such humanity then depends on the individual's "freedom from any but self-interested contractual relations with others" (Macpherson 1962:271–272). Members see themselves as equal (fundamentally more so than in any respects in which they might be unequal) because they are equally subordinate to market forces, understood as the best means of ordering human relations, if only by analogy. But the "centrifugal forces of a possessive market society" can only be offset by some "cohesion of self-interests, among all those who have a voice in choosing the government," sufficient to periodically determine the leadership of political community (Macpherson 1962:273). And yet that cohesion evaporates as the franchise is extended beyond the possessing classes to others.

Still, even as I reject it, the notion of possessive individualism usefully displays the problem of inequality for the project of self-granted human rights. Equality hardly follows from human rights as commodity relations, as the "rights of egotistical individuals of bourgeois society" in which the "equality of human rights expresses the 'equality' of the relations of exploitation" (Rancière 2006:17, 19).

---

[26] In this view, self-ownership entails the recognition of others' self-ownership, and self-ownership means nothing if not a right to self-determination. If one has a right to self-determination in that sense (namely because the individual owns him- or herself), then all persons would seem equally entitled to grant themselves human rights. In this approach, people "need" to own themselves as a condition not only of granting themselves human rights but also of having those rights recognized by others. Self-ownership would be constrained by the Lockean injunction to leave "enough and as good in common" for others: I may assign myself human rights only insofar as doing so does not deprive other persons of their self-assigned human rights (Locke 2005:288). Thus the human rights of one person must not render any other self-granting person worse off in terms of possessing recognized human rights.

I have no solution to these various inequalities in ability to acquire the capacity for self-assertion; I cannot resolve the inequalities in starting conditions that so often result in nonegalitarian lives. Until resolved, these problems constitute limits on the project of human rights addressees becoming human rights authors. But a project not perfectible in every way can still be viable, particularly in politics, where success is so often unlikely. And when success is had despite all odds, it is never complete or whole or everlasting. But if the project for self-granted human rights were realizable only in part, in just some communities, for even a limited amount of time, it still would have redeemed some part of its promise.

Whereas this chapter developed a cultural resource for human rights as social constructions, the following chapter uncovers the biological resource offered by emotional affect. To be sure, the possible deployment of emotions toward a free embrace of human rights will always involve culture as well. But emotions are not themselves social constructions, at least not in the sense of the "assertive selfhood" I advanced here.

5

Neurobiological Resources

Emotions and Natural Altruism in Support of Human Rights

In the seventeenth century, René Descartes famously upended age-old understandings by dividing man into mind and body. To this day we tend to think of mind in Cartesian terms: as independent of one's perception of it, corresponding in its operations to the way the world is, always consistent in its operations. Yet we now know that mind is largely unconscious, not literal but operating often with metaphor and symbol, logical only in part, and very much open to influences by values and interests. We've learned as well that reasoning has emotional aspects and that emotions are hardly devoid of reasoned features.[1] And if our emotions generate some of our reasoned beliefs and if we hold some beliefs emotionally,[2] then we must reject claims of an unbridgeable chasm between what Thomas Hobbes, in the seventeenth century, described as rational egotism or self-interest and what Adam Smith, a century later, called "sympathy." In the words of another leading light of Smith's time, David Hume (1966:30), to understand moral behavior as something completely rational, something "exclud[ing] all sentiment," is to miss the mark. We best "represent virtue in all her genuine and most engaging charms" by "approach[ing] her with ease, familiarity, and affection": as a "passion" (Hume 1966:118). Morality so construed will be "more correct in its precepts," "more persuasive in its exhortations," than if construed as purely rational, as entirely affectless (Hume 1968:621). Tellingly, one experiences emotion as a "site" of truth, in the same way

---

[1] Neurological research finds that the absence of emotion and feeling hinders – just as the absence of rationality hinders – our capacity "to decide in consonance with a sense of personal future, social convention, and moral principle" (Damasio 1994:xii).

[2] See Frijda, Manstead, and Bem (2000:4).

that one experiences belief. Hume was right (in part for reasons not available in his own time): the brain has "separate seats for emotions (the limbic system) and instincts (the brain stem)" but no "separate seats . . . for applying instincts/emotions according to . . . whether they are applied to the self, kin, non-kin, a familiar location, or a verbal abstraction" (Miller 1993:237). The emotion of fear, for example, is generated in the subcortex, whether fear for one's welfare in the current moment or that of the entire planet for millennia. It is more or less the same whatever its object.

What if this or that emotion were to take human rights belief as its object? Both the neocortex, which provides our capacity for abstract reasoning, and the subcortical emotional systems, which we share with other mammals, are in neurological play for our convictions – such as convictions about human rights. By "strengthening a particular belief, emotional feelings create conditions for belief-driven processing in which the likelihood of maintaining and using that particular belief should be increased" (Clore and Gasper 2000:30).[3]

Whereas the previous chapter explored a cultural resource for human rights as social construction, this one pursues a biological one: the possibility of an attachment to the human rights idea as an emotional object. I argue for (1) a conception of human nature as biological not metaphysical or theological and (2) a conception of human nature as *personality* structure integrated with *social* structure. (3) I assert that reason and emotion are intertwined in ways potentially helpful to the human rights project – that emotions can shape the way we think about rights. And I contend (4) that emotions positively associated with fictive kinship (which, like biological kinship, can be altruistically motivating) promote an embrace of the human rights idea. (5) These steps further emotion-relevant goals of the project for advancing human rights globally. (6) I conclude by showing how a human rights embrace via emotion is possible without being manipulative.

Human Nature as Biological Not Metaphysical or Theological

By *biological human nature* I mean several of the bases for human behavior that evolved through natural selection. I contrast human nature

---

[3] Emotions influence beliefs along several dimensions. They can influence beliefs currently held, strengthen or weaken the force with which they are held, and even encourage the development of new beliefs. See Frijda and Mesquita (2000: 45).

so understood with theological or metaphysical conceptions that invoke transcendental truths about the world, available through divine revelation or the contemplation of timeless essences or teleologies.[4] By *culture* I refer to socially constructed normative guides to behavior. Both natural and cultural phenomena are germane to the human rights idea even as each involves very different kinds of truth claims. Because biological nature is given not made, valid propositions about biological nature are valid for everyone, regardless of competing convictions, traditions, or ignorance. Cultural artifacts, by contrast, are constructed; hence they are valid only for those communities that fully embrace them. And yet aspects of biological human nature can support the human rights idea, itself a cultural artifact whose validity could become everywhere embraced, if only eventually and contingently.

Aspects of human nature can encourage particular cultural artifacts because what man creates culturally is never independent of what man is biologically. The ideas "our embodied brains come up with depend in large measure on the peculiarities of human anatomy." Indeed, "even our ideas of morality and politics . . . are created and carried out . . . by the neural anatomy and connectivity of our brains" (Lakoff 2009:10). At the same time, individuals are capable of experiencing "group-mindedness," a phenomenon with aspects both biological and cultural.[5] The capacity for social cooperation evolved "mainly from interactions within the local group" that involve individual neural anatomy as well as group-mindedness (Tomasello 2009:100). To be sure, group-mindedness can equally generate strife and suffering between and among groups, a point that challenges this proposal and one that I address at chapter's end. This double-edged-sword aspect of socially constructed norms returns in both Chapters 6 and 7, which implement a social constructionist approach to human rights that cannot guarantee that human rights will be deployed only to good effect or without unintended negative consequences.

I seek an institutionalized, emotion-based group-mindedness supportive of the human rights idea. As social constructions, human rights may

---

[4] Chapter 1 critiques theological grounds; Chapter 2, metaphysical grounds.

[5] For example, altruistic belief and behavior might be encouraged by biological means (e.g., via kin-based feelings) or by cultural ones (e.g., via symbolic representations of political, religious, or cultural community) and likely by both. From an evolutionary standpoint, emotions that encourage survival-related behavior are themselves likely to be passed down. The individual's survival, at least as genome, is tied not only to reproduction but also to the care of certain others: those to whom he or she is emotionally attached.

be possible as a sort of "brain work" because the brain's evolved systems may generate the bases of any community's values just as they generate bases for human emotions. This line of thought does not reduce the phenomenon of human community to the experience of human emotion, however. The connection I draw does not entail that we can intuit norms of moral right and wrong from the fear, anger, hate, love or other emotions that course through consciousness. Nor does it suggest that natural emotions entail "natural values." Human nature biologically understood guarantees nothing in a political way or otherwise in a value-driven sense.[6]

Cultural values cannot be deduced from biological givens; biology cannot do the work of culture; biological knowledge will never be knowledge of human rights.[7] Nor do I propose ethical naturalism. The project to construct and spread human rights is historical and cultural, not biological. Yet in the form of emotion, biology in addition to culture offers an unrecognized resource for that project. This chapter shows that affective support of human rights might be facilitated through patterns of everyday socialization. And it argues that integration into institutionally preserved funds of social solidarity can combine communal solidarity and human rights–supportive altruism.[8]

Encouraging Altruism Through Social Structure and Personality Structure

The existence and enforcement of human rights depend on two structures: the social institutions the individual regularly interacts with (from

---

[6] The argument that cultural values cannot be deduced from biological givens runs against a long tradition of political thought, from Aristotle to Aquinas, according to which natural law (metaphysical or theological) can be deduced from facts of human biology. Closer to our own time, Kant's *Critique of Judgment* would derive morality through teleological reflection on biological structure.

[7] Nor do ethical properties and ethical thought belong to the natural world; nor can ethical statements be reduced to natural scientific phenomena; nor can ethical questions be answered by science. Still, as I show, biological aspects of human nature are certainly relevant to the ethical sphere.

[8] I do not suggest that human rights fall within the category of altruism necessarily or exclusively. They might fall within the category of reciprocal selfishness, for example. Imagine a human right to self-determination articulated in terms of freedom from slavery, freedom of expression, and a freedom to private property. Imagine that I want the fruit of my labor, the use of my goods and property, or to speak my mind. Simply by the logic of reciprocity, not altruism, I am obliged to recognize your right to your labor, speech, and property.

the state down) and aspects of the individual's personality (his or her patterned behavioral characteristics). The first concerns political community with respect to its influences on social behavior; the second, the individual's psychological disposition insofar as it informs his or her political and moral behavior. For purposes of advancing the human rights idea, social structure and personality structure each needs to reinforce the other; neither by itself can author,[9] recognize, or advocate human rights. They *can* be mutually reinforcing at points where biology and culture meet up: in biologically based dispositions potentially supportive of human rights within culture and community.

Of particular relevance to human rights is altruism, an unselfish concern for the well-being of others. Altruism can be encouraged through the confluence of biology and culture, where *biology* refers to nurturance-oriented affect and *culture* to learned behavior (later I argue for a conception of emotions as learned performances). I draw here on the work of Michael Tomasello.[10] He studies processes of social cognition, social learning, and communication in human children and great apes. Evidently some of these processes facilitate the emergence in humans of altruistic thinking and behavior, at least in young children. Altruism in this context is *not* somehow imparted by culture (Tomasello 2009:xvii). From about one year of age, "human children are already cooperative and helpful in many situations." They "do not learn this from adults; it comes naturally." In later development, "children's relatively indiscriminate cooperativeness becomes mediated by . . . their judgments of likely reciprocity and their concern for how others in the group judge them." Such judgments "were instrumental in the evolution of humans' natural cooperativeness in the first place. And they begin to internalize many culturally specific social norms for how we do things, how one ought to do things if one is to be a member of this group" (Tomasello 2009:4).

To recognize human rights is to recognize persons we do not know and never will. The human child's natural and indiscriminate helpfulness toward others emphatically includes strangers. As an "outward expression of children's natural inclination to sympathize with others in strife," altruistic helpfulness constitutes a resource for encouraging an affect-based embrace of human rights (Tomasello 2009:13). Altruistic helpfulness is a kind of "mutualism," a "process primarily responsible for human cooperation in the larger sense of humans'

---

[9] Chapter 4 develops a theory of human rights authored by their individual addressees.
[10] As I do in Chapter 2.

tendency and ability to live and operate together in institution-based cultural groups" (Tomasello 2009:52). Mutualism originated in collaborative activities that provided a protected environment for initial steps in the evolution of such motives (Tomasello 2009:47). Efforts to spread the human rights idea might learn from this path, moving from "skills and motivations for shared intentionality" to degrees of trust and tolerance of others that far exceed what modern apes are capable of. Humans can be moved from the fear, anger, hate, love or other emotions that course through consciousness to collectively held norms that entail institutional practices (Tomasello 2009:54–55). This path might draw from a biologically based capacity for a uniquely human sense of "we." *We* refers to shared intentionality that offers a possible resource for encouraging cultural and political communities to freely embrace the human rights idea. The "sense that we are doing something together... creates mutual expectations, and even rights and obligations." Interconnectedness along various dimensions – biological, economic, cultural, environmental – constitutes "doing something together" (Tomasello 2009:58). In this sense it might also contribute to mutual rights and obligations, of which human rights compose a particular set.

Just how might a community cultivate interconnectedness that encouraged belief in human rights? The answer may depend on the answer to a different question: What conditions encouraged early humans to extend, again and again, their natural, helpful attitudes beyond the earliest and most local environments? I propose a speculative answer along two tracks. Along one, by internalizing social norms, the individual may be rendered vulnerable to emotions of guilt and shame when he or she violates norms. Internalizing norms is one means of coordinating the individual's behavior with group preferences and expectations. Vulnerability of this sort is "located" in the individual's personality (by which I mean his or her patterned behavioral characteristics). Along the other track, social norms contribute to the formation and perpetuation of social institutions by generating a communal background of trust. Along both tracks, developing a human rights–furthering orientation involves the integration of personality structure and social structure. It involves integrating the individual's disposition, insofar as it motivates his or her political and moral behavior, with the structure of some of the social institutions the individual inhabits. By *integration* I mean a mutually reinforcing relationship in which human nature and human culture "meet" in social norms, and in human rights norms in particular. To say that nature and culture "meet" means that the very young human being's natural altruism and natural mutualism might be encouraged, developed, and socially reinforced through the cultural artifacts of education and other socializing institutions. Here I conceive of human rights as achieving practical effect in certain kinds of "cooperative interactions governed by shared intentionality" (Tomasello 2009:106). Intentionality needs encouragement to survive the defensive, anti-altruistic behaviors that individuals learn early on (and continue to learn for the rest of their lives) in the face of repeated experiences as selfishness, deception, and betrayal, among other common features of life in human community.

Our initially nonlearned disposition toward altruistic behavior might be cultivated in a direction encouraging belief in the human rights idea. As their point of departure, forms of cultivation might begin with the fact that cultures are deontic: they promote certain norms and encourage normed behavior guided by this or that ethics of obligation. Forms of cultivation might operate along two further dimensions. Through imagination and symbolic communication, a cultural community might draw on young children's natural mutualism and altruism[11] but also on those aspects of local culture that already encourage such traits. And a community might draw on the fact that children generally want to conform to the group even when cooperation is not at issue, or the fact that children tend to respect social norms because children are sensitive, indeed vulnerable, to norms of authority and reciprocity (Tomasello 2009:40–41). Interaction of personality structure and social structure, culture, and biology mirrors – in human rights supportive ways – the possibility that biology may find encouragement in cultural communities: in the interconnection of reason and emotion. I turn now to that interconnection.

Reason and Emotion Intertwine

Some beliefs can generate emotion; some strongly held rational convictions can elicit strong emotions, which then encourage the individual to look for supporting convictions.[12] In this sense, emotions can lead to belief or validate the convictions at which they aim: "sensory feelings

---

[11] Even as the cognitive immaturity of young children entails a limited moral (for example, altruistic) capacity: "young children's moral judgments are determined primarily by information about the outcomes of actions rather than the intentions of the actor. This pattern . . . indicates a dissociation between two processes important for mature moral judgment" (Young et al. 2007:8239).

[12] Evaluative convictions may be accompanied by emotional affect that motivates the individual to seek rationally supportive grounds for the conviction. Compare Clore and Gasper (2000:25).

involved in the emotion may act as evidence" or subjective support of the "truth of that belief or commitment and of others consistent with it" (Clore and Gasper 2000:25). Some emotions can generate new beliefs. After all, emotions are appraisals "based on currently salient concerns" that can "turn into...long-term belief or commitment" (Frijda, Manstead, and Bem 2000:6). Far from precluding rational action, emotions may facilitate rational responses: "emotion focuses attention, crystallizes evaluation, and prompts action in circumstances in which reflection would be interminable, unfocused, and indecisive" (Posner 1999:310–311). These various forms of emotion work are possible along several dimensions.

First, some of our emotional experiences invest associated beliefs with credibility.[13] The individual is aware of emotions internally and directly, and the quality of this awareness allows emotions to be experienced as "accurate" or "true": "One can argue with logic, but not with feeling" (Clore and Gasper 2000:39). In fact, one *can* argue with feeling, but the point is that feelings often are powerfully persuasive, certainly to the person experiencing them. Thus one typically experiences emotions as beyond doubt. One's own emotions are believable in the sense that, for example, one's anger toward a person easily carries with it the conviction that the object of that anger is despicable. The quality of believability is no different from a love that blinds the lover to the beloved's faults; all the while, the lover is quite certain that his or her estimate of the beloved is quite accurate. Neurobiologically as well, love and hate are remarkably similar. If society as a whole or some part of it could harness the persuasiveness of emotions in this context (as that persuasiveness has already been harnessed in other contexts, such as marketing and advertising, political campaigns and appeals, to say nothing of cinematic film tracks), emotions might offer a heretofore unrecognized, untried resource for human rights advocacy.

Second, emotions can awaken, strengthen, or shape belief. They may color one's focus: "One tends to believe rumors that are consonant with one's prevailing emotional attitude" or "People despise those whom they humiliated" (Frijda and Mesquita 2000:46, 53). Sometimes emotions can change what one believes. They may stimulate the elaboration of beliefs,

---

[13] Moods convey believability to associated convictions or commitments. Whereas emotions are individuated in part by their object and often are associated with a particular stimulating event, moods generally have no object. Moods persist whereas emotions often are brief.

for example by drawing connections with information relevant to what one believes. Convictions may be generated to complement or complete an emotional context or circumstance or to rationalize one's feelings or emotion-driven judgments.

Third, emotions usually provide feedback to the person experiencing them. People are capable of "reading" their own affective feedback. The very capacity for judgment and decision is tied to such feedback, as is "emotional intelligence." Where emotions evaluate, their own feedback may either strengthen or weaken those evaluations. Emotions can be the experiential springboard for values: they can inspire and guide judgments (something already reflected in language, as in the English contempt/contemptible, respect/respectable, desire/desirable, admire/admirable). And emotions can influence rational convictions, as in a self-reinforcing circle of belief and emotion.[14]

Fourth, one associates what one fears with negative affect and what one desires with positive affect. Values are beliefs freighted with emotions as mental representations of positive or negative states of affairs.[15] Emotions can motivate behavior, sometimes powerfully: "What tends to 'drive' people . . . are their wishes, fears, and values," whereby "emotion is central to all three" (Westen 2008:81). Emotions can generate long-term goals passionately held; they can motivate value-guided behavior. In this context I ask: How might some emotions be deployed to advance a notion that certainly implicates emotion-laden values: the human rights idea? After all, human rights are not "weakened" by their connection to emotion, and separating them from emotions is an unlikely goal. Some legal, moral, or human rights are certainly suffused with emotions, ranging from love to hatred, shame to pride, disgust to attraction. Human rights can themselves be emotion laden, for example as a "passion for justice." Indeed, human rights might expand the menu of emotions to include a humanitarian ethos of compassion.[16] The question is: How can such emotional elements be deployed toward advancing human rights? I develop an answer in the next section.

---

[14] Affect, which is conscious, may provide private experiential feedback that supports public evaluations, which may be largely unconscious. The experience embodies a personal reaction even as it serves communal evaluations.

[15] Including values that reflect biologically evolved social orientations, such as norms against incest.

[16] "Only compassion sells. It is the basis of fundraising for humanitarian agencies. We can't seem to do without it" (Rieff 2002:55, quoting Jean-François Vidal, an official of the French aid group Action Contre le Faim).

Embracing Emotion-Based Human Rights via
Altruistic Fictive Kinship

Humans bond emotionally with mental abstractions, from creeds to histories to traditions, from gods to collective fates to principles legal, moral, and philosophical. Bonding of this sort may sometimes further altruism within the group, in which case bonding might be configured to favor an embrace of the human rights idea. But how? Fostering altruistic thinking and altruistic behavior is notoriously difficult. Return for a moment to Hobbes, for whom altruistic behavior is irrational from the standpoint of self-preservation. If man by nature is vulnerable, aggressive, and egotistical, as Hobbes supposes, whoever takes the first altruistic step risks death and destruction by those who decline to take a reciprocal step. If altruism is understood as something more affect based than rational, the more or less emotionally guided individual or group makes itself vulnerable to the more or less rationally guided one. In that case, political community is possible only as a social contract generated by the fearful calculations of egotistical individuals. Hobbes's political theory is distinctly modern precisely in this respect: it replaces metaphysical or theological absolutes with a normatively relative social construction. I embrace his modernity but not his rejection of the political plausibility of altruistic behavior.

Such behavior might benefit someone closely related, biologically, to the altruist. It might also benefit the altruist. For in both cases it might preserve a close genetic heritage (and possibly a genetic disposition toward altruism, if such exists: perhaps altruistic parents often make for altruistic children). Altruism can equally involve distant or unrelated persons. Kin-related altruism may still be egoistic but not non–kin-related altruism: for there is no familial gene pool for it to seek egoistically to preserve. An altruist of this sort is just what the human rights advocate hopes for. Hope of this sort is realistic to the extent that non–kin-based altruism, rather than family, is central to any political community of more than a few dozen persons.

Because non–kin-based altruism cannot depend on close biological links between altruist and beneficiary, it might instead be motivated by a "contagion of feelings" in the sense of secular, emotive appeals to humanity transmitted by cultural means. Lynn Hunt (2007) claims as much with respect to sentimental novels that encouraged empathy with neglected or despised others, or others ignored in their plight.[17] Enlightenment humanitarianism impregnates these books which, in the latter half of the 1700s, contributed to the explosive spread and wide popularity of sympathy for the downtrodden and socially marginalized (in fictional representation, at least).[18] Hunt speaks to the possibility of emotions transmitted by literary culture in particular. Sentimental reading not only transformed the sentiment of lettered Europeans, she argues; it transformed their very *capacity* for empathy across social boundaries. The novel-reading individual became more inclined to see other human beings – whether male or female, rich or poor, master or servant, citizen or foreigner – as possessing the same moral status as the reader. If other human beings have the same capacity as the reader for pain, suffering, and humiliation, the reader might possibly consider them morally worthy of what the reader takes to be his or her own right to be free from physical or psychological abuse. This contagion of feelings constitutes a peculiar kind of "we-ness," engaging perhaps the same primordial sentiments that incline humans to favor their kin altruistically yet now directed toward non-kin. This peculiar sense of species-wide identity might inform the human rights idea as an intersubjectively shared emotional state, especially if culturally reinforced in various traditions and institutions (some of which, for human rights purposes, might well require reinterpretation or reconstruction), in ways I suggest in Chapters 6, on cultural vernaculars, and 9, on the nation-state.

Because emotions are not restricted as to possible object, positive emotional regard might be oriented beyond one's relatives or friends to persons one doesn't know and never will. It might be oriented to persons far beyond one's political community rather than narrowly associated with kin.[19] If emotions are not restricted as to the object they attach to, and if any given object is generalizable, we might suppose that attachment to persons is similar to attachment to an idea. And if an emotional bond with a child or parent is not all that different from an emotional bond with an abstract principle, my proposal would appear the more plausible.[20] The

---

[17] Notable examples include Samuel Richardson's *Pamela* (1740) and Jean-Jacques Rousseau's *la Nouvelle Héloise* (1761). A century later and a continent away, the same effect might be attributed to some of the white Southerners who read Harriet Beecher Stowe's *Uncle Tom's Cabin* (1852).

[18] The genre was explosive in another sense: it tended to dissolve class-based and faith-based identities to allow readers to empathize with victims of other classes and competing faiths.

[19] Surprisingly, "kin recognition is not . . . a genetically coded trait" (Miller 1993:234).

[20] Note that the argument for generalizing emotional affect is not an argument for generalizing familial attachments to the community, a whole society, or the world entire (long

fact that emotions are not restricted in their possible objects suggests that referents of emotions are indeed generalizable. The generalization of kin-specific altruism to non-kin might be possible in ways pertinent to human rights–supportive behavior. Strong emotional attachment can equally characterize the face-to-face relationships within a family and the "imagined community" of the nation (Anderson 1991). Concern with the well-being of biological kin can be extended to concern with the welfare of "generalized" or fictive kin: that is, with members of the same political community or, in the case of human rights, members of (ultimately all) other political communities and (ultimately all) other "tribes," whether political, cultural, ethnic, socioeconomic, religious, or linguistic.

Here nature and culture meet in an additional sense. Biological altruism follows a logic of benefit exceeding cost over time. From a Darwinian standpoint, natural selection favors such altruism. Cultural altruism would follow a similar logic: life in community confers significant benefit to members in terms of protection, reproduction, and nurturance (and beyond, such as the comforts of religion and philosophy, art and leisure, technology and medicine). Emotions are prominent in both biological and cultural altruism; friendship and justice may feed off both; and human rights, if embraced on the basis of emotional affect, combine both.

Emotion-Relevant Goals of the Human Rights Project

The deployment of human rights–supportive affect pursues two goals: (a) identifying salient learning potential and (b) promoting emotions that facilitate social bonding.

(a) For most of their two hundred thousand year history thus far, *Homo sapiens sapiens* lived in "face-to-face groups probably numbering between 50 and 100 individuals in which cooperation with non-kin was probably limited to reciprocity with known partners" (Masters 1994:114). For thousands of years now, to the present, much of a human being's daily activities involve more or less normed behaviors[21] that bind him or her

an aspiration of utopian thought, from Plato to Rousseau). According to a prominent trope in political theory, beginning with Aristotle, the more familial relationships are generalized, the weaker they become. Closer to us in time, Tocqueville analyzes as weak and shallow the "general sentiment of humanity" that views all humans as equal and supposedly binds them to each other.

[21] Not only normal behaviors but also behaviors ranging from the acquisition, interpretation, and perpetuation of norms to their modification or shedding.

to an ever larger number of people he or she will never know, never see, never communicate with: not only fellow members of the extended political community, but members of other communities as well, such as one's profession, religious faith, language community, or ethnic group (each of course falling far short of the cosmopolitan standpoint of all human beings as such).

Under such circumstances, how might a human rights–relevant norm be facilitated by one or the other emotion? We know that emotions can be associated with reasoned convictions. Further, positive emotions such as affection likely entail an enhanced disposition to trust the addressee. Trust, in turn, offers a powerful support for cooperation. Human rights involve norm-guided behavior toward others and some of that behavior is distinctly cooperative. Cooperation, on an everyday basis, involves some of the ways that culture fosters agreement about norms. It may involve as well an emotional basis of core social goals of affiliation and attachment. So understood, cooperation is rational *and* emotional, based on reasoned ideas *and* positive affect.[22]

Given the brain's "biologically determined behavioral and emotional tendencies" that are "potentially modifiable by learning" (Panksepp 1994:116), how, through learning, might emotional tendencies be molded, modified, or directed? To the extent that human nature biologically understood includes antisocial elements, one key human rights goal for learning seems obvious enough: to cultivate the individual to constrain his or her egoistical dispositions. Addressees might learn dispositions of a different quality: they might learn altruism by learning to recognize human rights for others, including others who have granted themselves human rights.[23] Fostering socially constructed forms of altruism might proceed through emotionally charged examples, including altruistic behavior by parents and other potential role models (such as persons who perform public service),[24] or the learning of certain contents in educational settings (histories of oppression or studies of

---

[22] Such as reasoned identification via empathy, or grounded trust via affection, or reasonable happiness via informed enthusiasm.

[23] Chapter 4 develops a theory of self-granted human rights.

[24] In support of this example, see Perry (1997), who relates a public service motivation to parental socialization, religious socialization, professional identification, political ideology, and individual demographic characteristics. Evidence also suggests that "habitual behavior, encouraged by parents or other significant models," leads to "habits of caring that effectively became molded into an altruistic personality" (Monroe 2003: 408).

genocide, say), or through popular culture[25] or emotionally attuned rhetoric in the public sphere (such as fund raising for victims of war or natural disasters).[26] It might proceed through curricula and other paradigms of "emotional education" within school systems and beyond. Families, youth organizations, and political activism provide additional possible venues for fostering this kind of learning process. Important for the human rights project is the fact that educational content can be human rights specific in any of these venues.

I do not claim simply that rights need internalized cultural support for altruistic norms such as thoughtful parenting, good schools, and a rights-nurturing social environment. Rather, I propose a combination of natural affect and socially constructed norms, *not* as a new combination of emotions and moral theory but rather as a way of "doing politics" (as a way of advocating human rights). "Doing politics" would be informed by a recognition of how emotions and normative beliefs are always already combined. I propose enhancing those politics on the basis of our current understanding of neurological bases or supports for some kinds of social behavior.

Emotions offer a means to connect politically with many other human beings, as emotional creatures, across political and cultural borders and among different political and cultural communities. Surely some emotional affect is politically ecumenical, even given the historical variability and sociocultural specificity of its expressions.[27]

(b) Socially constructive emotions (*constructive* in the sense of human rights friendly) might be fostered by nurturing affect and incentive-based

---

[25] See, e.g., Utpal Borpujari, "Media, pop culture powerful tools in human rights advocacy," in *Deccan Herald* (Bangalore, India), 2 February 2010: "It began 10 years ago as an experiment using media and popular culture to advance the cause of human rights. The very first effort, in the form of the album and music video on women's rights, 'Mann Ke Manjeere,' was an astounding success with the album staying in the top 10 for six months on MTV."

[26] Consider this peculiarly American example: "Women's suffrage, the end of Jim Crow laws, and the recent advances in freedom and equality for gay people in the United States are also products of the politics of passion. In the course of American history, the sympathetic communication of sentiments has extended the generalized standpoint of moral sentiment so as to include the feelings and the concerns of many previously excluded groups in new ways. This expansion of moral sentiment has powerfully influenced public deliberation on matters affecting justice in this country" (Krause 2008:200).

[27] Compare Borutta and Verheyen (2010). Such qualities of emotionality raise the question: Would my proposal to encourage some emotions and discourage others require modifications if deployed in nonliberal societies – for example, in traditional societies, theocracies, and in many non-Western polities? One might pursue this question in terms of "emotional reframing," by analogy to the cognitive reframing I propose in Chapter 7.

altruism (as distinguished, say, from competition and dominance). Nurturant emotions and altruism-relevant emotions could contribute to political solidarity. By *solidarity* I mean an ecumenical effort to generalize, to "see others as the sorts of being who can suffer pain and humiliation in the same ways as 'we' do," to "extend our sense of 'we' to people whom we have previously thought of as 'they.'"[28] It addresses the very intersection of belief and emotion by expanding our notion of "we." Richard Rorty suggests something along these lines where he advocates "sentimental stories" as part of a "sentimental education" that "sufficiently acquaints people of different kinds with one another so that they are less tempted to think of those different from themselves as only quasi-human. The goal of manipulating sentiment is to expand the reference of the terms 'our kind of people' and 'people like us'" (Rorty 1993:122–123). In this approach, generating a sense of shared solicitude toward all humans need not always or only take the route of discursive, rational argumentation – "Why should I be moral?" – but rather an emotion-laden route that relates viscerally to some of the tasks of everyday politics: "Why should I care about a stranger, a person who is no kin to me, a person whose habits I find disgusting?" (Rorty 1993:133). The notion of "sentimental education" combines the rational and the emotional toward inculcating a conviction of shared responsibility that might take flight on emotional wings. Rorty's example is the "sort of long, sad, sentimental story which begins 'Because this is what it is like to be in her situation – to be far from home, among strangers,' or 'Because she might become your daughter-in-law,' or 'Because her mother would grieve for her.' Such stories, repeated and varied over the centuries, have induced us, the rich, safe, powerful, people, to tolerate, and even to cherish, powerless people – people whose appearance or habits or beliefs [or commitments] at first seemed an insult to our own moral identity, our sense of the limits of permissible human variation" (Rorty 1993: 133–134).

Solidarity in this politically ecumenical sense might be encouraged by communicating emotionally compelling accounts of hardship and suffering, and by doing so in ways that allow the addressee to imagine what it would be like to experience what is being described (as in the eighteenth-century novels I discussed earlier). So understood, a human

---

[28] Rorty (1989:192), who implicitly rejects Arendt's claim that generalization is an act solely of reason, never of emotion: Arendt (1965:88) speaks of "establish[ing] deliberately and . . . dispassionately a community of interest with the exploited and oppressed."

rights solidarity, generated through socialization in culture and institutions, would combine principled ethics with emotion-bound ethics (or an ethics without principles) as an attachment to the human rights idea that is both emotional *and* rational.

Is the Deployment of Emotion in Support of Human Rights Necessarily Manipulative?

The psychological or emotional manipulation of groups and individuals might itself constitute a violation of various possible human rights, such as rights to individual self-determination, say, or to freedom of belief and conviction. Might the project to advance the embrace of human rights by drawing on emotional responses of its addressees undermine itself in just this way?

The cognitive and ideational content of emotion offers one resource by which my proposal might control for emotional manipulation. Two features of the cognitive and ideational content of emotions are relevant: they are or can be (a) socially constructed with cognitive aspects and (b) constructed as emotional scripts that can be performed. An additional resource for controlling for emotional manipulation would involve ensuring (c) an individual's right of refusal in programs of emotional education, modification, or acquisition.

(a) If emotions are merely "bodily appetites," or moods with no determinate object (boredom, say, or melancholy); or merely physical sensations, such as blushes or tremors; if emotions are entirely natural, like blind, "fluid forces, pushing their way up through the psyche, accumulating, and eventually bursting through" (Solomon 1995:223–224); or if they are something that simply happens to us rather than something we might actively undertake – then they are without cognitive content. But to the extent that emotions can be regarded, at least in part, as social constructions, they offer themselves to the human rights project as a means toward realizing that project. And if emotions can be socially constructed, then perhaps socially destructive emotions can be deconstructed and perhaps reconstructed in ways supportive of human rights. That is, emotions might be "educated" to foster or guide thoughtful judgment and considered behavior. As something between a reflection without a motivational foundation and a fully rational basis for action, emotions might be "educated" to function as a component of strategic, action-oriented rationality. For example, they might be "tie-breakers in case of indeterminacy" (Elster 1999:284). Or in circumstances of great urgency, emotions might perform more quickly than cognition characterized by low emotional content (Landweer 2004:472). In ordinary circumstances, emotion might slip into the listener's mind the "belief or commitment that the emotion is about. . . . Presumably, it slips the beliefs into the listener's mind more easily, smoothly and unquestioned than would happen when the information alone was transmitted" (Frijda and Mesquita 2000:47).

Or emotions might be invested with other behavior-motivating content. Vengefulness, for example, might be turned from expression in bloodlust, vigilantism, or lynch mobs to a desire to repair broken social bonds, hence an emotion neither violent nor unreasonable, neither dangerous nor unlawful, even if it now seeks justified and measured punishment. Other emotions might be "educated" to reject negative expressions and to embrace positive ones: shame, for example, might be turned from a lashing out in anger to a remorseful renunciation of the disapproved behavior. Or an emotion invested with action-motivating content might result from a judgment about a situation or experience or about the intention of another person to act in a certain way.

(b) In a public sphere conceived as a kind of stage for public drama in which public emotions are often on display (sometimes challenging traditional divides between public and private spheres of life, at least where the public sphere is transformed into an arena for the display of emotion), people may "learn" to construct this or that emotion from an emotional script.[29] To "learn" in this sense refers to emotional knowledge: situationally appropriate emotional responses (when grief is appropriate, say, rather than indignation) and their implications for thought (what grief may tell us) and behavior (how to cope with grief in daily life). A script on disgust, for example, might construct the emotion as a means to demean this or that ethnic group as inferior, or it might construct the emotion as a form of collective disapprobation of invidious discrimination against any group. A script on love might construct homosexual and heterosexual couples as equally capable of romantic bonds; some

---

[29] A script might teach the "grammar" and "vocabulary" of an emotion in terms of a paradigm scenario, a kind of drama that enlists the individual's "natural capacities for emotional response," "drawn first from our daily life as small children and later reinforced by the stories, art, and culture to which we are exposed. . . . Paradigm scenarios involve two aspects: first, a situation type providing the characteristic *objects* of the specific emotion-type . . . and second, a set of characteristic or 'normal' *responses* to the situation, where normality is first a biological matter and then very quickly becomes a cultural one" (de Sousa 1987:45, 182).

scripts today construct homosexual couples as quite incapable of such bonds.

Group-based scripts and performances might sometimes generate "communities of emotion" that have the broad reach of public emotions. A group or movement might secure greater support for its cause by performances that appeal to common emotions (as in the case of movements for the abolition of slavery, for civil rights, or for the equal status of women at home, in the workplace, and in the public sphere). It might provoke or challenge the social environment, or win a hearing for its concerns, by performing discomfiting emotions. A group's emotional performance might generate bonding emotions, such as emotions of dignity, autonomy, solidarity, and hope; it might transform a stigmatized collective identity into a source of pride or political agency. And human rights claimants seeking recognition for the rights they assert likely experience a range of emotions, including pride, wherever they gain that recognition, and a different range when recognition is denied.

The notion of performance implies degrees of competency or incompetency. In this sense, scripts and performances might display levels of "skill" in "emotional discourse," for example in the selective display of this or that emotion in ways calibrated to achieve this or that effect or to transmit a particular message. The idea of human rights might be advanced through displays of emotional virtuosity. Virtuosity can be strategic: the human rights project might deploy emotional scripts strategically, advocating an embrace of the human rights idea or identifying and criticizing human rights violations. Scripts might be deployed to discourage persons, groups, or institutions that reject or violate human rights from doing so, perhaps by eliciting their sympathy or respect, or alternatively by generating in them some form of fear.

This account of emotional, script-based performance rejects the distinction between internal, private emotions and external, public emotions, and along with it a supposed dichotomy between the *experience* of emotions and the *expression* of emotions. It suggests that, in performing our emotions, we may self-reflexively evaluate our experience of them in terms of scripts. Scripts are cultural artifacts, and for this reason, among others, emotions may be culturally variable.[30] Thus recent historical

---

[30] Perhaps emotions are culturally variable because "moral goods do not vary randomly from culture to culture, but rather tend to cluster into three sets of related goods or three ethics, known as the ethics of autonomy, the ethics of community, and the ethics of divinity. Cultures rely upon the three ethics to varying degrees. The relative weights of the three ethics within a culture appear to affect the experience and expression of

research suggests that the people of the past spoke differently about their feelings and that they even conceived of them differently. The "emotions of the ancient Greeks were in some significant respects different from our own" (Konstan 2007:ix). The Greeks did not understand emotion as an inner impulse but rather as a response to the interpretation of the words, actions, and intentions of other actors. In contrast to our contemporary catalog of emotions, the only relevant emotions for Aristotle are those that emerge in the interactions of people. Emotions that appear to be independent of the perceptions of others, such as disgust or melancholy, have no place in Aristotle's *Rhetoric*.[31] Further, the ancient Greeks distinguished between anger and hatred or enmity in terms of what triggers each. They thought of anger, for example, as a response to an insult that demands revenge and that presupposes the actors' equivalent social standing.

(c) The deployment of emotions in support of embracing the human rights idea still confronts several problems in the context of determining which emotions to encourage and which to discourage or suppress. Problems arise in the context of establishing which rights are worthy of emotional support and which types of political programs deserve affective support, and by whose decision.

First, consider the problem of cognitive bias. Even (or especially) in a social world without moral absolutes (at least from the social constructionist standpoint on moral norms taken in this book), "bias" is a constant threat for reason and emotion alike: "when partisans face threatening information, not only are they likely to 'reason' to emotionally biased conclusions," but the "brain registers the conflict between the data and desire and begins to search for ways to turn off the spigot of unpleasant emotion" (Westen 2008:xiii). Indeed, emotionally motivated behavior can lead to cognitive bias. For example, to the person experiencing it, "Anger, like happiness, implies that the persons' own beliefs are valid.... [A]nger appears to be an emotion aimed at asserting one's own belief and perspective. Thus we might expect individuals who feel aggrieved to engage in belief-driven rather than data-driven processing" (Clore and Gasper 2000:23). The emotional person "no longer operates as a scientist carefully weighing the pros and cons of the belief or

emotion, as well as the way emotions are conceptualized by both local folk and local experts" (Shweder and Haidt 2000:408).

[31] The *Rhetoric* is concerned with the art of effective persuasion; and Aristotle's discussion of emotions is not, as we might expect today, in his text *On the Soul*.

commitment implied by the emotion" but is more like a "prosecutor or a defense lawyer seeking by any means to find evidence for the belief or commitment" (Clore and Gasper 2000:33). Emotions can influence rational convictions, as in a self-reinforcing circle of belief and emotion. Sometimes emotions become a negative spiral in which they generate beliefs that in turn support emotions.

Second, ponder politically dysfunctional emotionality. Affect-driven politics can entail behaviors that undermine social stability and its norms, from potential for deceit to a propensity for aggression to a political culture of hatred or anger. Further, evolution may have led to "layers of deviousness" within "those areas of the higher limbic brain which . . . interface between primitive emotional systems and higher cognitive systems" (Panksepp 1994:118). (Note that our ancient neuropsychological heritage – still with us – features emotions significantly older than self-conscious reasoning.) Or to "identify an enemy and charge that 'they' threaten 'us'" is often an effective "way to motivate people to collaborate and to think like a group" (Tomasello 2009:100). And then there are the "brutal opinions of the *hoi polloi*" that challenge the idea of a human rights idea capable of wide popular attraction (Solomon 1999:125).

Third, consider negative emotions that are nonetheless socially useful. Would my proposal require limits on self-aggrandizement in economics and politics? Would it require that some of the most powerful and materialistic of a community's members surrender some measure of their privileges? Might some of the emotions that are unattractive from a human rights standpoint still possess significant social utility? Do greed, selfishness, and materialism – and the "possessive individualism"[32] of the politically liberal communities of the West – facilitate the development and health of a market economy and the social wealth it can produce? If "greed, aggression, and the desire for power have . . . governed the politics of the past – more so than the other emotions," we might well expect that they will "continue to do so, even if we . . . address their sources within the human brain" (Panksepp 1994:117–118). There will always be persons who aspire to high positions in politics, the military, or the economy, for example. Some, whose service may nonetheless benefit society, will be egoistic, selfish, and ruthless in pursuing their own interests.[33]

---

[32] See Macpherson (1962).

[33] Aristotle's *Rhetoric* fleetingly suggests an argument that Hobbes develops at length: the idea that rational behavior is favored by fear and anxiety, understood as mechanisms for eliciting the best that individuals can offer in the way of prudent judgment and behavior.

In the face of such problems – of cognitive bias, politically dysfunctional emotionality, and negative emotions nonetheless socially valuable – the individual may sometimes need the protection offered by a right of refusal. He or she may reject emotional manipulation as an unintended and unwanted consequence of my proposal. A right to refusal would mean that the individual retains a right to the "wrong" emotions, to have emotions that the local community abjures. In that case, a human rights–oriented political community would not have a right to coerce its members to support human rights. Only by means of an individual's right to refusal could my proposal for encouraging some emotions and discouraging others be accomplished without infringing on individual rights (including, ironically, some conceptions of human rights).[34] Whether any given community offers such a right is entirely contingent, of course. Consequently a vital question relating to emotional manipulation concerns the political environment in which my proposal might be deployed. But at least we can see why such a right should be among the goals of a human rights movement. Likely it would take the form of a liberal right to individual autonomy – currently found, if found at all, as a civil right in liberal democratic communities. Few polities in the world today provide for civil rights in any robust sense. Where civil rights are absent, human rights advocates must ask themselves: What might move a political community or regime toward an interest in human rights? What might move it toward an interest that would facilitate the kind of emotion work I advocate and that in turn would be encouraged by such emotion work? I turn to this question in Part III.

Part II, which closes with the present chapter, identified cultural and biological resources for human rights as social construction. Part III illustrates two means of advancing the human rights idea: by translating it into local cultural vernaculars and by reframing it cognitively.

---

[34] To be sure, if encouragement or discouragement affects the individual's motivations subliminally, he or she could hardly realize any such right to refusal. But such a systematically distorted self-understanding would likely undermine the individual in all ways, under all circumstances, in all pursuits.

THIS-WORLDLY MEANS OF ADVANCING THE HUMAN RIGHTS IDEA

6

Translating Human Rights into Local Cultural Vernaculars

Part III now introduces two particular means of advancing the human rights idea conceived as social construction. Chapter 6 argues for human rights work of outside intermediaries and local participants, translating between local understandings and nonlocal human rights ideas in ways that preserve local "authenticity" and "legitimacy" – ways that resonate with local culture even as they also challenge it. Chapter 7 shows how a cognitive approach allows for human rights as rights *internal* to any given community's culture. It proposes human rights as a learning process that "cognitively reframes" local cultural and political elements in ways that render them more human rights friendly.

Both chapters develop something of a sociological standpoint. From that standpoint, as distinct from a theological one, world religions show themselves to be dynamic repertoires rather than fixed templates. Changes in aspects of religious belief have often entailed certain changes in political organization and commitment. How might religion's dynamic potential relate to the surrounding community's capacity for internal change? Specifically, would the spread of human rights in some cases depend on changes in the repertoires of some religions? Consider Islam, a faith of enduring geopolitical moment. From a sociological perspective focused on cultural changes that are human rights friendly, how might the following goal be pursued: a political context in which all ordinary Muslims enjoyed a culturally recognized, legally protected right to interpret Islam – to interpret with respect to its meanings and to the behavior that Islam promotes? In what kind of political context might ordinary Muslims ask themselves not "What is Islam?" but rather "*Which* Islam do we Muslims want?"

Perhaps few Muslims would find the idea of multiple "Islams" coherent. This is likely the case even as more than a few might be willing to entertain the possibility of multiple interpretations of what they take to be the uni-fied singularity of Islam.[1] Islam's spread since the seventh century from Mecca and Medina across cultures as diverse as those of Morocco and Indonesia generated multiple, even coexisting Islams. Given the cultural particularism and peculiar political sensitivities of each host culture,[2] multiple interpretations can be expected. But an outside observer's per-spective is not likely to be that of the ordinary individual participant in a particular locale. That is, probably few Muslims would choose among competing interpretations in terms of what they *want*, as if their faith were a matter merely of personal preference or private interest. Perhaps most would choose in terms of what they take to be the one *legitimate* or *true* understanding of their faith in their particular locale. Abbas Amanat and Frank Griffel (2007:1) suggest as much: "All normative discussions within Islam, as well as between Muslims and members of other faiths, center on the content of Shari'a." It treats a very wide range of issues, from acts of worship to marriage, divorce, and inheritance; from taxation and war to filial piety; from the legitimacy of violence or torture and just war to means of combating injustice.[3]

My point is that ordinary Muslims' cognitive openness to the possi-bility of plausibly competing interpretations is itself sufficient for par-ticipants to imagine alternatives to the status quo.[4] Cognitive openness marks a capacity for cultural change. Correlatively, a culture's capacity for change[5] in the form of learning, adaptation, or reframing depends on its cognitive openness. No culture in history has survived for long without such a capacity. Some ancient cultures, including the Egyptian, Chinese, and Roman, usually were constrained by their respective self-understandings to deny, camouflage, or play down the very changes that

---

[1] See Said and Sharify-Funk (2003).

[2] See Launay (1992) for a West African example.

[3] "Over the centuries of Muslim history a vast amount of literature has been generated discussing these normative questions. The first impression one gets from looking at this library is that of continuity and congruency. Legal authorities from many different centuries of Muslim history are quoted to determine the response of Shari'a to today's moral questions" (Amanat and Griffel 2007:1–2). Ramadan (2004:124) asserts of Islam a "singular ability to express its universal and fundamental principles across the spread of history and geography while integrating the diversity and taking on the customs, tastes, and styles that belong to the various cultural contexts."

[4] Even in the deeply religious conviction that fallible human beings may misconstrue infallible divine truths. See, e.g., Donohue and Esposito (2007).

[5] No socialized human being is independent of cultures, and there is no culture that is independent of socialized human beings. Rather, "people *live* culture in a *mutually constitutive* manner" (Gutiérrez and Rogoff 2003:21). *Mutually constitutive* means that people and culture each changes the other, continually.

guaranteed the long-term survival of each. By contrast, modern cultures embrace change. Science and other scholarship, for example, practice fallibilism, which anticipates and even institutionalizes change. Any propositions not challengeable, such as those of religious faith, are neither scientific nor otherwise scholarly in the sense of modern, institutionalized scholarship: valid knowledge excludes in principle all dogmatic claims. As for the modern embrace of change more generally, a global capitalist culture of consumerism and possessive individualism is driven by consumers' insatiable hunger for new styles, technologically more developed products, and the satisfaction of ever-new, market-generated needs.

Again, my point is that cognitive openness offers a significant, potentially noncoercive entry point even for some foreign concepts, schemes, or categories. Later I develop this entry point as "translation" and "reframing" and alternative "cognitive styles." In some cases, this sort of entry point may be sufficient for the ordinary faithful to take seriously the notion that a given construction of their faith is not the sole legitimate one. The historical record offers some examples. Hans Maier (1965) provides a compelling one in his study of the intellectual, political, and theological responses of French Catholicism to the French Revolution, to other global political and economic transformations, to changes in social stratification, and to the challenging intellectual influences of Jean-Jacques Rousseau and the Comte de Saint-Simon. These responses ranged from attempts to "baptize" the Revolution, to articulations of a liberal and democratic Catholicism, to a reactionary, defensive politics, to "social Catholicism," and finally to the ideational forerunners of Christian democracy. Consider another illustration, one that occurred in a later century and on another continent. Protestantism in Latin America transformed itself continually throughout the twentieth century. It did so in response to secularism; to the internal division and the challenges posed by fundamentalists, modernists, and Pentecostals; and to the political turbulence generated by the world wars and then the Cold War (Bastian 1994). In some cases historically, and likely in Islam today, cognitive openness at particular moments in time may be sufficient for the faithful to conclude that the legitimate construction of their faith is not the one currently preferred, observed, or enforced in their community or locale.

What cognitive openness might mean for theology can be imagined by analogy to what it has meant for jurisprudence, for the construal of legal documents is structurally isomorphic with the construal of religious texts I am proposing here. Indeed, in some cultures these were one and same text before the juridical eventually became differentiated out from the theological. Take interpretation of the American constitutional text, for example. Its interpretation has never involved the issue of cultural acceptance of human rights. But since 1787, any part of the historical path of its interpretation provides an analogy nonetheless apposite to a cultural capacity for cognitive openness. It does so not only for a tiny group of judicial elites but for the leaders and members of various social movements as well. This openness is sufficient to conclude that the best or legitimate construction of certain legal rules was not the one preferred, observed, or enforced at the time.

Cognitive openness in religious culture might be analogized to cognitive openness in legal culture in the following way: as of the 1960s, justices of the U.S. Supreme Court have interpreted the text of the Constitution's Bill of Rights of 1789,[6] as well as that of the Fourteenth Amendment of 1868,[7] to generate a jurisprudence of the individual's right to privacy. Surely the legislators of 1789 and 1868 never anticipated interpretations of their texts to prohibit the state from interfering with the sale and purchase of contraceptives by married couples,[8] or with a woman's choice to abort a fetus,[9] or with adults consenting to engage in sodomy.[10] Yet the notion today of a constitutionally guaranteed right to privacy is so embedded in American political culture that the justices might be said to have changed the way Americans understand or interpret their political culture. Or, in some cases, perhaps the understandings or interpretations of many citizens helped change the way justices interpret the law. The dominant understanding today is that of the individual's fundamental right to privacy, indeed as a right that is not some add-on to a more basic culture but a right always already at the core of American political

---

[6] The First Amendment forbids, inter alia, federal legislation that would favor any particular religion or prohibit its free exercise, or abridge the freedom of expression. The Third Amendment prohibits quartering soldiers in a person's house without his or her consent, and the Fourth, "unreasonable search and seizures" of persons, houses, papers, and effects without judicial warrant issued only upon "probable cause." The Fifth provides that the federal government shall deprive no person of life, liberty, or property without "due process of law." The Ninth states that the enumeration in the constitutional text of certain rights shall not be interpreted to preclude the existence of additional rights not enumerated.

[7] Which reads in part: "No state shall make or enforce any law which shall abridge the privileges or immunities of citizens of the United States; nor shall any state deprive any person of life, liberty, or property, without due process of law; nor deny to any person within its jurisdiction the equal protection of the laws."

[8] *Griswold v. Connecticut* (381 U.S. 479 [1965]).

[9] *Roe v. Wade* (410 U.S. 113 [1973]).

[10] *Lawrence v. Texas* (539 U.S. 558 [2003]).

culture, even if unrecognized as such for the first seventeen decades or so. This is an amnesiac imagining, however, for I think it unlikely that the justices simply uncovered rights latent in the spirit and culture of the Constitution. *Rather, reframing within a political and legal culture led to new cognitive styles, and new styles led to changed behavior.* That reframing was possible only in the context of some degree of cognitive openness. The logic of this process is no different from that of Islamic communities considering human rights today.

The openness of religious believers to multiple interpretations of sacred texts and teachings allows them also to consider, *from within their faith,* how different interpretations may entail different *political* consequences. But perhaps these ordinary persons are able to consider alternative interpretations only if social conventions allow them, without discouragement, to participate actively in the interpreting. Participation poses an alternative to embracing, as unquestionable dogma, the particular interpretations of religious authorities or other putatively "special persons." If this claim holds true, then the spread of human rights in many cases might require a prior liberalization of the individual's right to interpret his or her own culture – and specifically the *democratization* of the right to participate. How might a democratized right to interpretation (and the educational and other means likely necessary for individuals to be able to take advantage of democratic arrangements) affect Muslims? Even as they likely continue to disagree on many issues, might they nonetheless "share a view of Islam that emphasizes justice, human dignity and equality, the rule of law, the role of the people in selecting leaders, . . . consultative government, and the value of pluralism" (Feldman 2004:60)?[11] For it is this view of Islam that resonates with aspects of human rights, at least as widely understood in the West. (I return to the issue of the West's special role in the spread of human rights.)

Such agreement would seem possible among persons who believe that "ascertaining the will of God and coordinating quotidian social organization require human effort" (Feldman 2004:60). By contrast, a self-interpreting faith (that is, one constructed by this or that elite to be self-interpreting, or as not interpretable by humans) would be compelled to

---

[11] See also Kurzman (1998) for the work of thirty-two Muslims – from the Middle East, Africa, Asia, Europe, and the United States, the eldest born in 1877, the youngest in 1953 – on theocracy, democracy, rights of women, rights of non-Muslims, and freedom of thought.

reject a democratized right of the laity to interpret. Religious faith so practiced will always hinder the spread of human rights.

I argue that a democratized indigenous interpretation is possible in tandem with a religious worldview but only if democratized interpretation comes about as a "change from within" that worldview (Hashemi 2004:50). This liberalization would have to allow Islamic communities to remain largely religious even as it required a separation of mosque and state. But it would also allow interpretation of texts and other aspects of Islamic culture by the "millions of skeptics, agnostics, and atheists [who] currently live in the Islamic world" (Ali 2002:40). Under liberalized conditions, a secular court of law might rule on the request of a religion to be exempted from a general rule not itself aimed at religion yet nonetheless implicating some of the practices of this religion. For example, a secular court might rule on whether a person may receive unemployment compensation when he or she refuses the only employment available because it requires him or her to work on the Sabbath; whether a pharmacist, following his or her religion's proscription of birth control, may refuse to provide it to patients whose physicians have prescribed it; or whether women whose religion requires them to wear full facial covering in public may be exempted from a law requiring that state-issued ID photographs show the individual's full face. The courts so ruling would not inquire into religious doctrine. Rather, they would seek a resolution guided by a desire both to protect freedom of religious practice and to distribute fairly the imposition of general rules across a population diverse along any number of dimensions.

Democratized access to communally significant interpretations of an individual's own culture, including matters of religious belief and practice, would facilitate the development or expansion of cultural and religious pluralism. Any particular form of Islam grounding a community's political and legal system would have to accord the "right of all Muslims, both laity and religious scholars . . . , to 'perpetual reinterpretation' . . . of the Qur'an and tradition of the Prophet in light of 'ever changing human situations.'" A democratized right to interpretation would require, then, not a "traditional, static, and legal-formalistic Islam" but instead a "dynamic cosmopolitan . . . and pluralistic" Islam (Esposito 2004:99).

Under these conditions, what could "indigenous" mean? Muslims living in liberal, secular Western states are more likely than Muslims living in predominantly Islamic states or regions to understand Islam in the culturally liberal terms friendly to human rights suggested earlier (pages 139–40). Such persons might regard themselves, and their beliefs, to be no less indigenous than those of all other Muslims. By contrast, other Muslims might regard as indigenous, say, only Muslims living in the Middle East or in predominantly Muslim countries elsewhere. They might regard such "indigenous" Muslims as the sole culturally viable sources of "authentically Islamic" understandings. To be sure, for many Muslims the "Qur'an is a deep well from which Muslims may draw ... supplies of tolerance, pluralism, respect for diversity – even doubt" (Hashmi 2002:36). An Islam interpreted along the lines of tolerance, pluralism, and respect for diversity is an Islam that allows for broad understandings of "indigenous" and "authentic" interpretations. The spread of human rights within Muslim communities requires adherents to regard a traditional theological reading of the Qur'an as not more indigenous than one based, say, in historical sociology. It requires adherents to regard liberal readings as no less indigenous than "[n]arrow and illiberal readings of the Qur'an." Indeed, liberal readings "are not exclusively the province of fringe elements" (Hashmi 2002:32) but rather also the approach of some enduringly significant classical commentators.

To advance the project of human rights at points where they contradict some understandings of some religious faiths, I propose a way in which interpreters might find, *within* the normative understandings of their own culture, points developable into a more robust conception of human rights *within* that local cultural framework.[12] I seek a notion of "indigenous" interpretation that would be culturally authentic in contradistinction to "foreign imports tied to a colonial and imperial agenda" (Hashemi 2004:50). I show that this goal confronts the need for extralocal ideas and practices toward rendering some aspects of any particular religious culture more resonant with human rights. I develop this proposal in several steps. I argue (1) that translating between local understandings and nonlocal human rights ideas transforms the culture; (2) that transformation need not preclude local "authenticity" and "legitimacy"; (3) that transformation can simultaneously resonate with and challenge local culture; (4) that transformation at the local level is possible via "dual consciousness"; (5) that "dual consciousness" corresponds to a duality of roles, namely those of outside intermediaries and those of local participants; and (6) that this approach entails yet another dualism,

---

[12] I emphasize "developable" as marking the dynamic quality of any cultural community. By *cultural community* I mean a "coordinated group of people with some traditions and understandings in common, extending across several generations, with varied roles and practices and continual change among participants as well as transformation in the community's practices" (Gutiérrez and Rogoff 2003:21).

an uneasy one between cultural integrity and human rights.[13] I also show (7) that this approach has distinct limits.

Translation Transforms Local Culture

If the interpreter finds, within the normative understandings of his or her own culture, points *developable* into a more robust conception of human rights and *developable* within the local cultural framework, does his or her interpretation thereby maintain or transform that culture? If the interpretation maintains the culture more or less untransformed, then the translation can hardly be considered an act of cultural imperialism. This is the position taken for example by Jürgen Habermas. He argues that the "hermeneutic model of understanding, which functions in every-day conversations and which since Humboldt has been methodologically developed from the practice of interpreting texts," can be approached "beyond the boundaries of our own culture, of our own way of life and tradition" (Habermas 2003b:37). Interpretation needs to span some of the cultural and semantic differences that separate both sides, and it needs to span some of their respective pre-understandings. But it need not entail a methodological ethnocentrism. It need not require the assimilation of the interpreted to the standards of the interpreter. Nor need it expect that the interpreted convert to the interpreter's conception of the world.

In fact, human rights, for example as understood by the UN's 1948 *Universal Declaration of Human Rights*, are deeply particular as cultural commitments. The *Declaration* privileges, for example, the individual over the family as society's primary unit. It also favors rights over duties as the basis for interpersonal relationships. It supports legalism over reconciliation, repentance, or education as the basis for dealing with deviance. It elevates secularism over religion as the modus vivendi of public life. Core values of human rights so understood are likely preserved in the translation of human rights into the local cultural vernacular, not least because they are embedded in the laws and other legal instruments that make up "human rights law." But as Sally Engel Merry has found, the process of indigenization nonetheless remains pretty much a one-way street: "international perspectives are translated 'down'

---

[13] The dualism in steps 4 and 5 are the same, simply viewed with different emphases, and analytically distinct from that in step 6.

more than grassroots perspectives are translated 'up'" (Merry 2006: 216).

What changes, then, is the local culture; it changes in some of its aspects when human rights ideas are translated into it. It changes to accommodate a "distinctive modernist vision of the good and just society that emphasizes autonomy, choice, equality, secularism, and protection of the body" (Merry 2006:220). It changes if the local populace becomes persuaded that the state should be responsible for guaranteeing human rights and for punishing violations. And it changes if the local populace becomes persuaded that ordinary individuals are themselves responsible, in the sense of civic duty, to make rights-based claims against an ineffective or violative state.[14] These culturally specific claims favor individualism, rights, and legalism (Sinha 1981:77). At the same time, the various instruments of the "international bill of rights"[15] also recognize (but not without tension) such collective identities as family, nationality, religious belief and practice, organized labor, and even cultural life (Carozza 2003:46–47).

Because the distinctively modernist commitments of human rights are culturally particular to Western individualism, egalitarianism, legalism, and secularism, they inevitably challenge local culture wherever the latter's particularism differs from the particularism of human rights culture. Modernist commitments challenge indigenous patriarchy, for example, by reframing the socially constructed "normality" of sex-based violence. They frame patriarchy as a social failure to protect women from being victimized. They also frame it as a political failure to realize equality of the sexes. Such reframing deeply challenges local cultural understandings and, unless "indigenized," may generate local opposition and so undermine its own goals of human rights expansion. A quandary emerges: the more indigenized a new frame is, the less resistance it will meet. But it also meets with less resistance because indigenization may diminish its capacity to challenge the status quo. To "indigenize," then, is not to

---

[14] After all, the status of a country as a member of the UN, or as a signatory of human rights documents, does not predict whether it regards it citizens as bearers of human rights. See p. 31, note 17.

[15] The "international bill of rights" refers informally to one resolution of the UN's General Assembly (the *Universal Declaration of Human Rights*, adopted in 1948) together with two international treaties, both of which entered into force only in 1976, a decade after their adoption: the *International Covenant on Civil and Political Rights* and the *International Covenant on Economic, Social and Cultural Rights*.

transform a human rights culture. Rather, it is to transform the local culture. For example, the norm of sex-based equality, if indigenized, would transform a patriarchal community in profound ways. A culture of human rights would undermine aspects of some communities simply by being true to itself.[16] Is cultural imperialism therefore unavoidably an aspect of translation? If so, does it undermine the moral claims of human rights?

Transformation Without Precluding Local "Authenticity" and "Legitimacy"

The transformation of a local culture by nonlocal human rights ideas – even if the latter *are* forms of cultural imperialism – can be justifiable, and justifiable from a standpoint *within* the transformed culture itself. First, a capacity for translatability is not a quality added to the content of any particular culture. It is a feature internal to cultural understanding itself. The notion of an untranslatable cultural understanding is like the notion of a private language, one not sharable by two or more persons. If it makes no sense to speak of private languages, then it makes little sense to speak of untranslatable cultural understandings. More likely: to have any particular understanding is to already possess the capacity to translate into other, different understandings.[17] No cultural understanding X can be so different from cultural understanding Y as to preclude the translation of one into the other (where "translation" would mean that Y would understand X on X's terms).[18] The act of interpretation, which is a kind of translation *in nuce*, is common to all cultures. A particular interpretation might be imposed but not cultural interpretability as such. And a cultural capacity for interpretation is key to the spread of human rights.

---

[16] Even a diversity-respecting community "cannot be equally congruent with all values and ways of life." Indeed, it "should not try to be" because "it will quite properly support some and undermine others simply by being true to itself" (Carens 2000:101).

[17] On cultural translatability or untranslatability in general, see Benhabib (2002) and Valadez (2001). On creative reinterpretation within Islam in particular, see Emon (2004–2005).

[18] I am inspired by Davidson's (2001) argument that no language expresses thoughts so alien to other languages that one cannot be translated into the other, just as no idiom of the past resists expression in an idiom of today. But whereas Davidson speaks narrowly of differences between *languages*, I speak expansively of differences within *cultures* and within *ways of life*, as well as between local norms and human rights norms. Interpretation is bounded only by what is imaginable within any particular culture, tradition, or society. And what can be imagined in one can be imagined in another.

Second, as Habermas notes, interpretation between or across differences needs to be a two-way street:

> [The] very beginning of an interpretation . . . demands a hermeneutic effort since it makes participants painfully aware of the one-sided nature and limitations of their initial conjectures. Struggling with the difficulties of understanding, people must, step by step, widen their original perspectives and ultimately bring them together. And they can succeed in such a "fusion of horizons" by virtue of their peculiar capacity to take up the roles of "speaker" and "hearer." Taking up these roles in a dialogue, they engage in a fundamental symmetry. (Habermas 2003b:37)

Participants, in other words, go beyond their initial understandings to achieve a kind of shared intersubjectivity: by mutually taking the perspective of the other, each working his or her way to an understanding of the other's background assumptions. Mutual perspective taking casts participants in a symmetrical relationship with each other. Being symmetrical, that relationship is unlikely to be coercive, at least in the *worst* sense of cultural imperialism. I argue for a better sense.

Transformation Resonating with and Challenging Local Culture

Cultural imperialism is one form of "indigenizing" ideas foreign to a particular cultural community, translating from the foreign into the domestic in ways that coerce the latter. The possibility of imperialism points up an unavoidable tension even in nonimperialistic translations of human rights into local vernaculars. On the one hand, translation needs to resonate with local addressees, with the latter's local cultural symbols, narratives, images, and conceptions. On the other hand, locally resonant translations of nonlocal human rights cultures into local webs of meaning likely never reach full indigenization. The commitment of human rights cultures to the integrity of the individual's body, to individual autonomy and freedom to choose, and to the legal and social equality of persons *cannot* fully be indigenized into a cultural community that remains, say, patriarchal. Full indigenization would mean a profound transformation of the local culture and its understandings of religion, ethnicity, and place. A superficial transformation is more likely, and it is desirable insofar as it can still be effective.[19]

[19] Here I argue against much literature, including An-Na'im (1992a) and Coomaraswamy (1994).

Transformation via "Dual Consciousness" at Local Levels

Drawing on her foreign field research, Merry describes a phenomenon that might be called a "dual consciousness," that is, two different ways of thinking about personal injuries and injustices:

> Many women . . . attributed their injuries to their relatives' failure to abide by the norms of kinship and care. Local activists and reformers encouraged them to see their injuries as violations of their rights that the state is obligated to protect. In adopting this framework victims do not abandon their earlier perspectives but layer the rights framework over that of kinship obligations. These grass roots individuals take on human rights discourse through a double-subjectivity as rights-bearers and as injured kinsmen and survivors (Merry 2006:180–181).

The "framework" adopted by local people frames a "cognitive style."[20] That is, translation frames something local in terms of a cognitive style different from the current style.

Translation of human rights ideas into vernacular settings is a matter of framing local beliefs and practices in terms of a "human rights cognitive style." This style may resonate with a local culture such that the local population may appropriate it as a resource. What is appropriated is not imposed. A human rights cognitive style is a resource for identifying and communicating grievances in ways not only helpful in changing the local status quo but also in generating national and even international support of local causes. Rights language can be a resource at a grassroots level as long as it remains relevant to a particular situation and to the people operating within it.

Cognitive styles "frame" understandings according to which people think and behave. Frames are media of social change; frame change entails behavioral change. By "frame change" I refer in particular to the spread of human rights ideas and practice by changing a cognitive style currently prevalent within a community. Change in cognitive style is itself a kind of translation from one style to another.[21]

---

[20] Witkin (1967:234) defines a cognitive style as the "characteristic self-consistent modes of functioning found pervasively throughout an individual's cognitive activities (perceptual and intellectual)." These are patterns and preferences of thinking, learning, and behaving. Because they are complex and multidimensional, they can be consistent over time and across different contexts. Styles closely related to the dominant way of life find support in that environment and are more likely than marginal styles to be reproduced across generations. In Chapter 7 I further develop the notion of cognitive style, as cognitive reframing.

[21] Kuhn makes a similar argument with respect to natural scientists who, working within competing theories, might be said to work in different belief systems (what Kuhn calls

"Reframing" and "translation" are related, then, but they are not synonymous. At any given time, one always already has a frame (indeed, many). By contrast, one doesn't begin with a translation; rather, one reframes via translation. "Translation" refers to a revised frame, as when victims of local norms, practices, and understandings translate their grievances into a nonlocal language, that of human rights. They thereby reframe, say, a man's "disciplining" of his wife as spousal "abuse." A community's collective reframing can change a local-cultural perspective from viewing a particular behavior as a cultural necessity – say, as a necessity of traditional kinship – to viewing it as a violation of a human right.

Uncoerced translation is possible within a cultural community. Translation is not coercive where it resonates with a local culture. Human rights ideas and practices may resonate if to some extent framed in a local cultural vernacular. This occurs in East Asia, for example, when wife battering is reframed as violative of Confucian precepts about marriage (Merry 2006:220).

To be sure, a human rights cognitive style also challenges local culture. It does so, for example, when it reframes abusive behavior in terms of human rights rather than, say, the prerogatives of kinship as traditionally understood. A rights framework might be layered over a framework of kinship obligations.[22] This is one of the ways in which local groups and

---

"worlds"): "In so far as their only recourse to that world is through what they see and do," "after a revolution scientists are responding to a different world" (Kuhn 1970:111). What they accept as true is distinct from what they formerly held to be false: the sentence they now accept is not the same sentence they earlier regarded as false. After a revolution, it is a sentence of a different language, that of the new paradigm. No theory-neutral reality provides a viewpoint from nowhere from which we can compare different concepts, schemes, or categories; all claims about reality are theory-driven and standpoint-committed. Different claims are not made within some metaphorical "single universal space;" each is made from within its own particular "space." Still, the "distance" between some spaces may merely be words apart, words employed in particular concepts, schemes, or categories.

[22] Merry (2006:185) describes the experience of some battered women in the United States as the layering of a legally autonomous self over a self embedded in familial relationships: "In going to the law, a woman takes on a new subject position, defined in the discourses and social practices of the law. She tries it on, not abandoning her other subject positions as partner/wife, member of a kinship network that usually includes her partner's family as well as her own, along with other subject positions such as 'local,' Christian, and poor. She is, in a sense, seeing how it goes. The experimental subject position includes assertiveness, claims to autonomy, and mobilization of the power of the law.... There are risks: going to court typically precipitates an angry and hostile response from the partner.... As her partner struggles to reassert his masculinity through reestablishing his control over her, she may find her new subject position within the law an alienating and

grassroots organizations might relate to the human rights project. But this is no easy relation. It easily antagonizes local sensitivities and thereby exposes proponents to charges of dishonoring cultural, familial, or religious obligations, and perhaps even to charges of "cultural disloyalty."

By contrast, translation from global to local is translation from extralocal narratives to local ones, from nonlocal programs to local circumstances. It might be translation from declarations of international instruments to which a national elite may be signatory, to understandings at venues where ordinary people live and work. The embeddedness of human rights ideas in particular cultural assumptions about human nature, about norms of social interaction, and about the state can impede their translatability. If vernacularized too little, human rights ideas may have minimal impact on social transformation; if vernacularized too greatly, they may sacrifice their capacity to challenge the status quo. They will be ineffective if they blend in all too well with the very power relationships they ostensibly seek to transform.

A human rights cognitive style can work only if it can span the consciousness of local imperatives and the often competing consciousness of human rights ideas. It can work only as a "dual consciousness." This duality can be identified by answering two questions: Who does the translating? Who does the reframing?

"Dual Consciousness" and Duality of Roles: Outside Intermediary and Local Participant[23]

The spread of a human rights cognitive style challenges communal self-determination at various points. After all, the translating is undertaken not only by local participants but also by nonlocal intermediaries. In the case of translation by local participants, "to frame" can be an act of significant individual agency with respect to a framer's indigenous culture or the culture of others. This act of framing can avoid the common equating of culture with race, ethnicity, language preference, or national origin. To equate culture with ascribed qualities entails "overly deterministic, static, weak, and uncomplicated understandings of both individuals and the community practices in which they participate" (Gutiérrez and

---

empty one. It may disrupt her relations with her kin and her partner as she is pressured to leave him and turn to a new source of support in social services and legal officials."

[23] Again, the duality of this step is the same as that of the previous step (transformation via "dual consciousness" at a local level) but with different emphases.

Rogoff 2003:21). *To participate* in a cultural community is different from *being a member* of a racial or ethnic group. The former is active; the latter, passive. The former is chosen by an individual; the latter, simply given.[24]

Framing can be an aspect of the framer's self-determination. In a sense, he or she "emerges," culturally, through framing: the "structure and development of human psychological processes emerge through participation in culturally mediated, historically developing, practical activity involving cultural practices and tools" (Gutiérrez and Rogoff 2003:21).

I turn now to translation undertaken by nonlocal intermediaries. Important to note is that although cognitive styles strongly relate to indigenous *norms*, they are hardly indifferent to social *institutions*. A human rights cognitive style does not seek global human rights through global agreement about the best or most appropriate forms of government. Instead it focuses on behavioral standards under any number of different social, economic, political, and cultural circumstances. But it does champion greater individual agency and in this way encourage institutional arrangements for greater individual agency. Above all, it favors and encourages democratized access to cultural interpretation.

In many communities, a human rights cognitive style likely comes, at least in part, from outside and beyond a local venue; in many cases, it comes in part from the West. Human rights are widely understood in the West primarily as civil and political rights, by contrast to economic, social, and cultural rights. Human rights in the Western sense demand an individual's right to participate in a democratized interpretative environment but do not extend to demanding "full immersion in a stable, supportive social order" (Nylan 2003:579).

Western human rights ideas are likely to be introduced first by intermediaries. As they engage in framing, intermediaries take the particular story of a person's or a group's treatment or condition and generalize it. If this treatment or condition is problematic, it is so for reasons that should be of concern to the entire community, not just to those directly affected. Intermediaries reframe a particular story as a communal

---

[24] Group membership is often regarded in absolute terms: either one is a member or one is not. By contrast, an individual's participation in a cultural community is more easily grasped in terms of degrees. To an extent, it might also be a matter of choice, even as people do not easily or often choose to move from one set of practices to an alternative set. An individual's personality structure and psychological makeup emerge more through active cultural participation than through static group membership (see Giddens 1991; Hogg, Terry, and White 1995; Jenkins 1996).

concern by articulating principles or standards that would seem to apply to all members of the community even as they are denied to some.

In this way, intermediaries may transfer human rights consciousness to locals, both those affected by a practice or condition and those unaffected. And they may generalize a belief that the state is responsible for enforcement. As intermediaries, framers likely have developed the "dual consciousness" that many locals may lack. Intermediaries are conscious of local grievances in all their particularity, and they are conscious of transnational social movements (such as the human rights project). They are conscious simultaneously of local and extralocal norms.

Dual consciousness allows an intermediary to capture the complexity of cognitive styles: to conceptualize a norm, practice, or understanding in multiple ways. Conceptualization allows an intermediary to express indigenous experiences in the language of rights. Intermediaries reframe a particular story as one that concerns more than just local participants and persons directly affected: the experience of one victim may be typical or representative of a whole class of victims, and it may be relevant to the entire community. Both local and extralocal consciousness are necessary to the project of translating human rights into local vernacular.

Intermediaries can translate from one set of norms to another set, back and forth. They *need* to do so across boundaries of socioeconomic class, levels of educational attainment, racial and ethnic divides, and so forth. To be sure, national elites and nonelite social activists are more likely than most ordinary people to appropriate nonlocal frames. But they are also more likely than complete outsiders to enjoy some degree of local legitimacy. Legitimacy allows them, unlike complete outsiders, to vernacularize new frames, such as domestic violence laws or counseling centers for battered women. In these ways, members of an oppressed group might come to see their plight in human rights terms, even if the group does not adopt human rights talk.

The argument that institutional support is necessary for human rights does not entail that specifically democratic forms of government are also necessary.[25] Thus Jack Donnelly (1999:68) goes much too far in his argument:

> The International Bill of Human rights rests on an implicit model of a liberal democratic (or social democratic) welfare state. The legitimate state, as envisioned by internationally recognized human rights norms, is democratic.... It is liberal.... It is a welfare state: recognized economic and social

[25] See Habermas (1994).

rights extend well beyond the libertarian right to property. And all three elements are rooted in the overriding and irreducible moral equality of all members of society and the political equality and autonomy of all citizens.

Against Donnelly I would argue that a human rights cognitive style is indeed possible within a liberalized culture that nonetheless falls short of state-based democracy. A style under these circumstances might, for example, secure "freedom and social justice for all individual persons and communities against the excess or abuse of power by the state," including a nondemocratic one (An-Na'im 2003:9). Here the salient distinction is not between democratic and nondemocratic communities but rather between liberal and nonliberal ones.

John Rawls makes just this distinction. He contrasts a constitutional liberal democratic community with a nonliberal but "decent" one. From its own standpoint, the latter community is just and regards as reasonable some of the norms dear to a liberal community. Its legal system would follow a "common good idea of justice that takes into account what it sees as the fundamental interests of everyone in society" (Rawls 1999b:67). Its judges and other officials would have good reason to sincerely believe in the justice of the legal system and to respect possibilities for dissent (Rawls 1999b:72). Such a community would also allow a "sufficient measure of liberty of conscience and freedom of religion and thought, even if these freedoms are not as extensive nor as equal for all members of the decent society as they are in liberal societies" (Rawls 1999b:74). It might privilege an established religion but not persecute any faith or intimidate its practice. Given the possibility of inequality in religious freedom, it would recognize a right of emigration and assist persons wishing to emigrate. Finally, it would allow citizens (but only as members of groups and associations) a substantial role in decision making through a consultative hierarchy.[26]

In Rawls's analysis, this nondemocratic society could very well observe human rights by its own, culturally internal lights. To that analysis I would

---

[26] A liberal but nondemocratic polity is not foreign to modern Western conceptions of politics. Hegel (1970:§308) advocates political representation of groups, not (as in liberalism) separate individuals. Where the liberal principle of one person, one vote tends to atomize the social fabric, groups (for Hegel, estates, guilds, and other associations) are more likely to consider broader interests of society. Consequently he criticizes direct suffrage as provided in the 1815 Constitution of Würtemberg: The "electors appear otherwise in no bond or connection with the civil order and the organization of the state. The citizens come to the scene as isolated atoms, and the electoral assemblies as unordered inorganic aggregates; the people as a whole are dissolved into a heap" (Hegel 1964:262).

add that a "decent" legal system does not require legislation enacted by a representative assembly. Respect for rights does not require that dissidents be allowed to participate in popular voting, which might allow them to raise the level of their popular support. Nor does it require toleration of opponents seeking to overthrow the government.

The kinds of culturally internal debates that might be opened up by a democratized right to indigenous interpretation, to reframing, and to translation could lead to greater cognitive openness locally. Human rights might seem to be more plausible in (perhaps even compatible with) this sort of culture, society, or political community than previously thought. Such openness requires a liberalized communal atmosphere but not necessarily a democratic polity. And a liberalized atmosphere is more easily achieved than a democratic order. The integration of China and Vietnam into the global market provides an example: economic liberalization can stimulate some social and cultural liberalization without necessarily entailing the development of a democratic order.

Uneasy Dualism: Cultural Integrity and Human Rights

A number of international instruments consider cultural integrity a human right, one that sometimes stands in tension with the extracultural forces needed for spreading human rights. The problem is that introducing ideas into a cultural community that are foreign to that community may violate communal self-determination. The introduction of human rights into local cultures – with the participation of nonlocal intermediaries – likely cannot be free of all cultural imperialism.

From the standpoint of human rights, cultural imperialism is morally defensible but only if its goal and consequence facilitate individual agency within a political community. It would be defensible, from the standpoint of human rights, if it facilitated equal agency of all members to participate in self-interpretations of cultural elements informing the political community. From this standpoint, cultural imperialism is defensible where it democratizes an individual's right or authority to interpret his or her own culture. But from the perspective of any non–human rights polity, this democratization cannot be defended in human rights terms, of course. The normative localism I detail here entails the improbability that human rights can be spread entirely free of cultural imperialism.[27]

---

[27] For a general theory of normative localism, see Gregg (2003a).

Still, the effects of cultural imperialism (understood in this narrow sense) might themselves be indigenized into a local vernacular. For if normative localism is all that there is, then state-based human rights might be the most culturally plausible form of human rights. After all, in this model, the state *is* "the local"; human rights valid for a state are valid locally.

The model finds less support in the *Universal Declaration of Human Rights*, which invokes natural rights universally valid a priori. It finds more support in the 1789 *Déclaration des droits de l'homme et du citoyen*, which reframed metaphysical natural rights as mundane, locally valid "political rights." As such, they could now "only be held within specific political regimes." They thereby became "increasingly useless as a notion in international or intercultural relations" because, as John Stuart Mill asserted, "only members of nations *could* have rights" (see Pagden 2003:190).

In other words, non-Western polities – including those that are liberal but not democratic – indigenize human rights as those polities assume a state-based identity[28] committed to human rights. Each one would do so in its own way. If human rights can in this way become part of a given polity's cultural vernacular, then they hardly reinforce a supposed global "superiority" of Western norms. Correspondingly, a human rights cognitive style need not conflate human rights with any particular notion of the good life (Koskenniemi 1991:397). Rather, each polity's particular human rights cognitive style would incarnate a notion of the good life all its own. A state-based identity of this sort, like a cognitive style widely shared within a polity, would itself be a product of democratized access to indigenous interpretation.

This point brings a "chicken-and-egg" puzzle into high relief. Democratized access to local interpretation capable of enhancing human rights already presupposes an institutionalization and guarantee of

---

[28] The concept of "identity" is both fuzzy and elastic. Still, for my purposes it remains better equipped than any alternative to mark the experience of political community as a repertoire of networks, social roles, and personal ties – represented publicly through shared symbols, rituals, and narratives. It marks as well the experience created by political entrepreneurs (including human rights activists) who would persuade individuals that they are in fact members of a political community with distinct interests, problems, and collective goals. As Brubaker and Cooper (2000:16) point out, the state is a "powerful 'identifier.'" This is the case "not because it can create 'identities' in the strong sense – in general, it cannot – but because it has the material and symbolic resources to impose the categories, classificatory schemes, and modes of social counting and accounting with which bureaucrats, judges, teachers, and doctors must work and to which non-state actors must refer."

fundamental political rights, such as freedoms of the press, of thought, of expression, perhaps even of access to basic education. Such freedoms provide conditions for the possibility of individuals taking advantage of an abstract right to interpretation.[29] In communities where such freedoms are curbed or nonexistent, democratized access to indigenous interpretation is unlikely to emerge. And where access is absent, fundamental political rights remain culturally implausible.

Limits of This Approach

As I noted at the outset of this chapter, there are distinct limits to my approach. First, it is itself culturally specific, for example in its embrace of individual human agency. In this respect, it cannot but generate conflict in political communities with alternative commitments. Second, the approach is open with respect to "direction": it could be deployed toward discouraging belief in human rights just as well as it could be deployed toward encouraging it. Third, the approach requires that existential claims of religion not supersede human rights; this requirement constitutes a significant challenge to some religions. Each of these points bears elaboration.

First, no culturally defined position can be culturally neutral. All culture is particular, including "cosmopolitan culture." A robust civil rights form of human rights is a cultural commitment to respect for rights, probably as some form of legalism;[30] a conviction that every individual has an inherent dignity; respect for legal equality and freedom from abuse; and tolerance of different religious faiths within society. Such respect, conviction, and tolerance are culturally modernist features that, as such, are more likely to appeal, for example, to "assimilated and highly educated Muslims in the United States, as well as [to] the relatively small number of highly modernized Muslims in the Middle East itself," than to millions of traditionalist Muslims around the world (Kurtz 2002:51).

The problem for my approach is not any particular culture; rather, the problem is a lack of liberalized interpretation within any particular culture. By advocating a "liberalization" in interpreting cultural elements,

---

[29] The argument in earlier pages for the possibility of human rights in a culturally liberalized but not democratic community does not solve the chicken-and-egg puzzle. *That* enigma is: Which needs to come first, democratized access to interpretation or the institutions required for democratized access?

[30] The rule of law is not the only form of such respect, of course, though it is the one favored by liberal democratic regimes. The rule of law may not be the form favored by a human rights regime that is tolerant of difference but not democratic.

whether religious texts, national history or any number of behavioral customs, my approach constitutes a modernist, non-absolutist, historicizing and contextualizing reading of a political community's cultural patrimony. Thus it is likely to be opposed "both by absolutists who do not, on principle, accept any historical contextualization of the Qur'an, and by their Western critics who lack the sympathy necessary to accept such contextualization" (Bilgrami 2002:63). After all,

> it by no means follows from the fact that the Qur'an exalts justice as primary among moral values that a tolerant Islam must be read into the Qur'an. What counts as "just" is notoriously contested, and it might as easily be claimed that the Qur'an's vision of justice is only realized by those who put aside their own moral predilections and adhere to the legalistic requirements of the literalist reading. (Bilgrami 2002:62)

Second, processes of cultural reframing and translation do not themselves guarantee any particular outcome. They do not, for example, guarantee a movement *away* from cultural and normative parochialism. Interpretation can go in either of opposing directions. A fundamentalist Muslim wishing to spread, to liberal secular democracies in the West, a code no less universalistic than human rights – namely Shari'a – could equally draw on the approach I propose. I intend the approach as socially liberalizing, but it could be used to equal effect by groups that reject the "idea that the liberal political system is the best arrangement for all human societies, regardless of their diverse and conceptual and material resources" (Mahmood 2004:76). Such groups assert with considerable confidence that a liberal political system is not the best or most desirable for all societies. My approach allows for this: for "tak[ing] the resources of the Islamic tradition and question[ing] many of the liberal political categories and principles"; it allows for rejecting "liberal conceptions of individual autonomy, human rights, and individual freedom" and for an Islam interpreted as opposed to such conceptions (Mahmood 2004:75).

Third, although my position does not entail that democratized access to indigenous cultural interpretation must supersede religion, it does require that the existential claims of religion not supersede human rights.[31] Any such requirement will always constitute a significant challenge to some religions.

---

[31] In my approach, all norms, including those of human rights, are particular cultural constructs. It rejects any norm that claims validity as a matter of supernatural revelation, or as a matter merely of tradition, or otherwise as a matter external to ideas *achieved* by the participants themselves.

The secularism of my approach will offend at least some theological alternatives, such as verses in the Qur'an that "sanction gender injustice and hostile and aggressive relations with non-Muslims" (Bilgrami 2002:63). The same is true of provisions that "as a religious matter, a man may marry up to four wives simultaneously" (Fadel 2004:83). Likewise, if one argues that the "ultimate good is salvation," then one would hardly "prefer a democratic state to a theocratic regime that teaches true doctrine" (Fadel 2004:83). Equally, anyone who believes that "justice itself [is] known only as a consequence of revelation" would also reject my approach (Fadel 2004:82).

These limits to reframing and translating specific ideas and practices between cultures need not defeat a project for the global spread of human rights, even as they clearly qualify it. Still, for many of the faithful, it must be quite a reach. But possibilities remain. For example, it is unlikely that all Muslims will ever agree on one understanding as the single "true" one. Such enduring nonagreement constitutes an interpretive space within Islamic culture. Interpretive space can become dynamic; it can allow opportunities for considering alternative interpretations; it can imagine modifications to a community's normative system. In this dynamic space opened up by abiding nonagreement, groups and individuals might reframe some of their culture's current understandings. Muslims might ask themselves: What are the various Islams (plural!) that we Muslims might choose to construct? This inward-looking question might also be the starting point for outward-looking discussions with nonlocal intermediaries about translating human rights into the local Muslim community's vernacular.

From the this-worldly means of advancing the human rights idea explored in this chapter, as translating between different cognitive styles, I move in Chapter 7 to a different but related means: cognitive reframing.

7

Advancing Human Rights through Cognitive Reframing

In the previous chapter I developed the first of two particular, practical means of advancing the human rights idea conceived as social construction: translating between local understandings and nonlocal human rights ideas. In this chapter I turn to the second practical means: reframing culturally particular ideas, such as human rights, in ways that render them more plausible or attractive to the local community.

No one, neither speculative philosopher[1] nor empirical anthropologist,[2] has ever shown human rights to be anything other than a culturally particular social construction.[3] Human rights do not appear to be natural, divine, or metaphysical, despite persistent allegations to the contrary. And if they are a social construction, then there is nothing otherworldly about them, "nothing entitled to worship or ultimate respect. All that can be said about human rights is that they are necessary to protect individuals from violence and abuse, and if it is asked why, the only possible answer is historical" (Ignatieff 2001:83).[4]

---

[1] Perry (2007), for example, whose efforts I critique in Chapter 1.

[2] Handwerker (1997) and Renteln (1988, 1990) argue that human rights are universally valid as such. They are persuasively challenged by Wilson's (1997) and Merry's (2001) respective claims that human rights are not a priori universally valid. As one of a number of the contingent historical processes of global import (including the development of capitalism, the spread of the nation-state, and the age of colonialism), the topic of human rights is one strand of a more or less global debate on the nature of morally binding norms. An-Na'im (1990, 1992b) and Cohen, Hyden, and Nagen (1993) challenge Handwerker and Renteln as well. They assert nonuniversal, that is, national and regional, understandings of human rights that somehow mediate between the universal and the local.

[3] From a constructivist perspective, the idea that human rights are "natural" is itself a construct: a product of history, internally contested, with ambiguous boundaries of definition and application.

[4] Although there is no single justification for human rights to satisfy all objections and doubt, and although not everyone in any given modern society believes that human

Because many a social construction appears parochial from stand-points outside and beyond the community of origin,[5] one wonders: On what basis might one parochialism ever justifiably trump another? Specifically, how might particular human rights be made widely plausible *from within* communities in which they currently appear implausible for local cultural reasons? The words "from within" already signal a central aspect of my thesis: a parochial idea is legitimate for the community that embraces it. Human rights can be legitimate for any community that comes to embrace them.

But how can particular human rights become persuasive within cultural communities tomorrow that today regard them as alien or misguided? The answer could have critical implications: conceptually for the sociology of culture; practically for the human rights project. My approach aspires to redeem both possibilities. As theory, it combines cognitive sociology[6] with normative philosophy.[7] With practical intent, it would facilitate human rights diffusion through a new conceptual insight. It construes human rights as a cultural phenomenon[8] and then emphasizes cognitive culture over normative culture as better suited for advancing human rights if they are, in fact, a culturally parochial social construction.

I develop my approach in several steps: (1) I reject essentializing approaches toward culture and instead (2) distinguish *cognitive* aspects of

---

rights are actual rights, large segments of societies worldwide do in fact subscribe to some vision of human rights (if not always to absolutist, otherworldly, "all-or-nothing" versions). Such persons might embrace some idea of human rights for, say, economic, religious, or political reasons. But the target of my approach is not persons who already embrace human rights, for whatever reason, but persons, political communities, and cultural groups that now reject human rights, wholly or selectively, for whatever reason. A social constructionist approach renders no ultimate normative grounds for human rights; it eschews such foundations in their theological or metaphysical presuppositions, as I indicate in Chapters 1 and 2. It attempts to ground human rights in the free, contingent embrace of their addressees, as I argue in various ways in all of the remaining chapters.

5 Of course, even a claim once parochial might become cosmopolitan as a matter of contingent historical development.

6 Cognitive sociology extends back to Émile Durkheim (1858–1917), Karl Mannheim (1893–1947), George Herbert Mead (1863–1931), and Alfred Schutz (1899–1959). I draw on later work, especially by Goffman (1922–1982), as well as the contemporary approaches of Zerubavel and Eder, respectively. Approaches in cognitive sociology today range from objectivist, naturalist, and explanatory to subjectivist, humanistic, and inter-pretive. For a typology, see Strydom (2007).

7 This chapter extends a theory I first developed in Gregg (2003a).

8 The question of how culture may generate group cohesion, indeed a cohesion marked by shared behavioral values, goes back to Johann Gottfried Herder (1744–1803), Wilhelm Wundt (1832–1920), and Benjamin Lee Whorf (1897–1941).

culture from *normative* ones. (3) I show how a cognitive approach allows for human rights as rights *internal* to any given community's culture. I then propose human rights as a learning process in two senses: (4) as a "cognitive community" and (5) as a social system. (6) These steps render human rights, understood in the theoretically least taxing way as merely parochial social constructions, nonetheless spreadable across cultural and political boundaries – through a technique of "cognitive reframing."

Against Essentializing Approaches to Culture

Throughout history, and to this day, many societies attach themselves to various transcendental or otherworldly "truths" (most prominently proffered by religion and metaphysics). Examples include "national destiny" (Napoleonic France), "historical fate" (colonial America as the proverbial "city on a hill"), or "civilizational superiority" (premodern China, ancient Rome, the British Empire, and perhaps the American hegemon today). Such "truths" feed off an essentializing approach to culture.

There are many kinds of essentializing approaches; consider two. Essentializing is the notion of culture as a kind of "biology." From this perspective, cultural communities "have" culture in the sense that humans "have" a genome. Just as genomes are inherited without human will and consciousness, culture, in this view, is perpetuated largely without participant will and consciousness. But whereas genomes unconsciously determine people, people (always already embedded in culture) to some extent *consciously* perpetuate, modify, and create culture.[9]

Human genomes adapt over long evolutionary periods to the natural environments of human habitation (generating differences among populations with respect to, say, skin pigmentation, lactose tolerance, or resistance to malaria). In a very different sense of adaptation, humans develop and adapt aspects of their cultures in response to new social environments or to changes in existing ones. Thus the shift from an agricultural economy to a modern, urban-based industrial economy was accompanied by the replacement of the extended family with the nuclear one.[10] But whereas biological adaptation is a material process, cultural adaptation is a cognitive one, an act of human imagination. The plasticity of a material process is different from the plasticity of a cognitive one.

---

[9] Note the circular structure here: cultural artifacts influence the creators, often across generations, who in turn influence those artifacts by interpreting, modifying, or replacing them.

[10] Compare Jackson (1995).

Here we find the most salient difference for the human rights project: cognitive adaptations can be conscious and may be guided along distinctively normative dimensions. These cognitive features are multiply relevant to the human rights project. They are relevant if human rights are construed as social constructions embedded in an open-ended learning process permanently subject to self-reflection, self-correction, and re-formulation. Such features lessen the distance between inventing this or that human right and the various, oftentimes widely diverse environments of application.[11]

Essentializing in another sense is the notion of culture as a set of identities internalized by each member. "Internalization" constructs individuals as if they were computers that, as a community, download the same set of files from a shared listserv. The downloaded software then provides each individual "computer" with the same framework for mutual understanding among members of the listserv. Essentialism of this sort presupposes that political communities are – or should be – homogeneous along cultural dimensions. It regards homogeneity of members as necessary for social integration and cooperation, and both integration and cooperation, in turn, as necessary to the successful coordination of beliefs and actions.

And yet no cultural community is entirely homogeneous, and no community is sharply bounded from all others. Like cultural integrity, cultural identity is always plastic, always dynamic and changeable rather than static and fixed. Globalization only increases heterogeneity along some dimensions (such as that occasioned by the flow of peoples across borders) while increasing homogeneity along others (including popular culture, youth culture, and some consumption patterns).

Here we have the antiessentialist upshot: sharing among a community's members, and their coordination of belief and behavior, does *not* require shared, distinct norms. For the human rights project, then, no single version of human rights is necessary for the spread of human rights. Indeed, insistence on a single version could be counterproductive. To ignore the social, cultural, political, and economic particularities of any local community is to forsake possible change undertaken by a freely persuaded community. One alternative, the force of unilateral foreign interventionism, is morally and politically problematic and possibly ineffective as

---

[11] Cultural norms are permanently in need of interpretation: at *this* particular time, under *these* particular circumstances, how is *this* particular norm to be understood and applied toward what particular goals?

well, given the local resentment it generates. I discuss specific examples momentarily.

Correspondingly, human rights themselves are forever open-ended with respect to definition. Efforts to define and apply human rights will change over time, as the world changes, and as influential political theories wax or wane or undergo internal revision. And thus – to anticipate my discussion of "cognitive frames" – there is no single human rights frame. One frame might be oriented on individualistic human rights, for example, and another on group-based human rights.[12]

By "open-ended learning process" I mean something along the lines of Ignatieff's argument that, if human rights are the "language through which individuals have created a defense of their autonomy," it is "*not* an ultimate trump card in moral argument. No human language can have such powers" (Ignatieff 2001:83–84). A frame is similar: it renders "what would otherwise be a meaningless aspect of the scene into something that is meaningful.... Each primary framework allows its user to locate, perceive, identify, and label a seemingly infinite number of concrete occurrences defined in its terms" (Goffman 1974:21). But no frame is an ultimate trump card in cognitive argument. And just as "other languages for the defense of human beings could be invented, but this one is what is historically available to human beings here and now" (Ignatieff 2001:83–84), so other frames conceivably are possible for making human rights plausible from within a local culture. There the defense of a particular frame can only be contingent or historical anyway.

In short, in both its mechanical and biological forms, an essentializing approach to culture precludes precisely those features crucial to human rights as an actionable political vision. One actionable vision would be a self-reflexive learning process. Such a process is open to self-doubt, constant self-examination, considerations of criticism and alternative visions,

---

[12] Although no single culture is embraced by all the world's communities, some cultural elements, symbols, and idioms are spread far more widely than others. Meyer et al. (1997) even speak of a general world culture ("general" as distinguished from "universal") that coexists with local cultural elements, symbols, and idioms. The very notion of a general world culture presupposes that different cultural communities are neither uniformly distinct nor profoundly isolated from each other. To be sure, no political community operates in terms of a universal culture even if technology, natural science, modern medicine, and even aspects of capitalist economics appear uncontroversial across most political boundaries in the world today. From a sociological or anthropological standpoint, the notion of a "universal culture" can only describe a possible, contingent future, not a structurally given functional necessity (let alone an otherworldly truth). But it might someday describe the end state of a historically contingent expansion of overlaps across particular cultures.

and the humility taught by attention to history. (From the perspective of later generations, any society appears morally flawed in significant ways).

In later pages I redeem this critique in terms of a cognitive approach that does not essentialize culture. My alternative involves "re-framing." First, however, I turn to the notion itself.

Cognitive Aspects of Culture as Distinguished from Normative Aspects

I distinguish "normative rules," which guide conduct along moral principles, from "cognitive rules," the non-normative rules behind normative rules. An individual holds a particular normative rule on the basis of having been socialized into one or more cultures, a process by which he or she internalizes dominant social norms.[13] Cognitive rules,[14] by contrast, are acquired through a process of imitation or mimesis.[15] They involve a network of symbols, scripts, and routines generating behavioral templates or strategies of action, such as "common definitions of the situation" (Scott 2001:39) or "filters for interpretation, of both the situation and oneself, out of which a course of action is constructed" (Hall and Taylor 1996:947).[16]

[13] Durkheim (1893) and Parsons (1951) are representative of approaches to social integration that emphasize the production of shared rules and norms.

[14] DiMaggio and Powell (1991:63–64) offer one of the most influential accounts of social integration by cognitive means, one that, in analyzing organizations or institutions, shifts the analytic focus "from object-relations to cognitive theory, from cathexis to ontological anxiety, from discursive to practical reason, from internalization to imitation, from commitment to ethnomethodological trust, from sanctioning to ad hocing, from norms to scripts and schemas, from values to accounts, from consistency and integration to loose coupling, and from roles to routines." The range and diversity of this litany gives depth and texture to the distinction between normative and cognitive.

[15] Berger and Luckmann's (1966) claim that organizations structurally reflect socially constructed reality is an argument from imitation or mimesis. DiMaggio and Powell (1991:67–77) build on that argument with their typology of pressures on organizations to conform to the local institutional environment. Coercive forces derive from political or regulatory institutions, from normative forces, or from occupational or professional constituencies that norm participants' behavior. Mimetic forces, which are cognitive, guide organizations unable to map out their own policy or approach (perhaps because the participants' socialization into dominant norms fails to guide). Participants are then likely to copy successful organizations.

[16] Sociological approaches, from ethnomethodology (Garfinkel 1967) to the new institutionalism, stress cognitive components of behavior over normative ones. DiMaggio and Powell (1991:35, n. 10) define cognition (as distinguished from affective or evaluative thought) as "both reasoning and the pre-conscious grounds of reason: classifications, representations, scripts, schemas, production systems."

Normative and cognitive rules coexist and interact. People use both as cultural resources to "strategically act in ways that are independent of social structure" (Thornton 2004:40). Individuals and organizations generate these strategies both normatively, through socialization to cultural values, and cognitively, as "cultural competencies" or a "tool kit or repertoire" from which actors select symbols, stories, rituals, and worldviews for "constructing lines of action" (Swidler 1986:277).[17]

I use cognitive rules to decipher how normative rules might be interpreted and deployed. I analyze cognitive rules as "frames," as the cognitive rules "behind" or "underneath" a certain kind of normative rule, human rights.[18] Frames are one feature of an individual's cognitive membership *in the collective experience* of his or her various cultural communities. Frames link the individual's orientations to the world with those common to his or her communities.

A frame approach is one among a number of contemporary cognitive sociologies, and here Erving Goffman's (1922–1982) work is seminal.[19] He characterizes frames as "definitions of a situation," definitions "built up in accordance with principles of organization which govern events – at least social ones – and our subjective involvement in them" (Goffman 1974:10–11). Often actors may be unaware that they are employing this or that frame. Often they need not be aware: we "personally negotiate aspects of all the arrangements under which we live, but often once these are negotiated, we continue on mechanically as though the matter had always been settled" (Goffman 1974:2). The individual may well be unaware of "such organized features as the framework has and unable to describe the framework with any completeness if asked, yet these handicaps are no bar to his easily and fully applying it" (Goffman 1974:21).

Even so, individuals can always become conscious of employing frames, and this possibility is crucial for the human rights project. They can employ frames by conscious design, much as a competent speaker can speak without knowing explicitly the grammatical rules he or she is following. The individual can always learn the rule descriptions that he or

[17] In this view, culture is not some "unified system that pushes action in a consistent direction" (Swidler 1986:277). Rather, groups and individuals constantly modify culture by drawing on different tools (and different combinations of tools) in these kits.

[18] Rules behind or underneath other rules are "meta-rules."

[19] Strydom (2007:350) regards Goffman as the "most central and influential figure in cognitive sociology." I draw on two of his many lines of influence. One is Zerubavel's notion of "social mindscapes" (1997), which gives a cultural spin to Goffman's discussion of frames as "schemata of interpretation." The other is Eder's (1996, 2007), which extends the notions of both frame and "interaction order" into a theory of communicative action.

she has already mastered implicitly. The project of advancing human rights via frame change requires participant consciousness because the project requires, for its moral integrity, participant free will and critical judgment.

The method of reframing I develop here is not some passive internalization. Rather, it involves "some degree of explicit discursive articulation" (Brubaker and Cooper 2000:18), some degree of self-conscious agency. Any frame can be self-reflexive.

I develop the notion of frames as a notion of controlled cognitive change.[20] Such change is not teleological; indeed, it is quite reversible. The process that brings a person to adopt any particular "mindscape"[21] can just as well bring him or her to adopt alternative mindscapes.[22] Such change may be political inasmuch as the introduction, interpretation, or revision of a mindscape occurs within one or another social field of power. Some mindscapes become institutionalized in powerful ways, prominently in the law, economy, and political system. Here change is uncertain: it may be frustrated by various obstacles; it may fail; it may succeed but only partially.

In three respects I take the notion of frames in a direction not Goffman's, namely toward human rights. First, a frame is a distinct interpretation of the world (or at least of one or more issues). It influences how participants view social phenomena. Correspondingly, a human rights frame is a distinct interpretation of the world: it deploys the specific normative terms of human rights. It is a *cognitive* frame for a particular moral vision.[23]

Second, a frame is perspectival:[24] "When participant roles in an activity are differentiated," the "view that one person has of what is going on is likely to be quite different from that of another. . . . [W]hat is play for the

---

[20] Goffman is not particularly concerned with frame *change* beyond the sense of everyday accommodations or "repairs" to an ever changing interaction order. I open up frame analysis to cognitive change that advances the human rights idea.

[21] To use Zerubavel's (1997) term.

[22] The argument in Chapter 6 is structurally similar: that processes of cultural reframing and translation can move in either of opposing directions: away from cultural and normative parochialism, for example, or toward it.

[23] The distinction between normative and cognitive aspects need not exclude one from the other; it could mark a division of labor between them.

[24] Perspectivalism may be analyzed only from a point itself perspectival. A human rights frame is perspectival because claims to human rights are themselves "optically" relative or culturally parochial. This circular logic does not doom the possibility of knowledge: "without any danger of contradictions or antinomies emerging it is possible to express the syntax of a language in that language itself, to an extent which is conditioned by the wealth of means of expression of the language in question" (Carnap 1967:3).

golfer is work for the caddy. Different interests will...generate different motivational relevancies" (Goffman 1974:8). Correspondingly, any
human rights frame is perspectival. There have always been competing
understandings of what human rights are (and in Chapters 1 and 2 I
argue that they are not "natural" but instead socially constructed). There
have always been competing accounts of their foundation (in Chapters 3,
4, and 5 I argue that they are this-worldly not otherworldly, for example).

Third, frames can motivate and guide behavior in the strong sense of
political activism. They "provide background understanding for events
that incorporate the will, aim, and controlling effort of an intelligence,
a live agency....Such an agency is anything but implacable; it can
be coaxed, nattered, affronted, and threatened. What it does can be
described as 'guided doings.' These doings subject the doer to 'standards,' to social appraisal of his action based on its honesty, efficiency,
economy, safety, elegance, tactfulness, good taste, and so forth" (Goffman
1974:22).

Correspondingly, a human rights frame can motivate and guide behavior with strategies of individual or collective action.[25] If it can change
behavior, it may be able to change aspects of the local social and political
order.

Rendering Human Rights Internal to a Community's Self-Understanding

By reinterpreting frame theory in this fashion, I not only reinterpret Goffman. Against a tradition extending three hundred years from Thomas
Hobbes (1588–1679)[26] to Talcott Parsons (1902–1979),[27] I also argue
that cognitive meta-rules, as distinguished from deep moral norms, can
generate social order independent of moral norms. I do not mean that
social order is possible entirely without moral norms. On the contrary,
cognitive rules allow people to understand and use norms to create social
order.

A human rights frame is not itself moral; rather, it may orient the
individual's moral empowerment from *within* a given community in ways
that facilitate human rights practice. Moral empowerment in the form
of human rights is a cultural prescription and, in principle, a possible

---

[25] See Khagram, Riker, and Sikkink (2002:12–13) for examples.

[26] Hobbes (1909) posits community as the product of egoistic individuals seeking refuge
from other egoistic individuals. Political community then appears as a refuge from human
nature because it constrains egoistic individualism by political norms.

[27] See, for example, Parsons (1951).

prescription for *any* culture. Human rights can become a "language" of moral commitment *within* any particular culture, even if not wholly in terms of that particular culture – indeed, even if in terms that challenge one or more of its aspects.[28] This moral capacity is cognitive, as a kind of grammar of social life: human rights that come to be embraced by individuals as an aspect of their *own* social system.

But a human rights frame can empower individuals only by "enabling social systems to learn in a way that individuals cannot" (Eder 2007:403). To the extent that human rights can be expressed in any language, they can be indigenized in any culture. That is, they can be configured as a *native* language of any particular political community in the sense of a social system that can learn a "human rights grammar."

Native here means "something acquired" but also "something freely assented to," a feature central to my approach. Cultural practices to which communal members can freely assent likely possess a legitimacy *internal* to the community. A human rights frame challenges internal practices most compellingly as an idea internal to that community. Internal legitimacy is created at the level not of individuals but of the social system, as a cultural artifact intersubjectively generated and maintained.

An idea once external can become internal through system-level learning, learning that makes the human rights standard *internal* to the community. An idea internal to a community can criticize practices within it. It constitutes a capacity for imminent social critique:

> [I]t is up to victims, not outside observers, to define for themselves whether their freedom is in jeopardy. It is entirely possible that people whom Western observers might suppose are in oppressed or subordinate positions will seek to maintain the traditions and patterns of authority that keep them in this subjection.... [A]dherents may believe that participation in their religious tradition enables them to enjoy forms of belonging that are more valuable to them than the negative freedom of private agency. What may be an abuse of human rights to a human rights activist may not be seen as such by those whom human rights activists construe to be victims (Ignatieff 2001: 73–74).

---

[28] Like any cultural convention, human rights can be introduced to cultural communities in which they are foreign, or in which they are indigenous but only marginally, or in which they are indigenous but different in meaning and practice from foreign versions. For instance, they can be communitarian rather than individualistic, as in the argument from putative "Asian values" (Bell 2006). Human rights are best introduced in cultures resistant to them as a language not of prescription but of free commitment and empowerment as Chapter 4 urges.

An embrace begins with articulating human rights in the "natural" cultural logics of local application. *Local application* refers to venues where, in any given instance, they are to be established, promoted, strengthened, or defended. To introduce into a social system a human rights frame of individual moral commitment and empowerment may challenge various systemic features. But once framed in the local cultural logic, human rights need not delegitimize that logic as a whole. Thus the "women in Kabul who come to Western human rights agencies seeking their protection from the Taliban militias do not want to cease being Muslim wives and mothers; they want to combine respect for their traditions with an education and professional health care provided by a woman. They hope the agencies will defend them against being beaten and persecuted for claiming such rights. The legitimacy for these claims is reinforced by the fact that the people who are making them are not foreign human rights activists but the victims themselves" (Ignatieff 2001:69–70).[29]

Still, once framed in the local cultural logics – that is, once "indigenized" – human rights will surely delegitimize *some* aspects of those cultural communities, and sometimes profoundly. Above all, a plausible understanding of human rights may challenge authoritarianism, patriarchy, and other traditional patterns of obedience. This particular understanding champions individual agency over group-based agency; it rejects group rights where they trump individual rights.[30] Such individualistically understood human rights challenge traditional and authoritarian social systems to "learn" greater individualism by "learning" entitlements and immunities for the individual *as such.*

But if learning means adopting or appropriating,[31] why settle on this particular understanding of human rights? Why interpret human rights as individual rights rather than as the interests of the community? One answer is because individuals are everywhere more vulnerable than

---

[29] Recall the argument of Chapter 6. Using Islam as an example, I show how interpreters might develop human rights *within* their own culture even as they draw on extralocal ideas and practices. They can do so despite points of significant conflict between the local culture and that of human rights; they can do so in ways that resonate with the local culture yet also challenge it. Translators can do this work if they have the "dual consciousness" of outside intermediaries and local participants.

[30] Thus authoritarians such as Lee Kwan Yu of Singapore argue that "Asian values" (Bell 2006) entail group rights that trump individual rights.

[31] What I have in mind is a community's or individuals' appropriation of human rights rather than their outside imposition. Appropriation is likely negotiated and partial as well as constrained by various factors, such as political and economic circumstances.

groups to human rights abuses.[32] The appeal of human rights is likely to be greater for individuals than for groups; although entire groups can be oppressed and persecuted, the primacy of the individual refers to the actual physical and mental point of suffering. Further, human rights obtain especially when the most marginalized individuals can avail themselves of human rights from *within* their own cultural and political contexts. For some communities, this would require greater individualism within. It would require that individuals freely define themselves and their experiences in their social environment in terms of individualistic human rights.

This is not to suggest that human rights are coherent only as fundamentally individualistic; such a suggestion is sociologically naive and empirically inaccurate. For the guarantee and realization of human rights of the individual always lie with the group, the community, and the social system, never with the individual. After all, rights are matters of recognition: a person has an effective right if that right is socially recognized. Rights in this sense are a kind of "group performance" rather than a "solo act."

Indeed, precisely in terms of local cultural logics, the commitment to human rights can only be effective if it is collective. Even as the "effect of human rights violations can only be felt by the individual and the consequences only suffered by the individual" (Montgomery 2001:85), an observance of human rights is communal or collective. In this sense, human rights are "impersonal." They are impersonal in another sense as well. Civil and political rights of the individual might be thought to be "closer" to the individual's selfhood (in some philosophical sense of self)[33] than collective cultural, social, or economic rights. In this view, political or religious expression may track the individual's selfhood more intimately than might commercial speech. Correspondingly, the

---

[32] But not in all cases. For example, the "right to freedom of religion is clearly based on membership in the (religious) community and benefits the community by protecting it from persecution" (Salmon 1997:59).

[33] Such as the individual conceived fundamentally in terms of his or her capacity for self-determination, whether in the clearly political forms offered by Kant or Rawls or even in the apolitical, existential form suggested by Kierkegaard's (1980:52–53) notion of healing "sickness unto death." Kierkegaard marks a path of despair: "in despair not to will to be oneself. Or even lower: in despair not to will to be a self. Or lowest of all: in despair to will to be someone else." Such despair comes of trying to flee the ethical responsibility of being one's "authentic self" (the self one is and the self one aspires to be). By realizing as much, one may gain the "will to be oneself" as a form of right living.

individual might realize him- or herself more profoundly in the polling booth than in the shopping mall. (Perhaps for that reason, the liberal democratic state can regulate commercial speech much more easily than political, religious, artistic, or scholarly expression.) Human rights in the vein of individualistic (civil and political) rights would then seem to be more personal, and human rights in the vein of collective (cultural, social, or economic) rights, more impersonal.

Human Rights as Cognitive Community, and Cognitive Community as Learning Process

For purposes of realizing human rights locally, through internal change rather than by foreign imposition, human rights might be conceived as a kind of learning process, one embedded in the social system itself. This conception presupposes a nonessentialized understanding of culture, culture as socially constructed rather than as a priori categories of human understanding or as given in some super-organic sense. It presupposes culture as internally dynamic not static, as open to outside influences rather than hermetic, as marked by differences and tensions within rather than as something homogenous and consensual, and as laced with power relations rather than somehow free of all such relations.

Embedded in a social system, a learning process can be thought of as an emergent "cognitive community." As I argued in Chapter 1, Georg Simmel (1964) provides an early and still insightful analysis of the cognitive constitution of the individual through the groups of which he or she is a member. Through an intricate socio-mental web of group affiliations, the individual becomes a member of many different multiple cognitive communities at the same time. The individual's very individuality lies in his or her unique and particular configuration of intersecting group affiliations. Yet individuality is itself always a group-based social construction.[34]

Important to the human rights project is the fact that each person's web of socio-mental affiliations is immediately communal. The web filters the individual's particular understandings and orientations into communally recognized ones. On the one hand, each person uses the same cognitive processes as every other. On the other hand, different people may

---

[34] The cultural possibility of being an "individualist" is itself a matter of membership in a cognitive community, no less than the possibility of being a "conformist."

use the same cognitive processes differently, in part perhaps influenced by membership in particular cultural groups, subcultures, or cognitive communities. Thus socio-mental affiliations are neither universalistic nor individualistic; they take place at a level above the idiosyncratic individual yet below universal features of human cognition. This is the meso level of persons as social beings, as members of one or more cognitive communities.

A century ago Karl Mannheim captured community in just this sense: "It is not men in general who think, or even isolated individuals who do the thinking, but men in certain groups who have developed a particular style of thought" (Mannheim 1936:3). The single individual does not think so much as he "participates in thinking further what other men have thought before him" (Mannheim 1936:3). Similarly, frames carried today were earlier carried by others. And they are carried not only by individuals but by entire communities. Communal life in the specific sense of shared understandings refers to communities that share various frames. The human rights project could be advanced by generating "human rights communities" within any given local culture.

A "human rights community" would be a community similar in some ways to others, from professions to institutions, from political movements to nations: communities "larger than the individual yet considerably smaller than the entire human race" (Zerubavel 1997:9). The crucial difference: unlike other communities, a human rights community could, in principle, eventually embrace the entire human race. As a mundane social construction, human rights could be expanded in mundane political ways, potentially without geographical or cultural limit.

Such expansion would depend on the kind of "intersectionality" captured by Simmel. Intersectionality would depend on what I call a "plurality of lenses." It occurs along any number of dimensions (very much beyond the three favored in so much contemporary analysis: race, class, and sex). It can include everything from age cohort, ethnicity, and religious belief to familial status, occupational group, geographic location, and national origin. As a member simultaneously of many intersecting cognitive communities, the individual is connected at least impersonally to the members of each of the shared communities. Each connection offers a kind of "lens" into the world of the person with whom the connection is formed. The individual has as many social lenses as he or she is a member of different communities. Multiple intersecting cognitive subcommunities "meet up" where they intersect in the individual: any one individual is a particular "standpoint" within a web of intersecting standpoints, likely with some understanding of each of those communities. That intersection could, in principle, always include a human rights community.

What is possible in principle could become real in fact through a kind of "learning" at the level of the social system: by adding human rights "nodes" with which individual affiliations might intersect. "Learning" in this context would take into account the fact that the individual sees the world through his or her cognitive connection to others (through which he or she also sees him- or herself: for his or her very identity is related to how he or she views the world). How he or she views the world cognitively is the point of access for the human rights project:

> "Looking" at the world from an impersonal perspective presupposes a certain cognitive ability to transcend our subjectivity and adopt others' "views" as if they were our own.... This presupposes some fundamental process of "optical" socialization where we learn to "look" at things in unmistakably social ways.... [I]t is an impersonal outlook which [people] acquire through their membership in a particular professional community (Zerubavel 1997:32–33).

What Eviatar Zerubavel calls an "impersonal outlook" I would call a lens, one neither personal nor random but rather collective (hence impersonal) and patterned. It is a generalized way of looking at the world. Lenses are plural.[35] In short, my approach does not entail that each individual has a wholly unique and personal cognitively ordered world or that all individuals cognitively order the world in the same way.[36]

---

[35] Cognitive diversity is "optical pluralism." Diversity has long been analyzed as optical pluralism. Marx and Engels's (1998) focus on the distinct interests of each social class provides an early example; Simmel's (1964) discussion of intersectionality offers a later example; feminist social standpoint theory furnishes a still later example (Hartsock 1983).

[36] Expectably, some cognitive lenses compete with others, and other lenses simply overlap. Diversity appears at points where there is no overlap, for example in political and cultural communities that are diverse within themselves and disparate when compared with each other. Here there may not be much of a shared cognitive world. Goffman suggests why: the "world we take for granted is a cognitively ordered world and ... we act together by making the presupposition that we share such a cognitive order" (Eder 2007:396). Hence one kind of "political strife" refers to the problematic experience, of groups and of individuals, of differences between or among cultural communities: where different cultural communities clash because of these differences. Clashes can place into question the basic presuppositions of the participants. Differences in presuppositions may correspond with the absence of overlaps between or among the cultures in question. Here

Human Rights as a Learning Process at the Level of Social Systems

The status of children is particularly sensitive with respect to human rights. As a subgroup usually unable to make responsible decisions for itself, most children lack autonomy in this respect among others. Children often require the protection of others. So do some adults, to be sure, but not because of the natural vulnerability and defenselessness of children as such.

Autonomy is a significant issue for my approach, which depends on the individual or community consciously and freely adopting one cognitive frame (a human rights frame) over alternatives. Even children who already enjoy human rights in practice are still less autonomous than their parents or caregivers. Relevant to a cognitive frame approach is the fact that children anywhere in the world today are likely to be exposed to, and are more or less likely to adopt, their parents' or caregivers' views on, say, matters of religious faith and political orientation, among many other matters relevant to human rights issues. Many parents regard their worldviews as core to their identity and expectably want their children to share these views. Even the liberal democratic state allows a great deal of parental autonomy in terms of parents' raising their children according to the parents' worldviews. It guarantees each individual's right, upon reaching majority age, to embrace and express his or her own convictions. Many individuals embrace in adulthood the viewpoints into which they were socialized as children.

Thus even liberal democratic communities share with traditional authoritarian societies the experience that socialization influences many persons, to some degree at least, over the course of their entire lives. The social and psychological consequences of such influence often run so deep that legal and political-cultural guarantees of individual freedom for adults in many cases may be an unneeded resource by the time the individual attains majority (where, at the point of majority, the individual may freely choose). Even an individualistically oriented constitutional community like the United States, which guarantees freedom of conscience and expression, does not provide for childhood socialization that is "neutral" or "unbiased" in the sense of "free from parental preference." That exemplary expression of liberal democratic

the human rights project fails. To be sure, the absence of overlaps may be benign. But often enough it contributes directly or indirectly to ethnic conflict or other problems of a multicultural cast.

tolerance in the Western mold, the U.S. Constitution's First Amendment, very much allows for the socialization of children into their parents' or caregivers' particular worldviews.[37] It neither presupposes nor requires any "neutral" or "unbiased" standpoint on the parents' part.[38]

Its approach, in other words, allows for parental personalism. Yet as I earlier argued, human rights require a kind of "impersonalism" by analogy, say, to language. Language is inherently communal: it involves a concept-based approach to the world, to one's environment, to oneself. Concepts, unlike sense perceptions,[39] might be shared by all linguistically competent members of a language community. Concepts cannot be possessed exclusively by any one person or group. Further, concepts articulated in language are not wholly generated by individual minds, nor are they wholly modified by a single person's imagination. They are "located" at the impersonal collective level of the social system.[40]

At that level, relations among individuals are "emergent properties that result from individual actions but cannot be reduced" to the psychological makeup of individual participants (Eder 2007:403).[41] Similarly, language is carried by individual speakers yet cannot be reduced to its carriers. In this way, language makes communication and even understanding possible among diverse individuals. It allows them to interrelate despite manifold differences among individual lives. Development of cognitive competence has "collective effects and lead[s] to a 'culture' that is more than the sum of cognitively competent individuals" even as it is "contingent upon their properties" (Eder 2007:395).

---

[37] The Amendment (1789) reads in part: "Congress shall make no law...abridging the freedom of speech, or of the press."

[38] Indeed, its provisions for freedom of belief and expression would be otiose if, in all contexts, citizens were completely indifferent toward any given political commitment or religious convictions.

[39] Sense perception has "individualistic" qualities. For example, no observer can determine empirically the "accuracy" or "truth" of another person's claim to have an itch or pain.

[40] At the same time, the individual can articulate his or her own experiences, convictions, and demands precisely by deploying the common and impersonal medium of language. Indeed, the individual can grasp him- or herself individualistically only in the nonindividualistic medium of language. Doing so in no way compromises his or her uniqueness.

[41] Eder (2007:404) draws an illuminating analogy between social systems and individual psychology: "The 'brain' of social systems is...the social relations a society stores in the structures of its 'systems.' The mind of these social systems is their 'culture,' the semantic representation of its structures."

An impersonal approach is relevant to the human rights project insofar as human rights are necessarily a collective phenomenon and insofar as collective phenomena are impersonal.[42] The individual acquires impersonal perspectives through "optical socialization," that is, through learning certain ways of "framing" the world (from frame acquisition to continual frame maintenance to periodic frame adjustment). One impersonal perspective looks at the world from the viewpoint of others. To understand the other, especially the distant other, depends on the local, culturally *internal* plausibility of human rights to insiders, to the members of that locale. For the human rights project, to understand is to look at the world from the standpoint of the other's suffering as though that suffering were one's own.[43] For the outsider to look at the world this way is to see the world from the insider's standpoint. To be sure, the insider may not view the phenomenon in question as one of suffering. In cases where "suffering" might plausibly refer to a human rights violation, cognitive sociology can be deployed to advance a human rights frame from *within* the local cultural and political community.

"Looking at the world from the standpoint of the other" may help sustain certain political and moral interrelations among individuals. Some of them are cultural. Culture provides one logic of interconnection within ongoing communication. Through communication, individuals learn; groups of individuals learn together; and social systems also "learn" but in ways that cannot be reduced either to individual- or group-based learning (Eder 2007:403–404).[44] Here lies the political significance of the impersonal learning of a social system: systems can "learn" what many individuals, perhaps in part because of their socialization, may not be able to. "Learning" here entails adopting a human rights frame.

---

[42] Like all social constructions and ethical systems, human rights are intersubjective not subjective, and what is intersubjective can also be impersonal.

[43] As I suggested in Chapter 5 with regard to sentimental novels in the latter half of the 1700s that encouraged the reader's empathy with and sympathy for the downtrodden and socially marginalized may have enlivened notions of human rights.

[44] According to Eder (2007:404), "societies make choices that individuals experience"; those choices create "conditions for success or failure [that] are beyond the intentional reach of actors"; these conditions are "new environments for the self-organization of societies." This self-referential pattern is analogous to human rights as a social construction: cognitively competent individuals create human rights culture, are exposed to the culture they collectively create, and learn from their own collective creations.

Cognitive Reframing

Any given individual's capacity for agency is always already embedded in any number of normative and cultural commitments that surely affect how he or she might regard normative claims entailed by human rights. That capacity is embedded in commitments that likely affect how the individual deploys his or her agency (if not necessarily in ways always predictable). Children grow up in culturally pre-populated spaces, spaces that often influence many of them enduringly; like everyone else, they do not deploy their agency in a culture-free vacuum. Not only for children, but especially for them, agency constrained by its cultural environment may be agency strongly committed to that environment, whatever its normative tenets.

One precondition for the guided cognitive changes required by the human rights project (for children as well as for adults) is some degree of compatibility between individual agency and cultural environment. The individual's enduring embeddedness in deep and powerful influences, in cultural-environmental influences, hardly extinguishes individual human agency. It hardly extinguishes the individual's capacity to question aspects of his or her cultural socialization and environment or to adopt alternative political beliefs and cognitive commitments. Human rights–oriented social and political change depends on some degree of compatibility between the individual and communal levels, between individualism and communitarianism. Toward making the local cultural logic more human rights friendly, the impersonal social system level needs to resonate more with the individual's level.

Consider "childhood" as something on which there needs to be agreement if human rights are to be accorded to children. What cognitive horizon delivers agreement on the question: How is "childhood" best defined?[45] Most understandings of childhood are culturally determined and may differ widely across political communities, legal systems, and history. Not surprisingly, there is no global agreement as to what constitutes a "normal" or "desirable" childhood or even when childhood ends.

Further, current human rights instruments are insensitive to the culturally contextual nature of definitions of childhood. The Convention on the Rights of the Child,[46] for example, presupposes consensually accepted boundaries of childhood, boundaries fixed and unambiguous.

---

[45] Answers to some cognitive questions may have distinctly normative implications.
[46] See Muscroft (1999) for the text of the convention and analysis of its consequences.

It presupposes a notion of what a "normal" childhood is as a standard by which to measure abnormal childhoods in need of human rights redress.

Presuppositions of this sort imply that children's human rights, with respect to definition or application, are non-negotiable in any particular community. They imply that children's human rights must be the same for all communities given a presumption of globally valid understandings of "normal childhood."[47] And yet, in every society, the status and social identity of a child differs in one way or another from that of an adult. In short, how "childhood" is defined is highly relevant for the human rights project. If, for example, "we reject an arbitrary age of eighteen and accept local norms, the view that all early marriage is wrong becomes untenable.... [A] child marrying at fifteen in full accordance with traditional norms and local custom in India is very different from a child marrying at fifteen in the UK" (Montgomery 2001:82).[48]

Under such circumstances, how is frame change possible? In particular, what is possible by eschewing perspectives that essentialize local culture? Consider the following example of empirical research that challenges essentializing presuppositions. Studying child prostitution in Baan Nua, Thailand, Heather Montgomery (2001:94) found children's sexual exploitation negatively correlated to their desire to live with their families and within their communities. That is, the children valued the "right" to living with family above the "right" to be free from sexual exploitation. Engagement in the sex trade was a means for them to remain with their families – but only if framed in terms of a "cultural belief in supporting their parents and their sense of filial duty. This is not to claim that culture demands that they prostitute themselves. While their cultural environment makes it more likely that they will become prostitutes, it does not mean that it is solely because of culture that they do" so (Montgomery 2001:95).

In this case, evidently, the presence or absence of human rights is tied not primarily to culture but more to poverty and other factors in the participants' *inadequate agency* to generate alternatives to prostitution as

---

[47] Such presuppositions contribute nothing to resolving additional problems: that the assurance of one human right might be possible only at the expense of others, say, or that, in practice, rank ordering different human rights cannot be neutral with respect to culture, time, and place.

[48] If childhood is not a homogenous state, then which differences among the various members of the category "children as such" are significant for human rights? Which are significant with respect to adult expectations along dimensions of, say, sex, age, cohort, or position within the family? Decades ago, Ennew (1986) and La Fontaine (1990) suggested initial answers.

a means to staving off what children regarded as the worst consequences of poverty:

> Children undoubtedly gained satisfaction from being able to support their families and fulfill their kinship obligations, yet their agency was minimal and they remained socially and economically marginal. Their poverty and low social status consigned them to the edges of society, from where they had no structural power. With no welfare state or social security safety net, there were few options that enabled them to survive even at subsistence level (Montgomery 2001:95).

Child prostitution, then, is not some cultural cue that, under conditions of poverty, "surfaces" to motivate behavior.

A putative human right to be free of sexual exploitation evidently requires attention to *global economic* relations as much as to *local cultural* particularities.[49] This approach does not simply assume the universalistic normative position that child prostitution is morally offensive under any conditions that presuppose a human right to fundamental human dignity. For example, it does not assume the moral claim that prostitutes reduce themselves to the material value of their body, a value always below that of the nonmaterial, dignity-based value of a human being as such. Instead, this approach focuses on the fact that children are unlikely to be autonomous agents choosing prostitution.

Autonomy is at issue along several dimensions. One dimension is economic: if the children's families had sufficient income, the children's "right" to be free of sexual exploitation would not conflict with their "right" to live with their families and within their communities. The eradication of child prostitution might best be pursued not through cultural engineering (or through punishment of parents) but by "ensuring that their families could stay together and have a sustainable income" (Montgomery 2001:97).

Child prostitution is a matter not only of participants' economic condition, as Montgomery obliquely acknowledges: "Both children and their parents told me that they chose prostitution and that it paid better than other jobs, yet their explanations were not as unproblematic as they claimed" (Montgomery 2001:95–96). Also deeply problematic is the lack of autonomy on the part of the participants. Children clearly lack autonomy along several dimensions.

---

[49] According to Montgomery (2001:98), local consequences of Thailand's international political and economic position are "as important as cultural specificities in perpetuating . . . sexual exploitation."

One is access to information: the "people of Baan Nua allowed for no wider moral or political understanding. Whatever the children said about sex work, they did not have the complete knowledge to make a fully informed decision" (Montgomery 2001:96). A further dimension is cultural: "Parents placed overwhelming emphasis on their own cultural understandings and rationalizations and in doing so were unable to see the selling of their children in its wider political context" (Montgomery 2001:96). Yet a third dimension is the culturally undifferentiated approach of international human rights instruments and relevant NGOs: the "Convention and the NGOs who want Article 34 [concerning sexual exploitation and the sexual abuse of children] enforced at whatever cost, allow for no cultural specificity" (Montgomery 2001:96).[50]

Given problems of local access to information, local cultural understandings, and well-intentioned but locally unhelpful international voices, my approach to cognitive frame change might be deployed as an alternative. The questions are: How might we configure reframing so that it resonates with the local community? How might the idea of human rights, or of specific human rights, be brought to resonate from within the local community? Answers to these questions emerge from a different empirical example. Elizabeth Boyle examines the practice of female genital cutting (FGC).[51] FGC is locally framed in a variety of positive ways that depend on an entire belief system rather than on any single explanatory factor.[52] Single factors range from the cultural to the aesthetic, from the hygienic to the religious to the sexual.[53]

---

[50] See Muntarbhorn's (2007) analysis of Article 34.

[51] I use the term FGC to include three different practices: clitoridectomy (removal of all or part of the clitoris), excision (complete clitoridectomy plus removal of all or part of the labia minora), and infibulation (removal of the clitoris and labia minora, then the cutting and sewing together of the labia majora). FGC is widely practiced today in Burkina Faso, Chad, Côte D'Ivoire, Djibouti, Egypt, Eritrea, Ethiopia, Gambia, Guinea, Mali, Nigeria, Sierra Leone, Somalia, and Sudan. Between 100 and 140 million women and girls have undergone this procedure, and each year approximately 2 million face it as a prospect (World Health Organization 1999).

[52] The cultural quality of this procedure is immediately on display in that naming it one way or another is unavoidably a political act. The term "female genital mutilation" presupposes that the procedures mutilate (in ways that male circumcision or breast implants for women do not). The expression "female circumcision" analogizes sometimes drastic and harmful surgeries to the much more minor operation performed on infant males. By contrast, the term "FGC" does not rest on undefended presuppositions nor does it make false analogies.

[53] Including claims that a girl will not become a mature person unless her clitoris is removed; that a woman's external genitalia have the power to blind birth attendants, cause the infant's death or deform it physically or mentally or cause the husband's death; that FGC

How might FGC be reframed toward facilitating greater individual autonomy along some of the various dimensions of autonomy I earlier identified as crucial with respect to human rights for children? The individual's capacity to critically reconsider local norms is of course aided by his or her capacity to imagine alternatives to those norms. Boyle (2002:151) found that exposure to alternatives facilitates the cognitive reframing of local norms by women – usually the mothers of girls targeted for FGC – in ways that deviate from traditional or dominant social practices.

Formulations of alternatives begin with critiques of the status quo. In terms of my approach, FGC might be reframed negatively, as a matter of injury, pain, possible illness, and deprivation of sexual pleasure; as a feature of the patriarchal family; or as one element of a general religious or political structure that systematically subordinates women. And it might be reframed as a violation of the individual's right to bodily integrity and decisional autonomy.

The procedure could also be framed from the perspective of women who have been cut and who then drew conclusions from the experience at odds with dominant local norms. One factor relevant to a participant's openness to extralocal frames is whether the girl's mother had undergone the procedure.[54] Women who, as girls, underwent the procedure are less likely to reframe their view of FGC (particularly with respect to the next cohort, their daughters) than women who have not. But women who underwent the procedure and later come to reject its local norms are likely to be the procedure's strongest critics.[55]

Boyle's (2002:147) work also suggests (in my language, not hers) that women who experienced FGC and later reject it for their daughters are more likely than women who have not undergone it to frame their objections as a cognitive claim, as a self-conscious local rejection of a local norm. One of the most significant local norms concerns the social and legal status of women. Anti-FGC measures might be framed as empowering local women and, by extension, their daughters, at least in the sense of allowing them to be free, as children, of a procedure they may not be

---

ensures virginity, a prerequisite for marriage and a woman's access to land and security; that a woman's sexuality needs to be, and can be, controlled through FGC; that the external genitalia are ugly and dirty and will continue to grow; and that FGC is linked to spiritual purity or some religious command.

[54] Compare Boyle (2002:150).

[55] Compare Boyle (2002:151).

able to evaluate as well as an adult.[56] "Empowerment" would mean the right and capacity to reject aspects of their cultural environment, such as FGC.

I argue that the local understanding of women's' social and legal status can be reframed individualistically, in terms of protecting and enhancing individual agency. Reframing of this sort makes significant demands on the local cultural community. Only if that community can accept a more individualistic view of rights might members be able to freely embrace a cognitive style that regards FGC as a human rights violation of individual rights to bodily and decisional autonomy. It is clear that in the case of mothers who support FGC for their daughters, an individual's capacity and readiness to reject a significant belief or practice of the local culture renders the framer more inclined to draw on extralocal frames to explain and support opposition.[57]

It is no less clear that such frames first have to be "indigenized" for the women – but not only for them. Toward making the local cultural logic more human rights friendly, reframing cannot proceed only at the level of the individual, ignoring the impersonal social system. Reframing the local status of women in terms of an individual right to bodily integrity (which then provides local grounds for rejecting FGC or child prostitution) entails deploying a cognitive rule that revises local normative rules that

[56] Reframing is a cognitive technique and can serve any normative purpose. For example, anti-FGC efforts might themselves be reframed as hypocritical. After all, women in affluent societies (particularly in the West) may respond to cultural frames that valorize particular body types and other specific aspects of physical appearance by undergoing breast implants, Botox injections, and tummy tucks. Young women in particular may respond by anorexic behavior. Further, in the West, infant males are routinely circumcised, also a form of "cutting." But the charge of hypocrisy cannot be sustained if it rests on comparing apples with oranges, in two respects. First, FGC is generally performed on young girls without their consent; breast implants and Botox injections are chosen by adult women. One might think that these Western women are similar to African mothers who would subject their daughters to FGC, but only if one thought that both were victims of "false consciousness" perpetrated by local culture. But my position, as culturally relativist and normatively localist, rejects that notion as presupposing some universally valid, objective, or acultural form of human consciousness. Second, analogizing male and female genitalia generates a dubious standpoint inasmuch as it cannot generate widely persuasive answers to such questions as "Is FGC more like male castration than male circumcision?" and "Does male circumcision benefit the health of the male (and perhaps that of his female sexual partners), whereas FGC can only harm the woman's health?" For a counterargument, see Abu-Sahlieh (2006). For other voices critical of some anti-FGC arguments, see Gruenbaum (2001) and Gilman (1999).

[57] Thus frame theory does not proceed from some neutral normative standpoint; there is none, anyway. As an approach to political and social change, frame theory offers itself equally to someone who champions FGC.

justify FGC. Because human rights–oriented social and political change depends on some compatibility of the individual level with the group or communal level, the alternative frame would need to be "indigenized" more or less for the whole community.

The approach to the whole community might be piecemeal. One might build on the empirical observation that the likelihood of cognitive reframing can be affected by the degree of parental conformism. Key is whether the child's family conforms to local norms. The greater the degree of conformism, the greater the degree to which the procedure will be framed according to prevailing communal norms. Uprooting local conformism *as such* is not the issue. Although cognitive reframing would challenge FGC-supportive conformism, it could also advocate human rights–supportive conformism. The issue, then, is: Conformity to what kind of local norms?

Norms themselves can be reframed in any number of ways, of course. FGC might be reframed as a technical, medical issue, for example, rather than as a normative human rights concern.[58] The procedure might be rejected from a medical standpoint (because it provides no medical benefit and very possibly causes medical harm). Local culture is challenged less, or less frontally, where the relevant belief or practice can be reframed locally as "narrow" or acultural.[59] And to reframe a cultural issue in acultural terms is to travel the route I advocate: advocacy of the cultural particularism of the idea of human rights yet without essentializing it or any other cultural phenomenon.

I turn now to Part IV, which considers human rights as they might be socially constructed in the future, in line with reconceptions of both human nature and political community. Nature might one day soon

---

[58] To reframe in this way is to presuppose the acultural quality of medical science and procedure. Medicine and natural science are themselves cultural constructs, of course. But unlike, say, deep culture in the sense of institutionalized religious faith or the metaphysics of nationalism, natural science and medicine appeal to the natural environment for confirmation or correction, rendering them "thinner," that is, more easily generalizable across cultural and political boundaries, than the "thick" norms of deep culture. In Gregg (2003b) I offer a general theory of thick and thin norms.

[59] See Boyle (2002:138) for supporting evidence. Issues framed as acultural can nonetheless have significant cultural consequences. Correspondingly, a cognitive approach can realize normative goals. If reframing FGC as a medical issue – and if, as a medical issue, the procedure could be modified (lessened in severity or even eradicated) – then the consequence fulfills a human rights norm: a right to bodily integrity or freedom from sexual exploitation, particularly of children who, as children, lack the intellectual and emotional maturity (and the information needed for decisional autonomy) to make informed and responsible decisions.

be construed in terms of cultural choice, specifically with regard to manipulations of the human genome: where genetic choice replaces genetic chance, thereby raising its own set of human rights questions (chapter 8). And political community, in the form of the nation state, might be reimagined as a human rights state that replaces the former's exclusive logic of sovereignty, which discourages the project for human rights, with a boundary-crossing logic of inclusion that might advance it (chapter 9).

PART IV

HUMAN RIGHTS, FUTURE TENSE: HUMAN NATURE AND POLITICAL COMMUNITY RECONCEIVED

8

Human Rights via Human Nature
as Cultural Choice

In Chapter 9 I argue for the human rights state as an alternative to the nation-state that we know today. The nation-state is not the state in which human rights most likely are available because it conceives of rights as granted by the state, a grant that depends on state sovereignty (the state need not grant rights to noncitizens, for example). Hence human rights in practical terms depend today on the nation-state, which, from empirical observation, in most cases today does not grant its citizens human rights. The human rights state, by contrast, understands people as human rights bearing as a matter of cultural choice rather than political membership (membership in the nation-state, indeed, in a particular nation-state). To make this choice, or to evaluate the choices of others, one must know when a human rights–bearing person is first present. At any stage along the biological development path prior to birth, for example? Any answer will presuppose a conception of man that justifies human rights assigned solely by virtue of being human. What conception of man renders human rights plausible in a way not dependent on a gratuitous grant of the nation-state? What conception corresponds to and facilitates the human rights state that I introduce in Chapter 9?

To anticipate the answer I develop in this chapter: a wholly naturalistic conception that takes human nature as biologically understood and eschews supernatural explanations, whether theological or metaphysical. That conception allows for cultural choice to construe people as human rights bearing. In a naturalistic conception, all rights are cultural constructions, as are all social institutions, from political communities to property rights to legal tender, from customs and mores to friendship and marriage.

The question "When is a human rights bearing person first present?" is then the query "At what point on a developmental continuum might political community so construct the human person?" To access this question in terms that will highlight what a political community may take to be valuable about human existence, I consider human existence not only as actual but also as potential. I analyze potential human existence with reference to current debates about the manipulation of the human genome. In this context I address the question: Might political community (and the human rights state in particular) construct human life at the pre-personal level as human rights bearing?

The question is urgent, even absent a human rights state, because technological means to artificially manipulate the human genome may become available within twenty years. Then, for the first time since its evolution 200,000 years ago, *Homo sapiens sapiens* may begin to remake its own biology at the genetic level. Genetic manipulation is a matter of human culture intervening in human nature. By *human culture* I refer to normative interpretation as well as to scientific-technical engineering;[1] by *human nature* I refer to humans biologically understood. Genetic modification concerns the biology of how some genes control some of the targeted organism's characteristics. It equally concerns the cultural dimensions that guide the selection of targets. The moral and legal evaluation of the benefits and dangers of genetic modification is itself a cultural act. By *genetic modification* I mean changes in the DNA sequence of a plant or animal resulting in detectable alterations in corresponding biological characteristics of the organism. In terms of natural selection, modification constitutes a response to changes in environmental conditions (a core aspect of the process of evolution). As artificial selection, by contrast, modification concerns reproductive isolation toward generating animal and plant species with characteristics attractive to humans, such as productivity, quality as a food source, or adaptability to targeted environments.[2]

---

[1] By *culture* more broadly I refer to products of the human mind that entail seemingly unlimited possibilities for the transformation of the natural environment but equally for mankind's dynamic and open-ended social self-transformation.

[2] Consider several examples. The dog, descendent of wolves, is the first animal species to be domesticated, at least 12,000 years ago. To date, artificial selection has resulted in more breed categories, 400, than for any other living animal. Humans have selected for specific personality traits, such as activity, aggressiveness, and obedience, to mold each breed to a specific task, such as tracking, herding, guarding, fighting, or companionship. Humans have also selected for body size, fur color, and appearance. Selected breeds range from those as small as the Chihuahua (from three to six pounds) to those as large as the Irish wolfhound (100 pounds or more). Humans began to domesticate livestock animals in the seventh millennium B.C.E. (Clutton-Brock 1999:51). After millennia of artificial selection of measurable phenotypes (visible characteristics), agricultural plants and livestock animals have become staple food sources for an ever growing human

Since James Watson and Francis Crick (1953) discovered the structure of DNA in 1952, research has identified a number of plant and animal genes encoded for specific phenotypes. The human genome sequence was first published in 2001. Research distinguishes between two categories of human genes: those related to characteristics that medical science targets for therapy and those related to characteristics that, in terms of this or that cultural norm, might be thought to "enhance" the recipient. Therapeutic targets are causal genetic mutations for diseases such as Down syndrome, cystic fibrosis, and Alzheimer's (the most common neurodegenerative disease in the industrialized world today). Characteristics that may enhance their carriers – such as physical appearance or intelligence – are selected on the basis of cultural preferences for a particular color of skin, eyes, or hair, or for heightened cognitive and other abilities.[3]

population. For thousands of years, humans genetically modified agricultural plants and animals by phenotype selection. In 1865, Gregor Mendel discovered that the inheritance of phenotype in an offspring follows a simple and highly regular pattern; that pattern involves the inherited combination of parental genetic factors. These were later identified as genes. Genes reside in a large molecule, deoxyribose nucleic acid (DNA). Watson and Crick's discovery of DNA's double helix structure inaugurated the modern era of genetic research. Since then, researchers have identified, in various plant and animal species, large numbers of genetic markers ("simple sequence repeat" and "single nucleotide polymorphism"). These markers identify the genomic region possibly responsible for the genetic variation in the desired trait. This process is called "quantitative trait loci mapping." It allows researchers to associate, quantitatively, genetic markers with desired traits. In this way it allows them to identify the specific regions in a genome that contain the genes causally related to the wanted trait. This "marker assisted selection" (MAS) allows for the relatively accurate selection of breeding stock with genetics responsible for desired attributes. MAS has accelerated the pace of artificial genetic modification in agricultural species. The most successful genetic improvement in the economic traits of livestock animals is milk production in the dairy cow. MAS selects sires that produce daughters with high milk productivity. The semen of the selected sires is used to fertilize, by artificial insemination, a large number of cows to produce high-yield daughters. By 2009 the dairy industry's use of genetic selection technology had increased milk production per cow more than 4.5-fold over the 1940 rate. Biotechnological development in the twentieth century has also revolutionized artificial genetic modification of agricultural species through the direct manipulation of genes causally related to the desired traits. The most significant examples are genetically engineered plants and animals.

[3] *(a) Pigmentation:* Among the most visible and identifiable characteristics of the human species, skin and hair color are determined by type and amount of melanin pigment produced by skin and follicular melanocytes, or pigment-producing cells (Thong et al. 2003; Liu et al. 2005). Using comparative genetics and a site-specific cloning approach, research has identified multiple genes that control skin color, eye color, and hair color (Sturm 2009). Genetic variation in these genes, detected by DNA sequencing or by a site-specific genetic test, can be used to determine the color of the individual's skin, hair, and eyes (Spichenok et al. 2010). A genetic test of preimplantation embryos may be able to predict the child's skin, hair, and eye color. *(b) Height:* Human communities

But a point is reached when genetic engineering for purposes of therapy begins to bleed into engineering for purposes of enhancement. On the one hand, with regard to genetic manipulation as *therapy*, no one proposes allowing patients to remain ill when they might be treated, even if not healed. If someone faced death unless treated, likely no community would legally or even morally prohibit the relevant gene therapy. But consider therapy that so modified the patient's genes that his or her children would not inherit his or her genetic disease. Or consider "remedial enhancement," in which parents' genetic characteristics could be classified along some dimensions as "below normal." What if they were allowed to have their embryo modified in ways that rendered that dimension "average" or above in the person who developed from that embryo?[4] Here, either therapy cannot be distinguished from enhancement or such distinctions are matters of cultural understandings not natural phenomena. In this way, among others, "human nature" can only be regarded as a matter of cultural choice. As such, the legal and moral regulation of genetic enhancement, or the question of when

apparently have long paid great attention to height or adult stature. In postindustrial populations, height appears to matter for both mate preference and mate choice (Sear and Marlowe 2009). According to a study by Herpin (2005), with identical educational levels, taller men generally enjoy better careers than short men because, for example, they tend to receive greater supervisory responsibilities. Height is also an important factor in various sports. One might well conclude that most people would prefer to be tall than short. A widely embraced hypothesis states that the height of the human body is controlled by a large number of genetic factors, each with a small effect on the overall phenotypic variation. Genome-wide association analysis has identified 47 single-nucleotide polymorphisms associated with adult stature (Lettre 2009), which explain only about 5 percent of variation in height. Larger studies to find additional common height polymorphism are ongoing. Within 10 years research may well be able to identify the causal genes for human stature. *(c) Intelligence.* Since the publication of *Heredity, Genius: An Enquiry into its Laws and Consequences* by Francis Galton in 1869, the association of genetic makeup with human intelligence has been a socially and politically sensitive topic, not only for scientists. The heredity of intelligence has been confirmed by several large-scale studies. With the completion more than 10 years ago of the sequencing of the human genome, several genome-wide association studies have identified 6 different chromosomal regions and 16 candidate genes associated with human intelligence as measured by IQ scores (Rizzi et al. 2010). Although most of these candidate genes need additional validation, association of intelligence with the genetic variations in two genes, *ATXN1* and *TRIM31*, has been confirmed in the samples ascertained for attention deficit/hyperactivity disorder (Rizzi et al. 2010). With accelerated technical development in neuroscience, research may identify the causal genes for human intelligence within a matter of decades.

[4] Parents' being permitted to genetically manipulate their embryo's genome for non-remedial enhancement need hardly entail that any individual's inherited features are therefore purchasable commodities, as Ludwig Siep (2002:113) argues.

human rights are first present in the sense of a human rights–bearing being, will find no guidelines in nature.

Genetic modification must then be understood, at least in part, as always also a political act. To modify a DNA sequence genetically is to change the genome of an individual – or an entire species – and is likely to be motivated not only by an interest in health but also by political, economic, and other cultural concerns. Take a common example in which technicians modify human DNA by selecting sperm or preimplantation embryos or by manipulating the embryo's genome. Selection is used in connection with various sex-linked diseases, and sex-sorting human sperm technology can reduce sex-linked diseases. But it can just as well facilitate parental preference in selecting the sex of offspring, where health is no longer the point.[5] Again, selection allows for screening embryos for genetic abnormalities but equally for their sex or for other factors of cultural preference. The stakes of cultural and political preference and commitment only increase with biotechnological development. Thus preimplantation genetic diagnosis (PGD), introduced only twenty years ago, screens for genetic disease–free embryos; couples at high risk for offspring with genetically inherited disease are screened prior to implantation.[6] Embryos without detectable genetic defects become candidates for transplantation into the mother's uterus for gestation.[7]

---

[5] In humans, X-bearing sperm has a DNA content that is 2.8 percent different from that of Y-bearing sperm. The DNA can be stained with a fluorescent dye and its content measured by the intensity of the fluorescence. On the basis of the difference in staining intensity, X and Y sperm can be sorted into different groups through flow cytometry. Using the sorted sperm for insemination, parents can select for a child of the desired sex. This approach has also been used to reduce sex-linked disease risk as well as to balance the sex distribution of children within a family. In 1992 the U.S. Department of Agriculture granted the Genetics & IVF Institute an exclusive license for a patented flow cytometric sperm-separation technology for development and use in humans. In 1993 the Institutional Review Board approved clinical studies to apply flow cytometric sperm sorting to couples at risk for having children with sex-linked disease. In 1995 the trial was expanded to couples for family-balancing purposes. From June 1994 to January 2007, a total of 1,125 pregnancies resulted from sex-sorted sperm. Of the 943 births, XSort resulted in 92 percent females, and YSort, in 81.8 percent males (Karabinus 2009).

[6] The procedure involves in vitro fertilization (IVF), embryo culture, and biopsy to obtain a single cell for a genetic test as well as a genetic test using markers to detect for genetic abnormalities.

[7] PGD is currently used to detect single-gene disorders and chromatin rearrangement. In rare cases, it is used to select for embryos whose HLA blood type matches that of a couple's child (sibling to the future child) who suffers from malignant conditions such as leukemia or lymphoma. The afflicted child's most effective medical option is a bone marrow transplant from an HLA-identical donor. To treat their sick child, some parents use PGD to select for embryos with HLA matching the child's. In other words,

Although PGD is now routinely performed in doctors' offices, selection for intelligence or physical appearance has yet to be performed.[8] Such an application one day soon could become routine wherever the relevant technology becomes available at locally plausible costs. Whether such an application should be permitted could be formulated as a human rights question: Might a human embryo be culturally understood as possessing a human right to be free of genetic manipulation, or free at least from genetic enhancement where enhancement can be distinguished from genetic therapy?

In three steps, I analyze the question "When is a human rights–bearing person first present?" in the context of genetic manipulation. (1) I argue

they seek to have another child who could then donate bone marrow to his or her sibling. Further, for single-gene disorders, PGD is most often performed to screen for autosomal dominant disorders such as Huntington's disease, myotonic dystrophy type I (DM1), neurofibromatosis, and Charcote-Marie-Tooth disease. It is also used to screen for autosomal recessive disorders such as beta-thalassemia/sickle cell disorders (with or without HLA typing), cystic fibrosis, and spinal muscular atrophy (SMA), and for X-linked recessive diseases (in which PGD is undertaken for a specific diagnosis) such as the fragile X syndrome, Duchenne/Becker muscular dystrophy, and hemophilia A and B. PGD is also deployed in cases of chromatin rearrangement or structural abnormality, a condition that often leads to developmental abnormality in the embryo. PGD allows parents to choose between terminating the pregnancy and giving birth to a mentally retarded child.

[8] Currently not technically feasible, several technologies in early stages of development may soon make such selection possible. Consider two: (a) Mediated site-specific genome modification is an artificial nuclease that can introduce double-stranded DNA breaks at specific sites of the genome toward facilitating DNA sequence replacement by means of homologous recombination. Zinc finger nucleases (ZFN) capable of recognizing different targeting sites can be engineered and produced in vitro. When a site-specific ZFN, together with the DNA fragment with the desired sequence, was injected into a mouse or rat embryo, the ZNF facilitated the exchange of the targeted genome site, leading to offspring with a modified genome. This approach to modifing the genome at a specific site has been successful in both mouse and rat models (Cui et al. 2010). It has also successfully modified the genome of human stem cells but much work remains to be done before it can safely be used to modify the human genome. (b) Meganucleases (MNs) (see Arnould et al. 2011), also called homing endonucleases, are enzymes that cut double-stranded DNA at specific sequence sites and in this way facilitate homologous recombination. First discovered in yeast, they have since been used for site-specific gene insertion or deletion in mammalian cells of several different species. These enzymes contain a DNA-binding domain and a DNA-cutting domain. The DNA-binding domain can be artificially engineered to recognize specific DNA sequences. These enzymes may be able to introduce DNA breakage at the specific site of a host genome and then allow replacement of the DNA fragment of the genome by the artificially provided DNA fragment. Currently in its infancy, such applied science, like ZFN engineering, may one day become the technology of choice for targeted human genome modification.

that human nature and human culture lie on a continuum such that, at points, each intersects with the other, increasingly so as we make human nature available to biotechnological design. The genetic engineering of human nature leads to a kind of "second nature" (which I define shortly). This occurs as genetic chance in natural reproduction is displaced by genetic choice through technology. In this normatively unchartered territory, political communities are challenged to identify cultural norms that might guide human intervention into human nature. If they find no guiding norms in nature, they may well be inclined to open themselves to the reenchantment of nature – so as to remoralize nature in an effort to prohibit, deter, or limit genetic enhancement. I argue for recasting "second nature," or human nature as human artifact, as something positive. That is, I conceptualize human nature not as that which limits us as a species in our choices, but rather as itself a cultural choice. (2) I view human nature as a cultural choice above all in deciding where, along the contiuum of the stages of natural development, to socially construct the threshold point at which political community might recognize an organism as bearing human rights. (3) To regard human nature as a cultural choice allows equally for two different conclusions: that pre-personal life is "human nature," or that it is not. In the latter case, pre-personal life is not a human being in the sense of bearing human rights, such as a human right against being genetically manipulated.

"Second Nature": Human Nature as Cultural Choice

The prospect of genetic modification is hardly the first time that political communities have sought to enhance human nature by unleashing the cultural potential of the species as a whole. One of the most powerful visions of culture over nature in any age was the European Enlightenment's project of "optimizing" both nature and culture. The *Encyclopédie, ou dictionnaire raisonné des sciences, des arts et des métiers,*[9] published between 1751 and 1772, captures this vision. It aimed not only to summarize the current status of all human knowledge but to critically evaluate it as well. In the words of its editor, Denis Diderot, it aimed

---

[9] With later supplements, revised editions, and translations; contributors numbered approximately 2,250; not surprisingly, the work overall conveys no single or unified vision.

to change the very way we humans think ("*changer* la façon commune de penser").[10] It regarded all men as equally capable of "optimization," culturally, but not only culturally. All men, the *Encyclopédie* implies, are equally capable of development *as nature*. To be sure, one might argue that humankind passed the milestone of developing nature through culture already, as early as the prehistoric era. For in a cultural sense, man has always already "made himself" through his control of nature no less than through cultural creations, from tools to norms to belief systems, and from institutions to traditions. Yet humankind taking control of its own *genome* – while hardly anticipated by the *Encyclopédie*, gaining that kind of control is certainly in its spirit – is indeed a historical watershed, a "Copernican Revolution." Copernicus destroyed the ancient geocentric worldview; Darwin, humankind's anthropocentric understanding of animal life.[11] Humankind was constrained each time to "decenter" itself as a species from the center of major systems of human experience at which we humans are so pleased to place ourselves, from the positioning of earth and sun to a "hierarchy" of forms of sentient life on this planet. Today we again face the prospect of decentering ourselves as a species in nature, this time by our taking control of our own genome. I argue that such control entails the displacement of nature by culture: that the reconstitution of human nature, biologically understood, renders it "second nature."

But first I review one tradition of thought about second nature. More than a half century ago, Max Horkheimer and Theodor Adorno took the term "second nature" as Hegel employs it and, following Marx, gave it a distinctly negative cast: what they called the "dialectic of Enlightenment." By retracing this path in the recent history of political theory, I provide myself a foil against which I develop my own notion of "second nature," as delivered through genetic manipulation, where the Enlightenment effort to enhance human nature need not turn into a dialectic of Enlightenment.

Hegel conceives of nature, understood in the most general terms, as a particular kind of "thought": one that instantiates externality (*Aüsserlichkeit*) as such. So understood, nature is "external to itself": it

---

[10] Diderot and d'Alembert (1966:642).

[11] Since 1995, each year astronomers detect hundreds of exoplanets, planets orbiting a normal star other than the sun. Given hundreds of billions of other suns, the ubiquity of planets, and the abundance of life's ingredients in the universe, life elsewhere seems likely. If it turns out that some of it is intelligent, humankind will experience yet another "Copernican Revolution."

is not self-aware in Hegel's sense, that is, not conscious of itself *as* a concept, as the concept of itself. For Hegel, the *truth* of nature would be the *concept* of nature. Only the human being can think this (or any other) concept; nature in general[12] can never grasp itself in thought. Nature remains external to the concept of nature, which is to say that it cannot recognize itself for what it really is.

From Hegel's perspective, that which *can* grasp itself in thought is thereby "the other" of nature: it is spirit or mind (*Geist*, which can be translated as either). *Geist* generates itself as "second nature" in two ways. First, it might realize itself in the form of a political community's system of laws. As a system of justice, the legal system constitutes one particular self-reflexive realm of actual freedom, freedom as it might be lived and experienced by members of political community.[13] The legal system then constitutes the world of mind or spirit as second nature.[14] Further, spirit or mind expresses itself in the encultured nature (*Gewohnheit*) of a community's morals, which is an additional form of second nature, in this case one that takes the place of human will as something "merely natural."[15] Second nature of this sort constitutes the core of a community's customs and mores.[16]

Marx recasts Hegel to analyze a terrible paradox in man's mastery over nature. Social conditions, he says, are nothing but the result of interactions among individuals. Individuals experience these conditions as the same "strange and unassailable power"[17] that nature once was for them. In the individual's experience, social conditions constitute a second nature, here in an ideological (or systematically distorted) form. As the demystifying power of knowledge and technology over nature leads to an ideological "naturalization" of society, the source of ideological consciousness shifts with it: from nature to society.

Georg Lukács then develops Marx's take on an unintended consequence of the human domination of nature. He surveys in modern capitalist society what he regards as the partial objectification of persons

---

[12] As distinguished from self-reflexive human nature.

[13] Hegel (1970:§4) speaks of "das Reich der verwirklichten Freiheit."

[14] The legal system "[hat] die Welt des Geistes aus ihm selbst hervorgebracht, als eine zweite Natur" (Hegel 1970:§4).

[15] Hegel (1970:§ 151) refers to "eine *zweite Natur*, die an die Stelle des ersten bloss natürlichen Willens gesetzt . . . ist."

[16] That is, "eine *zweite Natur*, die . . . die durchdringende Seele, Bedeutung und Wirklichkeit ihres Daseins ist" (Hegel 1970:§ 151).

[17] Marx (1969:21) writes of "eine durchaus fremde, allmächtige und unangreifbare Macht."

dominated by the economic system. According to Lukács, the domination of nature reflects processes that generate ideological consciousness
in the context of contemporary society, a society that privileges science
and technology over other orientations toward both the natural and
man-made environments. Objectification, domination, science, and culture again and again burst the various bonds of nature and exceed them,
in that sense ostensibly "freeing" man from the bonds of nature.[18] And
yet political community, as a kind of second nature, confronts its members with the same relentless regularity that earlier confronted them in
the forces of nature: man's escape from nature into civilization ends with
no freedom after all.[19]

Adorno and Horkheimer then sharpen this idea of the reduction of
domination within society to man's instrumental control over nature.
They sharpen it first into the idea of a "dialectic," an irony, in man's
domination of nature. They further sharpen it into the notion of man's
self-domination through labor. Finally they sharpen it into the claim that
reason, as manifested in human society and culture, in fact unintentionally deforms human community and the individual lives of those who
inhabit it.

I would suggest that viewing the historical course of the Enlightenment
in this way – (a) as inherently repressive and (b) as leading to the repressive qualities of discursive thinking – undermines the very foundation for
making such claims in the first place.

(a) If control over nature is somehow always allied with repressive domination, then it can hardly redeem Enlightenment claims to reasoned
progress and moral advance through understanding and manipulating
nature. So understood, the control of nature reveals a treacherous logic:
human labor, driven by an inner motivation to dominate, leads away
from pre-Enlightenment myth – yet, under the spell of Enlightenment
myth, reverts to domination. Ever greater control of nature actually contributes to the very evils from which man, through labor, would free
himself. Indeed, through labor, man generates the second nature that *is*

---

[18] Such that people in capitalist society "in ständig steigendem Masse die bloss
'naturwüchsigen,' die irrationell-faktischen Bindungen zersprengen, ablösen und hinter
sich lassen" (Lukács 1968:307).

[19] Lukács argues that the subjugation of human life within modern political community
(a kind of second nature) in some ways parallels the subjugation of human life within
nature: "andererseits aber gleichzeitig in dieser selbstgeschaffenen, 'selbsterzeugten'
Wirklichkeit eine Art zweite Natur um sich errichten, deren Ablauf ihnen mit der-
selben unerbitterlichen Gesetzmässigkeit entgegentritt, wie es früher die irrationellen
Naturmächte ... getan haben" (Lukács 1968:307).

modern society.[20] Even as I think this argument is mistaken, I also think the notion of "second nature" captures the dilemma posed by the human species eventually taking control of its own genome.[21] To be useful in analyzing that dilemma, however, the notion first needs to be freed from the reductionist spin given it within the Hegel-to-Adorno tradition.

By "reductionism" I mean that Horkheimer and Adorno take the idea of a dialectic of Enlightenment to its logical extreme. Extending the idea of second nature further than Hegel, Marx, or Lukács before them, they argue that man's ever greater domination of nature strikes back at man: by objectifying and dominating external nature, man brings about his own objectification. That is, even as he conquers nature to ever greater degrees, man is himself conquered by repressive qualities in that conquest that are incorporated into society and absorbed by political community. The control of nature – including genetic enhancement, viewed as the engineering of life that might be construed to have a human right to be free of alien manipulation – then assumes an ominous form: control *as* second nature.[22]

(b) The idea of second nature as itself a product of domination, a product that then necessarily reproduces domination, casts an ominous image. Second nature so understood negates the very mind and spirit that created it. *Self-negation* means: second nature, itself the product of a repressive process, represses human society from within the very members of that society. *Self-negation* also means: as second nature, the mind or spirit of humankind undermines itself.[23] The thesis of a self-negating control of nature marks an unintended dialectic: the human subject, realizing him- or herself by dominating nature, becomes an object of that very domination. The subject's power over a natural object – such as a human embryo – eventually comes to confront the subject in such a way that it objectifies the subject him- or herself: genetic manipulation as the undermining of human nature, where "human nature" is construed as something "natural," something vulnerable to violation and

---

[20] Labor contributes "durch ihren Fortschritt immer mehr mit an dem Unheil, vor dem sie behüten wollte"; it contributes to "jener zweiten Natur, zu der die Gesellschaft gewuchert ist" (Adorno 1966:75).

[21] The dilemma is marked by incongruity and irony and in that sense is "dialectical": "Unter dem Zwang der Herrschaft hat die menschliche Arbeit seit je vom Mythos hinweggeführt, in dessen Bannkreis sie unter der Herrschaft stets wieder geriet" (Horkheimer and Adorno 1969:49).

[22] Or the "Sieg der Gesellschaft über Natur, der alles in blosse Natur verwandelt" (Horkheimer and Adorno 1969:211).

[23] "Geist als zweite Natur … ist die Negation des Geistes" (Adorno 1966:350).

decimation through manipulation driven by cultural choice. In the context of genetic engineering, the thesis reads: by managing and altering its genome, mankind (as subject) manages and alters the human species itself, transforming man from a *subject* exercising power, to man as an *object* demeaned or subjugated by that power.

I cannot share this view of second nature. To construe the human relationship to nature in this way is to take, in politically and morally unpromising directions, a view I do share: the idea that nature and culture flow one into the other. First, this view reenchants nature, including "human nature," as though it were in fact somehow supernatural in the manner of a theological or metaphysical approach. Second, the argument undermines its own normative claims. For if all culture is repressive, then from what cultural standpoint might one possibly launch such a critique, inasmuch as any critique requires the existence of some space itself not infected by what is being criticized? Here we have the self-defeating logic of any totalizing critique: domination appears to be absolute when the critic projects it absolutely.

To rescue the idea that nature and culture flow into one another (an idea useful to my analysis of genetic manipulation), I would replace Horkheimer and Adorno's aporetic conception of the nature-culture continuum with a very different conception. My approach does not reduce human nature to human culture in the genetic self-transformation of the human species; it does not equate human nature with the biotechnological manipulation of human beings. I oppose reductionism because only if we, as a species, can presuppose that nature (and the human genome in particular) cannot be reduced to culture, can we then construct some notion of culture as the normative standard we need. We must have a notion of culture by which to critically evaluate our manipulation of nature. We also need to construct our standard ourselves if we are to eschew the otherworldly approaches of metaphysics and theology. We require such a standard because genetic manipulation poses a dilemma with respect to the question of human rights: it upends our understanding of "natural" and "unnatural." One might argue that the genetic self-transformation of the human species is, in some sense, "unnatural." In that case, one could imagine constructing a human right to be free of genetic manipulation. Or one might contend that our very nature is precisely to take control, by cultural means, of our natural environment, and by extension of our own genome, as a part of nature, and to manipulate our genome in whatever ways we believe may be to our benefit. In that case, the genetic self-transformation of the species appears quite "natural," in which case a human right to freedom from manipulation might seem inapposite.

Whatever choices political community makes, those choices likely will be guided by whether the community views enhancement as "natural" or "unnatural." How it views enhancement may in turn rest on how it chooses to differentiate among the various stages of fetal development. That genetic manipulation should appear "natural" from one perspective, and "unnatural" from another, parallels the fluid transition between categories of nature and culture. The differentiations among the various stages of fetal development are indeed fluid. Consider distinctions between the fusion of nuclei, on the one hand, and the embryo, on the other, or between embryo and fetus, or among different stages of fetal development, or between nonsentient and sentient life – and then between sentient life as such and an individuated person in particular. Such distinctions are certainly biological, yet only in part, for in part they are also cultural, not least where they might guide us in normatively binding ways.

Political community will make its decisions based on how it answers certain questions: Up to what point on that continuum should genetic manipulation still be allowed, for what reasons, to what ends?[24] Where exactly lies the threshold between morally permissible genetic manipulation and manipulation that is morally unacceptable? And why is it located precisely *there*? The answer to these questions presupposes a continuum between nature and culture, *not* the reduction of one to the other (the mistake made by the Hegel-to-Adorno tradition). But if there is a continuum, from which end is it best approached? The normative evaluation of genetic manipulation can proceed either from the cultural end or from the natural end. I consider first the one and then the other.

To understand human nature as something "sacred," whether theologically or metaphysically, is to proceed from the cultural end of the culture-nature continuum. Here the embryo appears as something "natural," in which case one might claim that it has a human right to its "naturalness" or to its "natural qualities," given its nature *as nature*. If one construes the embryo as unborn human life, one might regard human "naturalness" as something vulnerable to violation by human artifice, to

[24] Our cultural evaluation of the different stages of developing organic life, on a continuum from fertilized egg to sentient being to personhood (either before or after birth), is indeterminate. Ontological claims about points along that continuum, some of which might bind political community with respect to limits to genetic intervention, say, or to abortion, appear to be arbitrary.

technical intervention, or to culturally guided engineering. One might think that intervention or engineering constitute a turning away from the "naturalness" of man and the random chance and contingency of nature. This approach connects one claim, that the dignity of human beings is inviolable, with another, that the human genome is equally sacrosanct. To immunize human nature from further technical intervention and manipulation, this approach once again "moralizes" human nature, in this way rendering it less available to human design than, say, human nature understood in terms of health and longevity (the position I take in later pages). This line of thought develops new social taboos that discourage the development and application of genetic engineering. Taboos of a theological or metaphysical cast render genetic manipulation (which only recently became available through scientific and technological developments) unavailable to medical practice and scientific inquiry.

By contrast, one proceeds from the "nature end" of the nature-culture continuum if one views human nature in terms of health and longevity. What normative force might the idea of human health possess? Might it provide a plausible boundary between morally acceptable and morally unacceptable manipulations of the human genome? In an Enlightenment spirit, I would suggest that we construct no such boundary (indeed, even the boundary between genetic therapy and genetic enhancement collapses at some points). For the Enlightenment project is all about transgressing boundaries. Positive eugenics (genetic enhancement, as distinguished from negative eugenics or genetic therapy) would render our natural destiny an Enlightenment project – precisely in the sense of the *Encyclopédie* – by "optimizing" our biological nature. Genetic enhancement approaches the body as it would any other phenomenon of the natural world: from an objectivating stance (which may disregard the self-perception of the adolescent or adult concerned, whereas an embryo has no self-perception, though it is on a developmental pathway that can lead to a self-perceiving human). For example, from this perspective, humans' average life expectancy might appear to be "too low," as defective and inadequate, even as a kind of "disease" to be cured. Note that such a concern is not with social, economic, or cultural factors that might shorten life; the concern is with natural, biological, even *genetic* factors that may limit its length. Human life so understood has no genetic limits; natural limits become arbitrary as the upper limits of the average human life span become matters of the current state of scientific knowledge and the technology it spawns.

If humankind reframes anthropological constants as technical options, what we humans *naturally* are becomes something to be decided *culturally*.[25] The Enlightenment project to "optimize" our natural fate renders human nature contingent on human will, imagination, and cultural preference. Nature becomes a cultural undertaking of society as it becomes a contingent expression of human will. We then "create" our own nature *as* human beings, and we do so across ever-expanding boundaries. With regard to the human embryo in particular, the Enlightenment project to enhance human nature renders it an object of medical intervention and technology; the project renders the embryo a piece of nature that yields to culture. The embryo may soon yield to such an extent that humankind achieves very significant and ever greater control over its own future as a biological organism. As human culture becomes the venue, workshop, and platform of man's technological imagination of himself, "human nature" becomes a design of human reason. To the extent that man remakes himself as second nature, human nature becomes human artifact.

Human Nature as Cultural Choice: Human Rights Instead of Re-enchantment

"Human nature as human artifact" may sound disconcerting and certainly is so in the view of Marx, Lukács, Horkheimer, and Adorno. But I beg to differ, at least in terms of a medical approach to the body guided by notions of health and illness. By disenchanting human nature, the therapeutic goals of medicine desacralize cultural constructions of human nature, overcoming cultural barriers to the technical manipulation of the human body with respect to health-related goals. Modern medicine is of a piece with the Enlightenment project where theological, metaphysical, ethical, political, and scientific taboos capitulate sooner or later in the face of medical treatment that alleviates suffering, prevents death, and cures disease.[26] In many cases, people initially regard new medicines and medical techniques as transgressing a boundary between the acceptable and unacceptable treatment of human bodies. Sometimes the claim is that invasive medical techniques somehow injure "essential" or even "sacred" aspects of the patient. The successful implementation

---

[25] In Spaemann's (2002:106) sense: "Was wir von Natur aus sind, wird entscheidungsabhängig. Anthropologische Konstanten werden zu technischen Optionen."
[26] Compare van den Daele (2000:25).

of new techniques usually defuse such claims. The boundary between acceptable and unacceptable practices then shifts. Such was the history of vaccination, beginning in the late eighteenth century; of cardiac surgery since the late nineteenth century (surprisingly, brain surgery had been successfully practiced already in the premodern era); and of organ transplantation in the twentieth century (ranging from the cornea, kidney, pancreas, liver, heart, lungs, hands, tissue-engineered bladder, face, jaw, arm, and trachea, to a baby born by means of a transplanted ovary).

In this disenchanting spirit, I advance two proposals: (a) to approach the nature-culture continuum in terms of health and longevity and (b) to regard nature as a cultural choice and then to decide what types of genetic manipulation should be prohibited by constructing a human rights–based freedom from those types of manipulation.

(a) Likely most people rank health at or near the top of their personal hierarchy of values. Health so understood has an almost transcendental import: without it, nothing else really matters.[27] On that basis I suggest that the parameters of allowable genetic manipulation, and advisable restrictions on genetic enhancement in particular, be set by goals and ideals of health and longevity rather than by notions of a reenchanted human nature. I advocate the nonmoralizing, technical attitude of Western medicine, itself an extension of science and technology, as distinct from a moralizing metaphysical or theological approach. This attitude does not invest the body with a normative quality vulnerable to violation by manipulation and control in medical contexts and for medical purposes. It is oriented on health, good nutrition, and a prolonged life span; that orientation does not treat the body as "sacred," as possessing a "metaphysical essence," or as protected by rights of some kind of transcendental provenance, such as natural rights or human rights understood as natural in kind. This is not to say, however, that it raises no normative objections whatsoever to health-related forms of genetic manipulation, as I show.

(b) The normative evaluation of genetic engineering involves a *cultural* interpretation of *biological* phenomena. We take a cultural stance toward nature when, from a normative point of view, we consider if we should regard nature as that which limits us as a species in our choices: as something we are constrained simply to accept, as we are constrained to accept biological chance, such as the chance genetic features of a human being as a consequence of sexual reproduction. In that case we might regard the individual's genome as determining his or her "natural

[27] To paraphrase van den Daele (2000:27).

fate." To speak in such terms is to contrast the biological with the cultural, as in the claim that the individual's socialization determines his or her "cultural fate." By *culture* I mean that individuals are molded prominently, although not exclusively, through lifelong socialization. By *socialization* I mean the acquisition – through learning and internalization – of culturally normed ways of thinking and behaving and of widely shared understandings and practices. Socialization is a lifelong process by which the individual continually shapes his or her personal identity as a cultural being. The carrier of that cultural identity is always a natural being, even if one genetically modified.

By contrast, we take a cultural stance toward *cultural phenomena* if we think of *nature as cultural choice*, for example with regard to features parents or others might choose for offspring through prenatal genetic manipulation. "Nature as cultural choice" is one of the ways in which nature flows into culture. I distinguish it from "culture flowing into nature," as when communities and traditions invest biological difference with cultural meaning. This happens when political communities draw cultural inferences from biological differences, for example between the sexes – as in traditions that regard men as superior to women and distribute social goods, such as education and employment, accordingly – or from differences in skin pigmentation among human groups, often as a criterion for the distribution of social goods and burdens (persons of the favored color tend to enjoy higher social status than those of the disfavored color). Natural fate and cultural fate intersect when investments of biological difference with cultural meaning socially privilege one group and deprivilege another.

Nature flows into culture in another way as well: when culture constructs all persons, on the basis of species membership, as equally possessing human rights.[28] We might well distinguish a person from a nonperson precisely with respect to human rights: people have them, nonpersons do not. By construing the term *person* not biologically but forensically (in the social constructionist manner I advocate), the community decides what a "person" is and who belongs in this category; it employs criteria that are not biological but socially constructed.[29] From

---

[28] Or when political community constructs all members as capable of possessing the same rights, and specifically rights against the nation-state.

[29] John Locke proposed more than 300 years ago to regard "person" and personal identity in forensic fashion, as a capacity to follow legal norms and to be legally responsible for one's actions (Locke 1975: bk. 2, chap. 27, para. 26). Those capacities are not biological but socially constructed and depend on recognition by other members of political community.

a social constructionist standpoint, a human right exists only if conferred (even if conferred by the individual him- or herself, even as it still needs recognition by others to be effective).[30] Here there is no moral entitlement in some metaphysical or theological sense.[31]

In any given case, the particular *kind* of political community is then of the greatest moment, because different political communities, and different kinds of political communities, accord different rights, and few accord human rights, at least in today's world. But if a community were to ascribe human rights, to what might those rights be ascribed? To an embryo from the first moment that its presence can be detected? Or perhaps only to a being unmistakably "human"? One might think, with John Searle, that "infants and small children have a right to care, feeding, housing, and so on, and similarly, people who are incapacitated due to injury, senility, illness, or other causes also have absolute rights to care." One might imagine a right of the helpless to be helped by other persons in a position to help, under circumstances in which the right is "necessary for the maintenance of any form of human life at all" (Searle 2010:193). Even here, however, a form of life is regarded as rights bearing only if socially constructed as such.

The idea of socially constructed human rights entails that there are no unconditional rights at the moment of conception or before birth (or even after birth) except those accorded by political community. Only then would pre-personal life enjoy a right to protection of life and physical integrity. The embryo is not a legal person in any a priori sense; it enjoys no legally relevant quality of "human dignity" prior to a political community's decision to that effect. If embryos are not regarded as persons, would they have no rights – and therefore be available for genetic manipulation? Not necessarily, if the status of an embryo as having no human rights did not necessarily entail that parents or others could therefore freely dispose over the embryo. Further, it does not follow that the good of the embryo, even if without human rights, could properly be weighed against some other, competing good, as though each was commensurable with the other, or calculable in the manner of material

---

[30] Chapter 4 generates a theory of self-granted human rights.

[31] The embryo is not necessarily without legal rights simply because it is not regarded as a legal person. Its use might be legally regulated, especially if such use benefited humanity in terms of scientific insight or medical therapy. Or it might be accorded legal protection in a "utilitarian consideration of beneficial outcome against moral feelings that human cells, though not identical with human beings, yet need to be treated differently from any other living matter" (Warnock 1987:13).

placed in the identical weighing pans of a scale, one of which holds an unknown weight while the effective weight in the other is increased by known amounts until the beam at whose ends the pans are suspended is level, signifying some kind of moral parity of the goods being weighed.[32] After all, legal protection due solely to preferences of others leads to a dangerous slippery slope. Consider by analogy: Should a pediatrician attempt to keep a neonate alive only if the sperm and egg donors desire as much? Might such a criterion ever be applied to infants, dependent adults, the elderly, or the handicapped? The idea here is that someone not wanted by anyone is therefore not a person. No one advocates this idea, however; likely everyone would accord each human a "weight" of his or her own, one incommensurable with any other weight and in this way would preclude any open-ended balancing of competing goods. But if parents (or other potential "wanters") are not permitted to decide whether their neonate lives, should they nonetheless be permitted to determine some of the neonate's genetic features? Or should the neonate be accorded some moral "weight" of its own, even if not that of a human being? One could answer yes only if something like "human dignity" (in the sense of human rights) might apply to life unmistakably human. Such an approach might be plausible if, from a moral or legal point of view, pre-personal life were available for manipulation under some circumstances but not others. But is a human embryo such a thing? Should it be constructed as "human" in the sense at issue here?

If we attempted to answer this question by consulting the will, desire, and plans of the being targeted for genetic manipulation, we confront the fact that, at the stage of an embryo, the targeted being has no will, desire, or plans. But if the embryo follows the developmental path to personhood, it will have all of these eventually. Should potential personhood qualify pre-personal life for the status of human rights bearer? Kant's support for the rights not of embryos but of children is instructive here. He views the obligation of parent to child as something not socially constructed: parents are obligated to respect the autonomy of the child, and they are so obligated not by their decision but by some quality intrinsic to the child. Kant regards the "act of procreation as one by which we

---

[32] A political community might choose to provide an embryo with a legal status of inviolable dignity, one that would include the embryo's physical integrity. In this way it would avoid having to weigh the rights and interests of one legal party against those of another. One might argue against such an approach on the grounds that it leaves the validity of the rights and interests of one party dependent on those of a second party, and so denies the autonomy of the first party.

have brought a person into the world without his consent and on our own initiative, for which deed the parents incur an obligation to make the child content with his condition so far as they can" (Kant 1996:281). Parents have an obligation "from procreation," and "children, as persons, have by their procreation an original innate (not acquired) right to the care of their parents" (Kant 1996:280). But what about, say, a child not yet born? A fetus? An embryo? Kant does not address the developmental pathway of sperm and egg uniting to create an embryo that develops over months before it might plausibly be regarded as a human person in any rich sense. At the beginning of the pathway, newly fertilized eggs, say, or blastocysts are not yet embryos and cannot be distinguished from the embryonic auxiliary tissue.[33] Kant only addresses the other end of the developmental pathway, where there is no biological question as to human identity (even as some communities might construe some groups as subhuman, although without biological support, which is one human rights–based reason why treating human nature as cultural choice would not reduce nature to culture). The space between these two ends of the continuum is wide and complex (just think of the range of complicated biological development that occurs there).

Kant's argument cannot account for the fact that, when sexual intercourse or in vitro fertilization eventually results in introducing a new person into the world, it is then only at a point along a developmental pathway. One act or another begins a chain of natural events that can lead first to fertilized egg, then to embryo, then to fetus, then to an unmistakable human being and, at some point along this continuum – where it clearly moves from nature to culture and finds recognition within political community – to human rights bearer. I have argued that recognized legal status remains a social construction; as such, it does not follow from any biological pathway. So I am not surprised that the obligation that Kant posits of parents toward their child implies nothing about early stages of the developmental pathway, and specifically at what point the organism in question might be accorded human rights. That point is not objective; it cannot be determined by a scientific understanding of nature; it remains a cultural question that can only be answered by the contingent perspectives and convictions of this or that political

---

[33] For the first two weeks following conception, identity is severely problematic also because of the possibility of "twinning" (producing two offspring at a time), "chimeras" (where the organism has two or more different populations of genetically distinct cells that originated in different zygotes involved with sexual reproduction), and "mosaics" (where the different cells emerged from the same zygote).

community. What emerges into view here is the paramount significance, from the standpoint of human rights, of developing a political community in the sense of the human rights state, which I introduce in Chapter 9.

I have argued that an intractable cultural question cannot be answered by reference to the potential of pre-personal life to develop into a person: the question of when, or at what point along the developmental continuum, the human self is first present, present with the legal and moral status of a human being in the sense of a human right to protection of his or her life. I refer to a human right not to be manipulated biotechnically, or a human right not to be "optimized." The same argument can be made on additional grounds. Semen's potential depends on its fertilization of an egg that is then implanted; an egg's potential depends on fertilization and then implantation. The potential of sperm and ovum at some point following fusion to *become* what is unmistakably a human being hardly entails that this potential of sperm and egg must *not* be frustrated (say, by legal or moral norms). Why should the potential of an embryo, or even a fetus, be regarded any differently? After all, unless implanted, the embryo (or pre-viable fetus) will die. The case is very different with viable fetuses or infants. In short, the biological developmental pathway is contingent on its human environments. That environment includes decisions by humans to place the embryo in vitro, for example, and subsequently in a womb, and so forth. Nature will or will not develop depending on culture.

And for its part, culture – as a capacity to bear human rights – presupposes the existence of something that can be a human rights bearer, something that comes about through natural reproduction. In this particular sense, culture "depends" on nature without implying a point along the developmental continuum at which nature "turns into" culture, or culture into nature. For human beings situated in political community attempting to normatively evaluate the problems and prospects of genetic manipulation, it appears that nature and culture are coeval or co-originary; they would seem always to flow one into the other. This conclusion urges a nonreductionist alternative to the tradition of thinking about second nature that leads from Hegel to Adorno.

The upshot is an analytic recommendation: do not differentiate among degrees of "human-ness"; do not distinguish between a "partial" and a "full" human being (whereby the lower level of "partial" might be regarded as so far from being a "full" human being that it could not plausibly be treated as a human being in the sense of a capacity for bearing human rights).[34] To do so turns what Adorno called "the spell of blind nature"[35] into the spell of blind culture. For it construes natural phenomena as though they were cultural phenomena – as if the sociological, philosophical, or legal meaning of "human being" could be given by nature. And it allows moral evaluation of genetic manipulation in terms of the end or "final stage" of development: an unmistakable human being. That is, if an embryo issues into what is unambiguously personhood, then, from the perspective of a reenchanted human nature, the embryo itself must somehow be regarded as a human being. That would be the conclusion of a Kantian metaphysics, which would consider human life before birth as an end in itself (a *Selbstzweck*). One could equally reach this conclusion from a theological standpoint that regarded human life before birth as something "sacred," something sanctified by a transcendent or otherworldly source of meaning and value. For metaphysics and theology alike, pre-personal human life is entitled by a "moralized" nature to a human right to a genetic inheritance free of artificial intervention; to the inviolability of its natural, physical incarnation; "to the life it has"; "not to be used as research material"; "to be implanted in the uterus where it may develop" (Warnock 1987:1); "to be given ... the *chance of* [human] life" (Warnock 1987:5).

Cultural Choice about Pre-Personal Life

I reject, then, the re-enchantment of human nature, that is, the endowment of embryonic life with some kind of metaphysical or theological "essence," perhaps as part of natural law or an ontological order vulnerable to sacrilegious violation.[36] I reject the essentialist claim that fetal life incorporates some destiny or purpose or quality that is "real," "actual," "true," "ultimate," "fundamental," or "original." Such a perspective renders "human nature," or the "naturalness" of man, as something *given*, something that has *developed over time* in distinction to something

---

[34] Thus the debate on genetic manipulation, as I understand it, is distinct from the debate on abortion. Whereas the latter asks: At what point? the former asks: What kind of manipulation? The issue, then, is not *when* the manipulation happens but rather *what* kind of changes the manipulation brings about.

[35] A "Bann der blinden Natur" (Adorno 1966:350).

[36] Further, if the embryo in vitro possesses basic legal rights, those rights collide with a possible right of parents to genetically modify their offspring, even in the earliest stages of development. This follows *if* the embryo is culturally construed as a legal person who possesses basic rights.

made or manufactured. Indeed, it invests nature with socially constructed meanings that deny their own social constructedness, giving a social construction a patina of "nature." For if human nature is construed as metaphysical or divine (such that genetic manipulation of pre-personal life could only be evaluated on metaphysical or theological grounds), then the genome's manipulation (whether as therapy for sick persons or enhancement of life not yet born) would constitute a violation of some sacred or essential limit to what mankind may permit itself in its dealings with the natural environment and with human nature in particular.

I advocate a different approach and see two different ways to realize it. Here's one: if political community grants no unique ethical standing to nature, then the embryo, *as something natural,* has no special moral status. It has no such status even if it lies on a developmental continuum with a legal, human rights–bearing person who inhabits a political community that grants and recognizes individual rights. This option does not view the fertilized egg as the start of a self-regulated biological process "programmed" to develop into a full human being. It does not regard the fertilized egg from the moment of fertilization as part of an evolutionary process leading to a potential person and hence to a subject possessing human rights. Instead it views the legal and moral autonomy of any organism solely as an artifact of society. It does not regard the embryo or blastocyst as autonomous in the sense of enjoying human rights protection from alien determination.

Alien determination of the embryo is politically relevant insofar as it concerns the *person who eventually develops from it.* Jürgen Habermas (2003a:87), who in his own way has sought to reconstruct the Hegel-to-Adorno tradition toward realizing its goals by avoiding its aporia, frames the issue this way: a "genetic designer, acting according to his own preferences, assumes an irrevocable role in determining the contours of the life history and identity of another person, while remaining unable to assume even her counterfactual consent." Here we presuppose "our capacity to see ourselves as the authors of our own life-histories, and to recognize one another as autonomous persons" (Habermas 2003a:25). Our presupposition entails a *normative status* for human nature, one that reaches back to the pre-personal predicates of a human being (even as members of any political community probably could not agree on the threshold between person and nonperson). By "normative status" I refer to a relational symmetry among persons: *symmetry* in the moral and legal sense of the equality of persons as well as mutual respect among persons. Symmetry of this sort implies the inviolability of the individual's genome insofar as the individual is a legal person, hence not all the way back along the developmental pathway to the embryo, which cannot be regarded as a legal person. Interpersonal symmetry, legal equality, and mutual respect are possible between and among beings who are unmistakably human persons, but not between personal and pre-personal life.

Whereas this first way of realizing my approach eschews the search for some threshold between non–human rights–bearing pre-personhood and human rights–bearing persons, the second way of achieving my proposal does not. It does not operate with thresholds at all; instead, it thematizes a person's body in terms of the phrase "to have" as distinguished from the phrase "to be."[37] It distinguishes the autonomy of *having a body* from the autonomy of *being a body*: the individual always has a body but may not always identify with it.

It works with two dissimilar senses of "to possess one's body." One sense is that of *having a body* prior to reflecting on it; indeed, such reflection presupposes the very fact of having a body. That is, a person's subjectivity presupposes his or her bodily objectivity; consciousness presupposes the *fact of physical embodiedness*. A second sense of possessing a body is recognizing one's body as "truly" one's own. For example, one might recognize one's body as one's own if it was not determined (through genetic manipulation) in any of its qualities by others (such as the parents or caretakers who direct the physician to modify their embryo's genome). This sense of possessing a body involves personal identity, something culturally contingent, the *cultural contingency of personal identity*. One facet of human cultural identity is one's relationship to one's own body. Someone who, for whatever reason, cannot identify with it likely is disturbed in his or her personal identity overall. For one's bodily incarnation is the topological seat of one's identity, the point from which one speaks when one says anything at all, the point to which one (implicitly) refers when speaking of oneself, and the point in terms of which one orients oneself in space and relative to all things, as well as the divide between the internal, psychological world and the environment, and perhaps as well as the divide between what is "self" and what is "other," my actions in

---

37 In Plessner's sense of "is" and "have": "Der Körper vereinigt ... die Eigenschaft, Subjekt des Habens zu sein, mit der Eigenschaft, Objekt des Habens (sein Körper) zu sein, dadurch, daß er zum Mittel des Habens wird," such that "Das Mittel des Habens, das der Körper hat, ist die Einheit von Haben und Gehabtsein, von Subjekt und Objekt am lebendigen Körper, ihre Vermittlung zu seiner Ganzheit" (Plessner 1981:250).

distinction to your actions. Even if one does not identify with one's body, one can still do all these things. But doing these things might always bring to mind the person's nonidentity with his or her own body. Perhaps one would do all these things *despite* one's troubled bodily identity. A much more important question is whether being able to identify with one's own body is a condition for one's sense of personal autonomy, perhaps even personal freedom in some sense. That is, more important is the question of whether individual human freedom in political community presupposes that one understands oneself as "grown" not "made," or that one understands oneself to be a product of chromosomal chance rather than biotechnological design.[38]

Such questions can only be answered interpretively; the answer in any given case would depend on how the respondent interprets the social and natural worlds. Would someone who had a body that had developed from a engineered genome *not* regard him- or herself as "possessing" a body of alien determination? Would he or she regard him- or herself as saddled with an unwanted body, or a body with which he or she could not identify, without recourse to change it? And what if someone with a genetically tailored body *did* identify with it and did not regard it as being of foreign determination? In that case, the objection to the manipulation of the embryo could only be an objection to replacing biological chance with technological choice. And what might be grounds for such an objection? That a human "grown" is morally preferable to a human "made"? Kant alludes to a distinction along somewhat related lines: the "offspring is a person, and it is impossible to form a concept of the production of a being endowed with freedom through a physical operation" (Kant 1996:280). But that distinction does not rely on the autonomy of whatever would be genetically manipulated. It does not rely on the freedom from having one's hereditary factors programmed by others. Nor does it depend on the chance fusion, in sexual reproduction, of the parents' sets of chromosomes and then their divisions.

It depends on interpretation. Throughout the historical record (and note that the human capacity for culture is a precondition for mankind's very creation of its historical record), humans have interpreted the natural and social environment, as well as questions about what it means to be human, or how best to live as an individual, or how best to organize

---

[38] Habermas (2003a:57–58) also raises some of these issues; I do not share his conclusion that not to identify with one's body renders one dysfunctional and perhaps incapable of full freedom in political community.

communal life. To imagine a particular set of norms – from those of a small community to universally valid human rights – is to interpret man's biological membership in terms of a cultural category. (In the case of human rights in particular, it is to interpret biological species member-ship in terms of cultural constructs.) We construct cultural membership in biological categories when we guide our behavior toward other human beings by the fact that they are fellow members of our species. In this way we generate normative guides for a piece of nature, namely for the evolved organism that we are. And in seeking norms to guide us in our behavior toward nature, culture meets up with nature. So any question about human nature is at once a question about human culture. This is the case even though humans are part of nature; even though they inhabit multiple natural environments; even though, for tens of thou-sands of years now, they have exceeded their merely biological existence through cultural creations and ways of life.

So the distinction between "merely" having a body and "truly" being one's body involves cultural choices about pre-personal life. It does not involve metaphysical or theological truths or principles. Suppose, then, that legally privileged persons (perhaps parents above all) one day soon make genetic choices for legally nonprivileged pre-personal life (for their unborn offspring). Only by particular social, cultural, and political def-initions could one say that the parents thereby assault the recipient's autonomy, with consequences written unalterably into the body, unless and until the recipient is recognized as a legal person. And only by particular social, cultural, and political definitions is such recognition plausible. These are questions for the community's public sphere, for they are political. And politics would be displaced if nature, and human nature in particular, were invested with supernatural, otherworldly, meta-physical or theological qualities that would bind the stance of political community toward it.

Both ways of realizing my alternative to the reenchantment of human nature – to the endowment of embryonic life with an essence, whether theological or metaphysical – agree on this: that political community must not displace politics. They agree that political community should embrace the political task of socially constructing an answer to the ques-tion, "What is a legal person, at what point is it first present, and how do we know, and what kinds of genetic manipulations should be permit-ted, which prohibited, and in each case: On what grounds?" If individual autonomy is without natural predicates, if it is not a natural feature of human life, if it is something cultural, then a community should not seek to preserve the contingency of biological chance by disallowing genetic manipulation in the name of an assumed, rather than socially constructed, personal autonomy of the possible recipient. A political rather than metaphysical or theological determination of "human nature," as a matter of cultural choice, is the approach taken by the human rights state, which I develop in Chapter 9.

9

The Human Rights State

Part II developed two different kinds of resources for human rights as social construction, one cultural and one biological. Now Part IV, in recasting two core elements of human rights, also takes a dual track approach. Chapter 8 followed a biological track with respect to human nature biologically understood; the present chapter pursues a cultural track with regard to the nation-state. The nation-state presupposes nationality, the subject of Article 15 of the UN's *Universal Declaration of Human Rights*: "Everyone has the right to a nationality." Is that because the nation-state is the basic unit of social and political membership? Does the possibility of human rights depend on it? Are there alternatives? Kant considers related questions in his 1795 sketch for perpetual peace among states. It distinguishes among three visions of legal status ("types of constitutions"). The first and third focus on individuals; the second, on states. Despite this difference, we might think of them as nested one in the other, like concentric circles. At the center is the individual's legal status, grounded in a *"civil right* of individuals within a nation." Move out one circle and we observe multiple states in peaceful coexistence: the *"international right* of states in their relationships with one another." Transfer to the outer ring and we find a putative "cosmopolitan right" of "citizens of a universal state of mankind" (Kant 1997:98n). In which of these circles might anyone, anywhere in the world today, recognize his or her political condition? For several centuries now, some people have been fortunate enough to lead lives within the first circle, where they enjoy at least some civil rights. Some live simultaneously within the second circle. Here individuals who carry a politically "strong" passport cross international borders more easily than those with politically "weak" ones, but even here, bearers of weak passports usually circulate more or less freely. Today all states expect all persons, citizen and foreigner alike, to reside in the first circle. Ideally all persons would reside in the second as well, as citizens of one Westphalian state among others, each state recognizing the sovereignty of the others. But who in our world today also resides in that blessed outer circle, the cosmopolitan condition of individual rights penetrating all national borders? Who can even say what it might mean to live in a universal state of mankind? Hundreds of millions of people today inhabit the institutions and political practices of the first and second circles. The third, however, remains obscure in meaning and difficult to imagine in practice; it also remains an idea of abiding fascination.

I analyze the third circle, a universal political condition, in one of its most prominent versions: as the idea of human rights. As in previous chapters, I would strip the human rights idea of its utopianism and drape it with the regular habit of vernacular life by constructing human rights as initially valid only locally. By *local* I mean state-based human rights as distinguished from human rights universally valid a priori that are then applied locally. Human rights in this context could be whatever a state took to be human rights, but given the intellectual and political history of the human rights idea, it is not implausible to assume that many states would fix upon some combination of one or more of the three "waves" of human rights conceptions: civil rights of the individual, economic rights, and group rights. Each locale would develop its own mix.

More empirically oriented scholarship on human rights often distinguishes "local" from "state based," "federal," or "national." I use "local" more flexibly. Locally valid human rights in my sense would be more than the rights of citizens; even as positive state-based law, they would treat the law's addressees as potential members of a world republic of shared moral claims. "Local" then refers to state-based rights but in the unusual sense of state-based *human* rights. "Local" is more than just an antonym of "global." In this sense, the United States is local, but California, a unit smaller than the state, is not. Each member of the EU is local, as each is a state, and the EU itself might be considered local to the extent that it constitutes a kind of super-state.

By "valid" I mean that which, within a culture, marks an idea, belief, or practice in ways that members to some degree recognize and identify with. This chapter works the following hunch into an insight: local political culture, if charged with protecting the human rights it embraces, is more likely than any nonlocal culture to be vigilant in protecting them. If it doesn't support them now, it might become supportive if human rights are built off features already present locally, as I argue in

Chapters 3, 6, and 7. To that end, I develop a conception of the state to ground human rights in institutionally plausible practices of positive law at the local level. As in previous chapters, I reject metaphysically implausible and institutionally impotent attempts to ground human rights in "human dignity." Such attempts are improbable and sterile for reasons I develop in Chapters 1 and 2.

Instead I embrace universally valid rights as rights of local provenance that one day may achieve universal embrace; they could be universally valid in a contingent sense if all communities at some point freely came to embrace them. I do not mean that political communities everywhere one day will simply realize that they "really do," after all, support human rights for their own local reasons. And the merits of what I develop as the human rights state do not trade on asking: "Wouldn't it be wonderful if human rights violators could find the resources in their own traditions to change their spots and support human rights?" The merits of my proposal emerge in the course of showing how my localist alternative accomplishes the task of creating a universal political condition where now there is none – and how that alternative addresses practical issues of recognizing, observing, and protecting human rights.

This proposal is neither utopian nor fantastical. It does not entail abolishing existing nation states but rather transforming them in ways I detail in five steps: (1) I argue that human rights are available only in political community but (2) not in the mold of the nation state as we know it. For human rights purposes, the nation state is inadequate because of what I analyze as its "exclusionary logic." (3) I offer an alternative to the nation state by solving Hannah Arendt's puzzle of a "right to have rights" and (4) elaborate that solution as the idea of a human rights state. The human rights state has an inclusionary logic that extends across its own borders. (5) I then show how such a state might secure the three types of individual autonomy that make some human rights possible.

Human Rights are Available Only in Political Community

The committee that drafted the UN's *Universal Declaration of Human Rights* in 1947 thought of itself as drafting universally valid propositions.[1] On

---

[1] The principle drafters were Canadian (John Humphrey), French (Rene Cassin), and the American representative to the Commission on Human Rights, Eleanor Roosevelt. The committee did not seek input from representatives of Muslim peoples or indigenous peoples or more generally from the billions of persons in whose names it drafted the *Universal Declaration*.

what grounds? Perhaps it felt reassured in its self-perception when respondents – canvassed from a variety of intellectual, spiritual, and political backgrounds – all pointed from their respective traditions to the "dignity of the human person" (UNESCO 1949). Even though the idea of dignity might be thought to stand at the core of each of the document's articles, the *Universal Declaration* nowhere defines it;[2] Hannah Arendt does. She discusses inalienable human rights as they were articulated in the American Declaration of Independence and then in revolutionary France's *Déclaration des droits de l'homme et du citoyen*. Understood as "independent of history and the privileges which history had accorded certain strata of society," human rights constitute a human dignity of "rather ambiguous nature": a "belief in a kind of human 'nature' . . . from which rights and laws could be deduced" (Arendt 1994:298). But rights are not the defining feature of humankind; after all, man "can lose all so-called Rights of Man without losing his essential quality as man, his human dignity" (Arendt 1994:297). That's because rights can only be social constructions recognized by members of the local community. For if the "defining feature of humankind" is political community, then the "loss of a polity itself expels" the individual "from humanity" (Arendt 1994:297).

But rights cannot be valid "if a human being is expelled from the human community" because the source of rights is membership not in humanity but rather in political community (Arendt 1994:297–298). For Arendt, the right to have rights must be politically secured and it can only be secured by "humanity itself." She couples the human and the political in a philosophical anthropology: she thinks of political community as the "defining feature of humankind" that equates membership in a polity with membership in humanity.

But her anthropology is in tension with her nonanthropological claim that human rights could be ascribed to all humankind only in the presence of a global political community. I decouple the latter claim, which is deeply political, from Arendt's philosophical anthropology. I adopt only the former and urge that, if human rights are derived from community, and if any given political community is contingent and particular, then human rights are themselves contingent and culturally particular: they cannot exist before politics or otherwise beyond politics.

---

[2] Without defining "dignity," the preamble speaks of "recognition of the inherent dignity . . . of all members of the human family" and of the "peoples of the United Nations [who] have in the Charter reaffirmed their faith in fundamental human rights."

But what if one concedes that rights can be recognized and securely enforced within political community yet insists on a distinction between potential rights and actual rights? What if one argues that the individual may lose the social and political context in which human rights are recognized and enforced without necessarily losing the potential for enjoying those rights should that context be restored? Would one would remain a "human being in general," with human rights yet without the social and political context to realize them? In fact, this objection only reinforces my claim that human rights are contingent: they cannot exist without the social and political context in which they are recognized and enforced. Even if one argues with respect to Arendt's approach that it is not one's humanity that is lost, but rather the *opportunity* to be fully human, one still acknowledges that "full humanity" is not given but rather is politically constructed. For example, to regard stateless refugees as not less human than citizens, but rather as humans whose human rights remain latent because of statelessness, is to acknowledge that human rights are always politically contingent. Rights that remain latent are pointless for the bearer; what matters is the politics of actualizing them. If latent right can only be actualized in political community, then outside that community one has no rights (if rights unrealized are, in effect, no different from nonexistent rights). Hence the common assertion that a person has human rights whether or not he or she is a member of a political community that recognizes and enforces them is "not political" in the sense of "without practical effect." In that sense, to lose one's political community is to lose not only one's domestic rights but one's human rights as well.

The Political Community in Which Human Rights Are Available Is Not the Nation-State

I do not claim that all political communities ought to generate certain basic rights or that all have the capacity and commitment to generate human rights in particular. Rather I ask: In any given community, just what kind of political community and political membership might generate human rights for persons as I defined persons in Chapter 8? I answer by way of reconceiving the nation state. I begin with how the *Universal Declaration*, as a particularly prominent element in the global politics of human rights advocacy, takes the nation state for granted and even favors it by presupposing several decidedly nonuniversal institutions and various cultural preferences that are state-based:

- Rights to life, liberty, and personal security require the *state* as enforcer.
- Other rights imply a particular kind of *legal system*, one that recognizes a person in his or her legal equality, such as a right to remedy by competent tribunal and to a fair and public hearing, or a right to be considered innocent until proven guilty.
- Other rights can only be realized through *institutions of political participation* allowing for peaceful assembly and association, free elections, and participation in government.
- Still other rights require various kinds of *economic institutions*: a right to own property, to social security, to desirable work and trade union membership, to an adequate standard of living, and to rest and leisure.
- Some rights assume distinct *cultural commitments*, whether to certain institutions (marriage and family, education) or to shared forms of culture (a right to participate in the cultural life of the relevant community).
- The rights to free movement in and out of any country, or to asylum in other countries as protection from persecution, imply a more or less liberal international order composed of somewhat liberal states.

The *Universal Declaration*'s construction of individual autonomy precludes the political culture of hierarchically organized societies, that is, societies that allow all members some say in their community's organization but that systematically favor certain groups over others in a hierarchy of social standing and power, such as members of a particular religion, ethnicity, language group, or family; men in general; or elders.

In short, the *Universal Declaration*'s vision of human rights as universally valid is clouded by its delineation of rights some of which are particular only to some cultures and some of which are particular to the nation-state. The *state* is a legally defined organization of divided powers and formal procedures for deciding everything from political representation to public policy. The *nation*-state embraces the pre-political solidarity generators of blood, ethnicity, language, religion, or beliefs about a shared fate. It does not matter whether any of these features are real; what matters is the presence of a shared political identity conceived in normatively thick terms (as distinguished from, say, the normatively thin terms of a liberal democratic constitution). Even an immigrant polity such as the

United States embraces pre-political solidarity generators in its myths, such as "a city on a hill" in which "all men are created equal," guided by "manifest destiny," and descended from "huddled masses yearning to breathe free."

The *Universal Declaration* intertwines nationhood with statehood; its twenty-nine fundamental rights presuppose nothing less than the nation state. To possess human rights is not only to possess membership in a state; it is to be a member of a *nation* free from foreign domination.[3] If a person has no nation state, he or she has no such rights. At least this is Arendt's conclusion.

What exactly does Arendt mean by membership in political community as the only venue where rights are possible? As I've shown, she offers two understandings, one anthropological, one political. The latter is promising whereas the former is problematic in its metaphysical constitution. To be "human," she says, is to be "political" in the sense of having responsibilities to one's political community. Anyone outside political community is but a "human being in general," a being in an existentially diminished condition with respect to status, rights, and dignity: "without a profession, without a citizenship, without an opinion, without a deed by which to identify and specify himself" (Arendt 1994:302). Arendt makes this point repeatedly: to be reduced to "nothing but [one's] ... own absolutely unique individuality" is to be "deprived of expression within and action upon a common world" (ibid.). A "man who is nothing but a man has lost the very qualities which make it possible for other people to treat him as a fellow-man" (Arendt 1994:300).

In short, to lack political community is to lack even the possibility of human rights. For only in political community are human rights available – if at all; only there are they effective – if at all. I argued earlier that political community can only be particular and local, and Arendt would appear to agree where she says that the "fundamental deprivation of human rights is manifested ... in the deprivation of a place in the world which makes opinions significant and actions effective" (Arendt 1994:296). Such a place can only be concrete and particular; few persons' opinions and actions matter anywhere beyond a local venue (if they matter even there). A specific place, as a "framework where one is judged by one's actions" (ibid.), where one is recognized by others, is one of particular customs, traditions, understandings, culture, and history. Today

---

[3] Thus when Arendt (1994:288, n.44a) says that "every individual is born with inalienable rights guaranteed by his nationality," I take her to mean the nation-state.

that place is the state (and spheres within the state: family, community, profession, and so forth).

Hence the most basic right is not to universal or abstract political community but rather to a particular context for public behavior. Most basic is a right to a political context for responsibility to one's particular community (but perhaps not to others) and for recognition within it (but perhaps not in others). That context is the state, such that to be stateless is to be rightless in the sense of lacking a right to have rights. Evidently all the various particular individual human rights reduce to a kind of *Ur-Recht*: the *human* right to have rights, which in this account means a human right to state membership, to citizenship – not for principled or metaphysical reasons but for entirely practical ones. Of all the venues where one's opinion might matter and where one's actions might be of consequence, the community constituted by state membership is the most important. It is, in principle, better placed than any other venue to provide human rights. *In principle* means many a state as a state *could* come to observe human rights even though only some do so today. In fact, many states today are the single greatest obstacle to their citizens' possible human rights. As for those states that do not embrace human rights, one might say that they fail the normative potential of statehood: to provide and protect human rights. They fail the standard of a right to have rights. But is that standard universally valid today? Absent a universal political community on which it could be based (such as a world state or a confederation of states), it cannot be.

The idea of a right to have rights is a puzzle, then: it is a universalism ambivalent about itself, one that calls itself into question. Arendt (1994:298) believes that the "right to have rights or the right of every individual to belong to humanity, should be guaranteed by humanity itself" because humanity has "assumed the role formerly ascribed to nature or history." Because humanity *cannot* guarantee such rights, however, we end up with a puzzle again: an approach to human rights that is both universal and particular, as the putatively *universal* right to a state membership that can only be a *particular* right.

Solving the Puzzle of a "Right to Have Rights": An Alternative to the Nation State

If we take a different tack, one based on the distinction between morality and legality, we might break this impasse. Absent a world state that legislates a *legal* right to belong to humanity, such a right can only be a *moral* right. By contrast, a right to citizenship can only be a legal right because border controls and citizenship restrictions are matters of domestic law – and a state with open borders, and without privileges for citizens over noncitizens, would quickly cease to be a state. But the moral and the legal coalesce (if in curious fashion) in the notion of a right to have rights. In speaking of "a right to have rights," let us call the first usage a "*humanity membership* right" and the second a "*state membership* right." A humanity membership right is a moral imperative that is independent of the state: an imperative to treat all persons as members of some human community entitled to its protection. As a moral imperative, it enjoins all persons to recognize the membership of all persons in a universal moral community of "humanity." By contrast, a state membership right refers, at most and at best, to civil rights. Civil rights can follow from membership in some legal communities. Civil rights generate legal obligations among a community's consociates: members are bound to each other by reciprocal rights and duties,[4] Legal obligations, unlike moral imperatives, are enforceable within the state.

And that's not all. A humanity membership right can be a vehicle for abstract principles of human rights. By contrast, a state membership right is always a matter of jurisdiction: it concerns the territorially bounded sovereignty of a particular state. No one knows where a putative humanity membership right might come from; theories of such rights are plural and incommensurable, with uncertain claims to validity or legitimacy. By contrast, the source of a state membership right is clear to all: the state's legislature.

Arendt argues that an individual's humanity membership right entitles him or her to a state membership right. Be that as it may, I would argue that a state membership right does not entitle anyone to a humanity membership right. Of course, one cannot be a member of a particular state without being human, but a right of state membership, because it applies to humans (biologically understood), hardly entails humanity membership. For humanity membership is not simply membership in a biological category; it is membership in a particular cultural category, the category of socially constructed human rights. Human rights need not be constructed to include all persons with state membership – or even all humans because, as I argued in the previous chapter, "human"

---

[4] Think here of the classical Greek *polis* and the *isonomy* of citizens endowed with civil and political rights.

itself is a contested term: for example, does it apply to pre-personal life, such as an embryo? One cannot be said to be entitled to a humanity right by the fact of being a human unless "human" is understood in the sense of "humanity" – and inevitably some candidates for "human" will lie somewhere along the developmental pathway leading from a fertilized egg to life that is unmistakably human.

One might argue, with Kant, that a "right of humanity in *every* individual" implies your obligation to enter civil society with other individuals as legal consociates equally entitled to civil rights.[5] But even then, legal equality within civil society hardly entails equal membership in humanity. The various qualities or rights of state membership cannot be universal because the state can only be particular; even a right to state membership cannot be universal because no state is obliged to grant membership to outsiders, let alone to everyone, yet if there were a right to state membership, presumably it would be enjoyed by everyone. And even if the source of cosmopolitan norms (such as a humanity membership right) lies beyond state boundaries, the validity of those norms can hardly reach within state boundaries without state consent and cooperation.

To be sure, stateless people have sometimes had their (putative) human rights enforced for them, but such cases are exceptional and more like emergency stopgap measures than what I seek here: the local, free embrace of human rights to render them part of one's everyday experience. This conclusion dismisses the possibility of cosmopolitan norms, norms not state based. On the one hand, a cosmopolitan norm dismisses the idea that someone must be a member of a particular state to enjoy cosmopolitan rights. On the other hand, a cosmopolitan right of humanity in one's person implies nothing about one's rights as a member of a particular political community. If one enjoys a right not to be deprived of life, liberty, or property without due process of law, then only because of the state that legislates and practices legal proceduralism.

I find support for my claim about cosmopolitan norms in the famous third "definitive article" of Kant's *Perpetual Peace*: "cosmopolitan right shall be limited to conditions of universal hospitality." By hospitality (*Wirtbarkeit*), Kant means the "right of a stranger not to be treated with

---

[5] In line with Kant's moral law: "So act that you use humanity, whether in your own person or in the person of any other, always at the same time as an end, never merely as a means" (Kant 1998:38).

hostility when he arrives on someone else's territory" (Kant 1997:105).
Hospitality in this sense does not regulate domestic civil society; it does
not regulate relationships among citizens. Rather, the individual enjoys
hospitality as a potential participant not in the host state but in an imagined world republic. In terms of my analysis of an Arendtian right to
have rights, a right of hospitality is a *humanity* membership right, not a
state membership right. It can regulate the relation between insiders and
outsiders, between members and nonmembers, with narrow scope; for
example, the right to temporary hospitality from the host state is no right
to immigration.

In terms of a humanity membership right, the right of hospitality
cannot be refused *if* a humanity membership right is understood as
a moral claim with *legal* consequences – namely, where refusal would
violate the refused person's legal rights. But we have a problem here:
in this context, the notion of a moral right with legal consequences is
incoherent. For even if hospitality entails reciprocal moral obligations
on the basis of our mutual humanity, it is not a legally enforceable norm
of behavior within the sovereign nation-state. Even if hospitality were
an international obligation, its violation would hardly be sanctionable
against sovereign states (or at least, no political community has ever
been sanctioned by another, or by some international organization, for
refusing hospitality to outsiders). The right of hospitality can only be
a moral right without domestic legal consequence. (What international
law could possibly be enforced here?) If the state observes hospitality at
all, then it does so only as a gratuitous grant to the guest, a kind of benef-
icence – one is lucky to be a recipient, and this poignant need for luck
marks the absence of any right. In short, even as Arendt ties a human
membership right to a state membership right, each precludes the
other.

Alternative to the Nation-State: The Human Rights State

Here I see an alternative, one more likely to be effective in the promotion of a local embrace of human rights than various institutions have
been, such as the United Nations or the International Criminal Court.
Whereas such institutions operate largely on a universalist understanding
of human rights, I've argued that human rights need to be established
and enforced at local levels as locally valid norms. They might be locally
established and locally enforced only if Arendt's postulate of a right to
have rights is possible in a form correspondingly nonuniversal – and

nonuniversal because state-based, where the state is the venue for locally embraced human rights.[6]

A surprising conclusion? After all, precisely the nation state creates the problems to which many human rights would respond: refugees, expelled from their homeland; stateless persons, whose former states withdrew their protection and nullified state-based rights; displaced persons, in the form of refugees or stateless persons that no state will take in as members; and certain minorities (including asylum seekers, guest workers, and immigrants) that the nation state regards as "foreign bodies" within the community. Here we need to look more closely at the political condition of those in need of the host state's hospitality. Consider stateless persons. They do not enjoy "those rights which had been thought of and even defined as inalienable, namely the Rights of Man" (Arendt 1994:268). Ironically, only as an offender against the law can the stateless person gain protection from the law, namely as someone who, by becoming an offender, finally registers on the host's legal and political "radar." To be stateless is not only to lack a mechanism for enforcing any putative right, including a right to have rights, but also to lack all rights. Upshot? That a putative "right of asylum, the only right that . . . ever figured as a symbol of the Rights of Man in the sphere of international relationships . . . continue[s] to function in a world organized into nation states" – even as it "conflict[s] with the international rights of the state. Therefore it cannot be found in written law, in no constitution or international agreement. . . . It shares . . . the fate of the Rights of Man, which also never became law but led a somewhat shadowy existence as an appeal in individual exceptional cases for which normal legal institutions did not suffice" (Arendt 1994:280–281). In other words, if asylum is a human right, then it is one whose source can only lie *within* the host state. The same holds for naturalization: it can only be an act of the sovereign state. Even if undertaken by the UN or even by NGOs, repatriation can succeed only if the target state agrees to it. The same holds for statelessness: created by *particular* states, only *particular* states can solve it. There are "only two ways to solve the problem: repatriation or naturalization" (Arendt 1994:281).

---

[6] Just as individual autonomy has no natural predicates, just as it is not a natural feature of human life but something cultural (as I argued in Chapter 8), so a right to have rights is not natural but cultural. Just as individual autonomy cannot be assumed, metaphysically or theologically, but must be constructed politically, so, too, must a right to have rights. The human rights state, as a social construction, works with a thoroughly naturalistic conception of human beings, whose rights are socially constructed.

Both solutions are state based; more precisely, both are based in the nation state.

But why should the contemporary nation state be the last word? Consider an alternative that redeems the promise of locally valid norms. In the absence of an institutionalized *universal* mechanism for regular and consistent human rights enforcement at any level of political or social organization, human rights might be established and enforced at *local* levels, by *local* norms. This is possible if Arendt's notion of a right to have rights can be realized in a form correspondingly nonuniversal because it is state based. With regard to a right to have rights, I earlier argued that possession of a *humanity* membership right presupposes possession of a *state* membership right. But a right to have rights also means that to deny people a state membership right would thereby deny them a humanity membership right. Hence an empirical insight: a right to have rights has never featured in nation state membership. It has never rested on some universal confluence of humanity in the person of each member.

Consider, then, a very different kind of state, one that relates the individual's "humanity" to a territorialized legal status: what I call a "human rights state." A human rights state would inscribe the universal within the particular; it would include the excluded "within the circle of addressees of the universal" (Benhabib 2004:182). It would register a humanity membership right *within* a state membership right. It would transform the status of those outside its sovereign territory from a moral status (a humanity membership right) into a legal status (a state membership right). It would do so by adopting, as state-based law, the otherwise merely moral principles of human rights. It would juridify what, in the nation state, is only a moral recommendation: that the humanity or dignity in the person of the individual *should* find legal recognition in a particular political community's legal framework. For whether one has rights "depends on receipt of a special sort of social recognition and acceptance – that is, of one's juridical status within some particular concrete political community. The notion of a right to have rights arises out of the modern statist conditions and is equivalent to the moral claim of a refugee or other stateless person to citizenship, or at least juridical personhood, within the social confines of some law-dispensing state" (Michelman 1996:203).

When a state provides its citizens with human rights, it achieves what I earlier called the "normative potential of the state." In doing so, the state constrains its own sovereignty. The human rights state does even more: it discards the nation state's nationalism – its exclusionary logic – for a different kind of political solidarity: the principle that all persons, those inside state boundaries as well as those outside, are legally equal with respect to state-based human rights. Then, one might object, why have a state in the first place? After all, doesn't the state have compelling reasons for its exclusionary logic? Polities disagree about the nature, implications, and extent of rights. Although various nation-states provide, say, a right to political participation, to hold office, and to vote, would not such commitments undermine state sovereignty if they entailed that members of one polity could equally exercise such rights in all polities with the same commitments?

That objection makes sense if directed at the nation state. But the human rights state is different. It attaches what John Searle calls "status functions" to any unmistakable human being (to use a distinction I introduced in Chapter 8). In its creation, in its imposition or acceptance, and in its recognition within a community, a status function is a social construction, a work of collective intentionality, and nothing natural, and it requires neither theological nor metaphysical grounds or props. Humans can "impose functions on objects and people where the objects and the people cannot perform the functions solely in virtue of their physical structure" (Searle 2010:7). The "performance of the function requires that there be a collectively recognized status that the person or object has, and it is only in virtue of that status that the person or object can perform the function in question" (Searle 2010:7).[7] Thus legal tender and private property, institutionalized marriage and rights of various sorts, citizenship and state sovereignty, as well as the position of prime minister or police officer are all status functions.

Status functions carry what Searle calls "deontic powers": "they carry rights, duties, obligations, requirements, permissions, authorizations, entitlements, and so on" (Searle 2010:8–9). Deontic powers are "positive" as rights but "negative" as obligations. They are essential to social life: once recognized, deontic powers "provide us with reasons for acting that are independent of our inclinations and desires" (Searle 2010:9). When we are born into a particular community, we are born into any number of already existing social institutions with status functions that carry deontic powers.

---

[7] The collective recognition of the status is not necessarily approval: "Acceptance . . . goes all the way from enthusiastic endorsement to grudging acknowledgment, even the acknowledgment that one is simply helpless to do anything about, or reject, the institutions in which one finds oneself" (Searle 2010:8).

Human rights may be conceived as deontic powers deriving from assigned status. The status of being human, biologically understood, carries no status function; no biological fact does. But understood politically, the status of being human can become an institutional fact and carry whatever status function the community assigns it. That status, politically understood, could entail rights justified by the purpose of the relevant institution, such that to be denied human rights would be to deny the status function and the deontic powers it carries. But what might that relevant institution be? Not the *Universal Declaration of Human Rights*, which offers a set of mostly negative deontic powers imposed on all (unmistakable) human beings. The *Declaration* has never been able to overcome the exclusionary logic of the nation state. Because the human rights state is not based on an exclusionary logic and thus operates differently than the nation state, it also operates differently than the *Declaration*, which claims that everyone everywhere is entitled to the recognition of human rights that have always already existed. The human rights state, by contrast, urges everyone everywhere to craft for themselves Arendt's "right to have rights," that is, to construct rights and rights-recognizing institutions that in most places in the world today do not exist and never have existed.

For the human rights state, human rights (as well as "human duties") attach to one's position or status within institutions and the rules that define them. Status, institutions, and rules are all social constructions; they can generate "institutional facts" in the sense of someone's possessing rights or citizenship, for example. Such facts obtain only within the institution: someone who has human rights has them because they are attached, institutionally, to one's position or status within that institution. The status of "unmistakable human being," as distinguished from, say, an embryo (let alone a tree or some inanimate object), would be combined with what in Chapter 4 I develop as a "field of recognition" (such as an institution) to provide the status of a human rights–bearing creature (as well as a creature bearing duties and obligations, for example to respect the human rights of other creatures with the same status).

The human rights state, unlike the traditional nation state, realizes the "normative potential of the state" by constraining its own sovereignty by replacing the nation state's exclusionary logic with an inclusionary logic. It assigns the status of "unmistakable human being" to all biological humans, but now in the political sense of claiming that each person is entitled to a right to have rights, and to have human rights in particular. The human rights state, as an institution of constitutive rules, facilitates the collective recognition within itself of the status function of all human beings, citizen and foreigner alike, both resident and nonresident, as carrying the status function of human rights. Both positive and negative deontic powers derive from that status, for all persons, those inside state boundaries as well as those outside. From the standpoint of the human rights state, all are legally equal with respect to state-based human rights.

A community of human rights states would be something like the EU zone of rights shared across the boundaries of individual member states – but for the community of human rights states only. By social constructionist lights, human rights exist only if recognized: the status function of human rights requires recognition; absent recognition, that status function does not exist. Of course, for the persons involved, there is no practical difference between retaining rights that are not recognized and not having those rights in the first place. Hence to claim that "the point" of human rights is precisely that they apply even and especially to nation-states that do not recognize them is practically meaningful mostly as a justification for the unilateral, likely military intervention in those states. Unilateral condemnation is effective only if it changes the target of that condemnation, and historical experience is not encouraging on this account. Marx's (1976) ninth thesis on Feuerbach is on point here: what matters is not to interpret the world but to change it.

The project for human rights, as I reconceive it in this book, then has two principle tasks: first, the transformation of some of the existing nation states into human rights states, and second, the gradual enlargement of the community of human rights states through the transformation of ever more nation states. Different states might generate schemes of human rights that, from state to state, would differ in some respects. Within a community of human rights states we would observe problems of jurisdiction at points where the respective lists of two states did *not* overlap. And even when there is overlap (say, they all recognize a human right to political participation), other problems would emerge insofar as that right is interpreted somewhat differently in each member state. Some of these problems would be resolvable in the short term. For example, cross-border political participation, at least at lower levels of the local political system, need not undermine the human rights state. And some of these problems would not be resolvable, at least not in the short term. For example, one human rights state might recognize an embryo as human rights bearing and another not, so that forms of genetic manipulation in the latter state would be prohibited in the former. But such differences need not undermine other areas of agreement and overlap.

After all, any domestic political community always contends with disagreement, at times significant disagreement, without peril or paralysis. Even the most authoritarian of regimes, such as China or Iran today, cannot suppress all disagreement. Liberal democratic communities cope better or worse with disagreement, but cope they must because at any given time, consensus on a host of significant issues remains beyond reach. The human rights state can hardly transcend this striking feature of political experience: that agreement on how best to understand, and how to resolve, issues of great social import is often only partial at best.

On the brighter side of the ledger, at points of overlap, even human rights grounded in the concrete practices of each state would be the same for all members of the community. But even on the more conflicted side of the ledger, much will have been achieved by the realization of my proposal to the extent that there are any overlaps, for any overlap would indicate that the same rights were embraced universally within the community of human rights states – a contingent, historically achieved universalism. A theologically or metaphysically based universalism offers no such promise. My proposal's promise depends on more and more states becoming human rights states, a prospect entirely contingent on many complex factors and enduringly open to failure.

Human Rights Secured Through "Thin Norms" of Individual Autonomy

The human rights state would be well placed to safeguard the individual's autonomy from culture, politics, and institutions that might compromise his or her human rights. It would safeguard individual autonomy as a matter of local political culture, and not as a matter of unilateral intervention or of declarations by international elites. The human rights state seeks political community as autonomous and self-determining, hence rights proffered by international declaration or secured by foreign intervention would be no rights at all, especially where they violated local autonomy with its practices, traditions, and beliefs.

Conversely, probably some of those practices, traditions, and beliefs violate human rights as locally understood. For human rights are possible only if they secure the individual's autonomy vis-à-vis the family, the community, and the state. One might argue that, from a human rights standpoint, the violation of local communal autonomy is mandated wherever necessary to secure the autonomy of the individual. A political rather than metaphysical or theological understanding of human dignity explains why. Human rights as inclusion in political community, within the circle of socially recognized rights bearers, entails the recognition of each individual as a subject of equal rights – even in the face of tensions between locally generated human rights and local civil rights.[8]

The moral meaning of such inclusion is the internal relationship between the politics of human rights and the politics of human dignity. The politics of dignity is secured through the politics of rights only where dignity politics becomes coercive law within political community. That means that all members – especially members of marginalized and underprivileged groups – are included in political community only if they enjoy human rights within and against that community. Locally generated, locally enforced human rights can be legitimate in the eyes of their addressees if all persons are respected as individuals, and only secondarily (if at all) collectively. To be sure, recognition of individual human rights may be won through collective efforts, through local social movements and political struggles. And local recognition can be reinforced through the institutionalization of this or that conception of human rights in the ICC, the European Court of Human Rights, and war crimes tribunals, as well as through various kinds of media presence, for example in annual reports that evaluate the human rights adherence of individual states. And recognition of individual human rights may be won through future struggles against "traditionally privileged groups such as the aristocracy and from advocates of an authoritarian state," including "representatives of the churches who feared that the emancipatory spirit of human rights would undermine the moral fabric of Christian society and the hierarchical structure of the clergy" (Bielefeldt 2000:97). Collective resistance to oppression and degradation can serve individual rights even as individual rights can be endangered by some collective rights.

But the surest route to individual human rights is collective, that is, through the sovereign state, but now reconfigured as the human rights state. That state is "normatively minimalist" or "normatively thin" in ways I explain below.[9] It would secure to the individual the most basic level of "equilibrium": the protection of his or her physical well-being (a right not to be killed, not to be subjected to gratuitous pain, or a right to the satisfaction of basic needs with respect to food, shelter, or basic medical

---

[8] Although human rights advocates are not primarily concerned with using transnational institutions to enforce human rights within regimes that already support them – Canada could always do better, but the real concern is the Congo – tension between human rights and civil rights is inevitable even within democratic constitutional states.

[9] See Gregg (2003b) for a general theory of "thick" and "thin" norms.

care). And it would secure the protection of his or her psychological well-being (personal liberties of speech, association, and conscience).[10] Such a list of the most urgent of human rights cannot be reduced to a deep cultural bias of Western provenance or to the very particular preferences of political liberalism. This is just what John Rawls claims of his own list: the "right to life (to the means of subsistence and security); to liberty (to freedom from slavery, serfdom, and forced occupation, and to a sufficient measure of liberty of conscience to ensure freedom of religion and thought); to property (personal property); and to formal equality as expressed by the rules of natural justice (that is, that similar cases be treated similarly)" (Rawls 1999b:65). Although the human rights state does not follow from Rawls's approach, I join him in omitting many of the *Universal Declaration*'s rights, including full legal equality of all persons; freedoms of expression, assembly, and choice of employment; equal wages for the same work; and education.

Normative minimalism in this context recommends itself for two reasons. First, the effort to make the list as short as possible is conducive to identifying the most basic of all possible human rights. Second, a list might be thought more likely to motivate the creation of a human rights state the more it avoids the *Universal Declaration*'s distinctly liberal, Western cast, including bright-line separation of law from morality; thoroughgoing equality of men and women and of members of all religious faiths as well as nonreligionists; and civil and political rights that trump social, economic, and cultural rights. To be sure, my approach is hardly acultural or culturally free-floating; it embraces the *Universal Declaration*'s emphasis on an individualistic legal order that trumps the community's social cohesion, an emphasis on individual rights over collective rights and on rights over duties (features often viewed as peculiarly Western).[11] This embrace follows from what, for the human rights state, is the imperative of autonomy. The moral dynamic is clear: if the local political and cultural order is oppressive, the individual should be able to deploy human rights conceived in ways that offer defense.[12] I turn

---

[10] Whereas beyond such basic rights might be, for example, a right to education, to free choice of employment, and to equal pay for equal work.

[11] Still, normative individualism of this sort does not necessarily entail a preference for liberal individualism or political liberalism over, say, some forms of communitarianism.

[12] And he or she would likely welcome the outside imposition of rights – on whatever basis. With the words "whatever basis" I would signal that, even as I argue that the state offers the most realistic foundation for human rights, contributions may also be made by trans-, cross-, quasi-, inter-, and substate institutions and practices.

now to defending this "should." I defend it in terms of autonomy, indeed three kinds of autonomy.

As for the first kind of autonomy: first-wave human rights refer to the *individual's* right to freedom from various evils, such as unjust discrimination, slavery, torture and degrading treatment, arbitrary arrest and exile, as well as from interference with privacy, family, and home. These are freedoms from the state, from third parties, and from other *external* forces. Such freedoms constitute forms of *external autonomy*. Such autonomy does not reject community; rather, it qualifies the community's actions toward its members. By qualifying community, external autonomy embraces community in the sense of members collectively giving themselves their own norms. Second, the individual's external autonomy is secured through his or her *public* autonomy as a legal person, above all as citizen of a sovereign political community. The first kind of autonomy (external autonomy) coupled with the second (public autonomy) privileges the individual over the group or community. A third type of autonomy is the individual's *internal* autonomy, his or her freedom to think and behave by his or her own best lights (within limits, of course, such as not harming others).

Within the human rights state, the three types of autonomy are possible simultaneously. The individual's public autonomy secures his or her internal autonomy as one feature of state-based human rights. A person's internal autonomy – the freedom to pursue one's own designs for a preferred way of life – must be more than simply a means for achieving one's external autonomy. Indeed, internal and external forms of autonomy presuppose and reinforce one another. Individual citizens cannot pursue their external autonomy if the internal autonomy of each is not equally secure. At the same time, the internal autonomy of each citizen is achieved through all citizens' reasonable exercise of their external autonomy. By guaranteeing the individual's internal and external autonomy, the human rights state can provide political equality without ethnic, racial, religious, linguistic, or national freight. That guarantee prevents all manner of abiding background differences among persons, beliefs, practices, and institutions from impeding the individual's internal autonomy within the state.

This conclusion returns us to my point of departure. I argued that Kant's first and second images of political life – civil rights within the state and international rights among states – are both state based. I claimed that the promise of the third image – human rights – might be redeemed only if configured *not* as cosmopolitan but rather as state based. Kantian "citizens of a universal state of mankind" can only be citizens of this or that sovereign state. And I argued that today the state remains the most plausible venue for rights of any sort, including human rights – although not just any kind of state but solely the human rights state.

In keeping with the normative minimalism I advocate, I would now add: the human rights state has no foundation other than itself, in a sense articulated equally from two very different perspectives, that of Richard Rorty and that of Hannah Arendt. If the individual's moral convictions are a product wholly of his or her culture, community, and traditions, says Rorty, then there is "no 'ground' for such loyalties and convictions save the fact that the beliefs and desires and emotions which buttress them overlap those of lots of other members of the group with which we identify for purposes of moral or political deliberations" (Rorty 1991:200). Social norms are simply appeals to "this overlapping, shared part" of oneself, "those beliefs and desires and emotions which permit" one to say of one's moral or political community, "'*We* do not do this sort of thing'" (ibid.). And what Arendt calls a "common world," culturally "common to all of us and distinguished from our privately owned place in it," is also political community without universalisms, as a contingent community with contingent norms and contingent foundations (Arendt 1958:52). As Arendt asks rhetorically: "How should one be able to deduce laws and rights from a universe which apparently knows neither the one nor the other category?" (Arendt 1994:298). The idea of the human rights state provides a practical answer: human beings, understood in a way wholly naturalistic, socially constructing human rights that are then recognized domestically by the state which, given its inclusive logic, also recognizes those human rights self-granted and socially constructed beyond its sovereign borders.

Coda

What Is Lost, and What Gained, by Human Rights as Social Construction

This book proposes an approach to human rights based on a wholly naturalistic conception of the human being. If humans are wholly natural, then so is human morality, or so it would seem, for natural beings are not likely to possess a capacity for generating otherworldly artifacts. "Natural morality" refers to a repertoire of biologically based mechanisms of cognition and emotion.[1] Throughout the individual's life, natural morality is open to learning through experience, by reasoning about experience, and in socialization, culture, and politics (even as very young children already display some signs of moral cognition and behavior, although they have had very little experience and cultural learning).[2] As a product of evolution, natural morality is an anthropological constant in the sense that, whatever it is, it characterizes all human individuals, across the entire span of individual and group histories, cultural preferences, and normative convictions. This wholly naturalistic conception of the human being comports with the social constructionist approach that guides this book. And as social constructions, human rights may well build on aspects of natural morality.

Still, one wonders: Is something lost by viewing human rights in these terms? For example, do we humans perhaps want or even need human rights to be the sort of theological and metaphysical entities that they cannot be? Such a need would not surprise; after all, we cannot evade our constitutional weaknesses and limitations, those which the young Marx well captured: "*Religious* suffering is the *expression* of real suffering and at the same time the *protest* against real suffering. Religion is the sigh

---

[1] As I argue in Chapter 5, the distinction between cognitive and emotional mechanisms is an artificial distinction, but one that is analytically useful.
[2] As Tomasello (2009), among others, has shown empirically.

of the oppressed creature, the heart of a heartless world, as it is the spirit of spiritless conditions" (Marx 1967:250). The otherworldly appeals of religion and metaphysics reflect something of the psychological fragility of the intrinsically needy and sensitive human being exposed throughout life to tragedies and disappointments large and small, to failures personal and institutional, to injustice and disregard, when finally "our little life / Is rounded with a sleep."[3] From this perspective, my approach surely entails multiple losses: loss of the psychological feeling of security provided by belief in a supernatural source or foundation; loss of the impression of freedom from all the weaknesses of human nature and all the limitations of human understanding; loss of the conviction that justice will prevail finally because theological forces either beyond this world, or metaphysical truths underlying it, guarantee inexorable justice.

But my approach is not deaf to the "sigh of the oppressed creature." In the face of losing all the doubtful promises of metaphysics and theologies, it invites humans to regard themselves as ultimately responsible for the generation of the meanings so important to life public and private. It urges them to deploy this-worldly meanings in place of otherworldly ones. To be sure, to take full moral responsibility for ourselves in this sense is to assume a heavy burden. Yet doing so would render us, as political communities, "producers" of our fate – if not always "masters" of it. For we can hardly master a fate contingent on particular values, a fate about which people always will disagree as to its meaning and significance and how best to confront it. Correspondingly, even thoughtful and reasonable persons may never agree on what human rights are in general, or how a finite list of core rights might read, or how best to realize this or that one in concrete cases, or which trumps the other when, inevitably, under particular circumstances, two conflict. Again, this can hardly surprise, inasmuch as even thoughtful and reasonable people are not likely to all agree on the properties of the good life, or of a life not misspent, or of all the necessary constituents of justice and freedom in political community.

The psychological experience of theological and metaphysical loss may also ennoble us morally if we assume the stance of active producers of our fate, as distinguished from the posture of passive "consumers" of otherworldly givens. In this way, we ourselves can become the generators of the "heart of a heartless world," sources of a "spirit of spiritless conditions," and especially authors of "protest[s] against real suffering." This much is gained by taking my approach. In arguing for human rights

---

[3] Shakespeare, *The Tempest*, act 4, scene 1, lines 157–158.

as social constructions, each of my chapters sustains this gain. Each, in its own way, argues that human rights as political achievements are not inherent in human nature metaphysically or theologically conceived. Each constructs human rights as something that we humans, in light of our nature biologically understood, can author. We could take upon ourselves the task of generating the validity of human rights in local community and expanding it in ever-wider circles, aspiring to an eventually universal validity, freely embraced.

First, with regard to norms that are local not universal: Chapter 1 rejects human rights as a theological expression of a supernatural realm for human rights as local constructions of limited but expandable validity. This approach affords greater moral agency to individual rights bearers. The embrace of human rights then reflects a politics of agency instead of political fiat. This is also the gain offered by Chapter 2, which replaces a metaphysics of personhood with a naturalist alternative: individual dignity as political achievement and personal identity through social integration that still allows for difference. Chapter 3 expands the scope for diversity even in the presence of human rights, allowing for a spread of the human rights idea that never succumbs to some form of cultural imperialism.

Second, Chapters 4 and 5 offer practical gains: this-worldly resources for human rights as social constructions. Chapter 4 constructs human rights as self-authored through a personality structure of assertive selfhood. It does so in ways sensitive to inequalities among persons, with regard to the individual's psychological disposition and the qualities of the particular political community he or she inhabits. Chapter 5 shows how emotions positively associated with fictive kinship may be altruistically motivating, promote an embrace of the human rights idea, yet not manipulate the individual.

Third, Chapters 6 and 7 offer practical gains in another sense: as a this-worldly means of advancing the human rights idea in ways that preserve a significant measure of cultural integrity. Chapter 6 does so by translating between local understandings and nonlocal human rights ideas to transform the local culture in human rights–friendly ways; and Chapter 7, by cognitively reframing local cultural perspectives and practices to advance human rights as a learning process.

Fourth, with respect to the long-term future, Chapters 8 and 9 address human nature and political community as open questions rather than as static givens, reconceiving nature and community in ways that further the political project for human rights. Chapter 8 analyzes the trend from genetic chance in natural reproduction to genetic choice through technology to show how we might best regard human nature: not as something that limits us as a species in our choices but rather as itself a cultural choice. Chapter 9 underscores a claim I make throughout the book: that human rights are available, if at all, only in political community. But it also shows that human rights are unlikely to be widely available in political community in the mold of the nation-state, given its "exclusionary logic." More likely they would be available in a human rights state, with its inclusionary logic that extends across its own borders. Mankind gains by taking responsibility for the fate of human rights by reconceiving both human nature and political community in appropriate ways, detailed in these two chapters but more generally in the book entire.

References

Abu-Sahlieh, Sami Aldeeb. 2006. "Male and Female Circumcision: The Myth of the Difference," in *Female Circumcision: Multicultural Perspectives*, ed. R. M. Abusharaf, 47–72. Philadelphia: University of Pennsylvania.

Adorno, Theodor W. 1966. *Negative Dialektik.* Frankfurt am Main: Suhrkamp Verlag.

Agamben, Giorgio. 2005. *Homo sacer: il potere sovrano e la nuda vita.* Torino: Einaudi.

Ali, Tariq. 2002. "Theological Distractions," in Khaled Abou El Fadl, *The Place of Tolerance in Islam*, ed. J. Cohen and I. Lague, 37–41. Boston: Beacon Press.

Amanat, Abbas, and Frank Griffel, eds. 2007. *Shari'a: Islamic Law in the Contemporary Context.* Stanford: Stanford University Press.

American Anthropological Association. 1947. "Statement on Human Rights." *American Anthropologist* 49:539–543.

American Anthropological Association. 1999. "Declaration on Anthropology and Human Rights, Committee for Human Rights, American Anthropological Association," at http://www.aaanet.org/stmts/humanrts.htm

Anderson, Benedict. 1991. *Imagined Communities: Reflections on the Origin and Spread of Nationalism.* London: Verso.

An-Na'im, Abdullahi Ahmed. 1990. "Problems of Universal Cultural Legitimacy for Human Rights," in *Human Rights in Africa: Cross-Cultural Perspectives*, ed. A. A. An-Na'im and F. Deng, 331–367. Washington, D.C.: Brookings Institution.

An-Na'im, Abdullahi Ahmed. 1992a. "Introduction," in *Human Rights in Cross-Cultural Perspectives: A Quest for Consensus*, ed. A. A. An-Na'im, 1–18. Philadelphia: University of Philadelphia Press.

An-Na'im, Abdullahi Ahmed. 1992b. "Toward a Cross-Cultural Approach to Defining International Standards of Human Rights: The Meaning of Cruel, Inhuman, or Degrading Treatment or Punishment," in *Human Rights in Cross-Cultural Perspectives: A Quest for Consensus*, ed. A. A. An-Na'im, 167–188. Philadelphia: University of Pennsylvania Press.

An-Na'im, Abdullahi Ahmed. 2003. "Introduction: 'Area Expressions' and the Universality of Human Rights: Mediating a Contingent Relationship," in *Human Rights and Diversity*, ed. D. Forsythe and P. McMahon, 1–21. Lincoln: University of Nebraska Press.

Arendt, Hannah. 1953. "A Reply." *The Review of Politics* 15:76–85.

Arendt, Hannah. 1958. *The Human Condition.* Chicago: University of Chicago Press.

Arendt, Hannah. 1965. *On Revolution.* New York: Viking Press.

Arendt, Hannah. [1951] 1994. *The Origins of Totalitarianism.* New York: Harcourt Brace Jovanovich.

Arnett, Jeffrey. 1995. "Broad and Narrow Socialization: The Family in the Context of a Cultural Theory." *Journal of Marriage and the Family* 57:617–628.

Arnould, S., C. Delenda, S. Grizot, C. Desseaux, F. Pâques, G. H. Silva, and J. Smith. 2011. "The I-CreI Meganuclease and Its Engineered Derivatives: Applications from Cell Modification to Gene Therapy." *Protein Engineering, Design and Selection* 24:27–31.

Balibar, Étienne. 1994. *Masses, Classes, Ideas.* London: Routledge.

Bastian, Jean-Pierre. 1994. *Le protestantisme en Amérique latine: Une approache socio-historique.* Geneva: Editions Labor et Fides.

Baynes, Kenneth. 2009. "Discourse Ethics and the Political Conception of Human Rights." *Ethics and Global Politics* 2:1–21.

Bell, Daniel. 1996. "The East Asian Challenge to Human Rights: Reflections on an East-West Dialogue." *Human Rights Quarterly* 18:641–667.

Bell, Daniel. 2006. *Beyond Liberal Democracy: Political Thinking for an East Asian Context.* Princeton: Princeton University Press.

Benhabib, Seyla. 2002a. *The Claims of Culture: Equality and Diversity in the Global Era.* Princeton: Princeton University Press.

Benhabib, Seyla. 2002b. "Political Geographies in a Global World: Arendtian Reflections." *Social Research* 69:539–566.

Benhabib, Seyla. 2004. "Kantian Questions, Arendtian Answers," in *Pragmatism, Critique, Judgment. Essays for Richard Bernstein,* ed. S. Benhabib and N. Fraser, 171–196. Cambridge: MIT.

Bentham, Jeremy. 1843. *Anarchical Fallacies; Being an Examination of the Declarations of Rights Issued During the French Revolution.* Vol. 2 of *The Works of Jeremy Bentham.* Edinburgh: William Tait.

Berger, Peter, and Thomas Luckmann. 1966. *The Social Construction of Reality.* New York: Doubleday.

Bielefeldt, Heiner. 2000. "'Western' Versus 'Islamic' Human Rights Conceptions? A Critique of Cultural Essentialism in the Discussion on Human Rights." *Political Theory* 28:90–121.

Bilgrami, Akeel. 2002. "The Importance of Democracy," in Khaled Abou El Fadl, *The Place of Tolerance in Islam,* ed. J. Cohen and I. Lague, 61–66. Boston: Beacon Press.

Blau, Peter. 1964. *Exchange and Power in Social Life.* New York: Wiley.

Blaydes, Lisa, and Drew Linzer. 2006. "The Political Economy of Women's Support for Fundamentalist Islam." Paper presented at the Annual Meeting of the Midwest Political Science Association, 20–23 April, Chicago, Illinois.

Borutta, Manuel, and Nina Verheyen, eds. *Die Präsenz der Gefühle. Männlichkeit und Emotion in der Moderne.* Bielefeld: Transcript Verlag.

Boyle, Elizabeth Heger. 2002. *Female Genital Cutting: Cultural Conflict in the Global Community.* Baltimore: Johns Hopkins Press.

Brubaker, Rogers, and Frederick Cooper. 2000. "Beyond 'Identity.'" *Theory and Society* 29:1–47.

Buijs, Frank, and Jan Rath. 2002. "Muslims in Europe: The State of Research." Essay prepared for the Russell Sage Foundation, New York.

Bunch, Charlotte. 1990. "Women's Rights as Human Rights: Toward a Re-Vision of Human Rights." *Human Rights Quarterly* 12:489–498.

Burke, Edmund. [1790] 1999. *Reflections on the Revolution in France.* Oxford: Oxford University.

Burn, Shawn, and Julia Busso. 2005. "Ambivalent Sexism, Scriptural Literalism, and Religiosity." *Psychology of Women Quarterly* 29:412–418.

Campbell, Tom. 1986. "The Rights of the Mentally Ill," in *Human Rights: From Rhetoric to Reality*, ed. T. Campbell, D. Goldberg, S. McLean, and T. Mullen, 123–147. Oxford: Basil Blackwell.

Carens, Joseph. 2000. *Culture, Community and Citizenship: A Contextual Exploration of Justice as Evenhandedness.* Oxford: Oxford University Press.

Carnap, Rudolf. [1937] 1967. *The Logical Syntax of Language*, trans. A. Smeaton. London: Routledge and Kegan Paul.

Carozza, Paolo. 2003. "Subsidiarity as a Structuralist Principle of International Human Rights Law." *American Journal of International Law* 97:38–79.

Chabal, Patrick. 2002. "The Quest for Good Governance and Development in Africa: Is NEPAD the Answer?" *International Affairs* 78:447–462.

Cheah, Pheng, and Bruce Robbins, eds. 1998. *Cosmopolitics: Thinking and Feeling beyond the Nation.* Minneapolis: University of Minnesota Press.

Clore, Gerald, and Karen Gasper. 2000. "Feeling Is Believing: Some Affective Influences on Belief," in *Emotions and Beliefs. How Feelings Influence Thoughts*, ed. N. Frijda, A. Manstead, and S. Bem, 10–44. Cambridge: Cambridge University Press.

Clutton-Brock, J. 1999. *A Natural History of Domesticated Mammals.* Cambridge: Cambridge University Press.

Cohen, Ronald, Goran Hyden, and Winston Nagen, eds. 1993. *Human Rights and Governance in Africa.* Gainesville: University Press of Florida.

Coomaraswamy, Radhika. 1994. "To Bellow like a Cow: Women, Ethnicity, and the Discourse of Rights," in *Human Rights of Women: National and International Perspectives*, ed. R. Cook, 39–57. Philadelphia: University of Pennsylvania Press.

Copelon, Rhonda. 1994. "Intimate Terror: Understanding Domestic Violence as Torture," in *Human Rights of Women: National and International Perspectives*, ed. R. Cook, 116–152. Philadelphia: University of Pennsylvania Press.

Cui, X., D. Ji, D. A. Fisher, Y. Wu, D. M. Briner, and E. J. Weinstein. 2011. "Targeted Integration in Rat and Mouse Embryos with Zinc-Finger Nucleases." *Nature Biotechnology* 29:64–67.

Damasio, Antonio. 1994. *Descartes' Error. Emotion, Reason, and the Human Brain.* New York: Grosset/Putnam.

Darby, Derrick. 2009. *Rights, Race, and Recognition.* New York: Cambridge University Press.

Davidson, Donald. 2001. "On the Very Idea of a Conceptual Scheme," in *Inquiries into Truth and Interpretation*, 2d ed., ed. D. Davidson, 183–198. Oxford: Clarendon Press.

De Sousa, Ronald. 1987. *The Rationality of Emotion.* Cambridge: MIT Press.

Dewey, John. [1925] 1981. "Experience and Nature," in *John Dewey: The Later Works, 1925–1953,* vol. 1, ed. J. A. Boydston. Carbondale: Southern Illinois University Press.

Diderot, Denis, and Jean-Baptiste le Rond d'Alembert, eds. [1751] 1966. *Encyclopédie, ou Dictionnaire raisonné des sciences, des arts et des métiers, par une société de gens de lettres, mis en ordre par M. Diderot de l'Académie des Sciences et Belles-Lettres de Prusse, et quant à la partie mathématique, par M. d'Alembert de l'Académie royale des Sciences de Paris, de celle de Prusse et de la Société royale de Londres.* Stuttgart: Frommann.

DiMaggio, Paul, and Walter Powell. 1991. *The New Institutionalism in Organizational Analysis.* Chicago: University of Chicago Press.

Donnelly, Jack. 1999. "Human Rights and Asian Values: A Defense of 'Western' Universalism," in *The East Asian Challenge for Human Rights,* ed. J. Bauer and D. Bell, 60–87. Cambridge: Cambridge University Press.

Donnelly, Jack. 2003. *Universal Human Rights in Theory and Practice,* 2d ed. Ithaca: Cornell University Press.

Donnelly, Jack. 2007. "The West and Economic Rights," in *Economic Rights. Conceptual, Measurement, and Policy Issues,* ed. S. Hertel and L. Minkler, 37–55. New York: Cambridge University Press.

Donohue, John, and John Esposito, eds. 2007. *Islam in Transition: Muslim Perspectives,* 2d ed. New York: Oxford University Press.

Drzewicki, Krzysztof. 1995. "The Right to Work and Rights in Work," in *Economic, Social and Cultural Rights: A Textbook,* ed. A. Eide, C. Krause, and A. Rosas. Dordrecht: Martinus Nijhoff.

Durkheim, Émile. 1893. *De la division du travail social.* Paris: Félix Alcan.

Dworkin, Ronald. 1977. *Taking Rights Seriously.* Cambridge: Harvard University Press.

Eckel, Jan. 2009. "Utopie der Moral, Kalkül der Macht. Menschenrechte in der globalen Politik nach 1945." *Archiv für Sozialgeschichte* 49:437–484.

Eder, Klaus. 1996. *The Social Construction of Nature.* London: Sage.

Eder, Klaus. 2007. "Cognitive Sociology and the Theory of Communicative Action: The Role of Communication and Language in the Making of the Social Bond." *European Journal of Social Theory* 10:389–408.

Eide, Asbjørn. 1999. "Article 28," in *The Universal Declaration of Human Rights: A Common Standard of Achievement,* ed. G. Alfredsson and A. Eide. The Hague: Martinus Nijhoff.

Elster, Jon. 1999. *Alchemies of the Mind: Rationality and the Emotions.* New York: Cambridge University Press.

Emon, Anver. 2004–2005. "Natural Law and Natural Rights in Islamic Law." *Journal of Law and Religion* 20:351–395.

Ennew, Judith. 1986. *The Sexual Exploitation of Children.* Cambridge, England: Polity Press.

Esedebe, P. Olisanwuche. 1994. *Pan-Africanism: The Idea and Movement, 1776–1991.* Washington, D.C.: Howard University Press.

Esposito, John. 2004. "Practice and Theory," in Khaled Abou El Fadl, *Islam and the Challenge of Democracy*, ed. J. Cohen and D. Chasman, 93–100. Princeton: Princeton University Press.

Fadel, Mohammed. 2004. "Too Far from Tradition," in Khaled Abou El Fadl, *Islam and the Challenge of Democracy*, ed. J. Cohen and D. Chasman, 81–86. Princeton: Princeton University Press.

Feldman, Noah. 2004. "The Best Hope," in Khaled Abou El Fadl, *Islam and the Challenge of Democracy*, ed. J. Cohen and D. Chasman, 59–62. Princeton: Princeton University Press.

Fetzer, Joel, and Christopher Soper. 2005. *Muslims and the State in Britain, France and Germany*. Cambridge: Cambridge University Press.

Finnis, John. 1993. *Natural Law and Natural Rights*. Oxford: Oxford University Press.

Fish, Steven. 2002. "Islam and Authoritarianism." *World Politics* 55:4–37.

Frijda, Nico, Antony Manstead, and Sacha Bem. 2000. "The Influence of Emotions on Beliefs," in *Emotions and Beliefs: How Feelings Influence Thoughts*, ed. N. Frijda, A. Manstead, and S. Bem, 1–9. Cambridge: Cambridge University Press.

Frijda, Nico, and Betja Mesquita. 2000. "Beliefs Through Emotions," in *Emotions and Beliefs. How Feelings Influence Thoughts*, ed. N. Frijda, A. Manstead, and S. Bem, 45–77. Cambridge: Cambridge University Press.

Gaita, Raimond. 1991. *Good and Evil: An Absolute Conception*. Basingstoke: Macmillan.

Garfinkel, Harold. 1967. *Studies in Ethnomethodology*. Englewood Cliffs, N.J.: Prentice-Hall.

Ghai, Yash. 1994. "Human Rights and Governance: The Asia Debate." *Australian Yearbook of International Law* 15:1–34.

Giddens, Anthony. 1990. *The Consequences of Modernity*. Stanford: Stanford University Press.

Giddens, Anthony. 1991. *Modernity and Self-Identity: Self and Society in the Late Modern Age*. Cambridge, England: Polity Press.

Gilman, Sander. 1999. "'Barbaric' Rituals?," in *Is Multiculturalism Bad for Women?*, ed. J. Cohen, M. Howard, and M. Nussbaum, 53–58. Princeton: Princeton University Press.

Glendon, Mary Ann. 2001. *A World Made New: Eleanor Roosevelt and the Universal Declaration of Human Rights*. New York: Random House.

Goffman, Erving. 1974. *Frame Analysis: An Essay on the Organization of Experience*. Cambridge: Harvard University Press.

Gregg, Benjamin. 1998. "Jurisprudence in an Indeterminate World: Pragmatist Not Postmodern." *Ratio Juris* 11:382–398.

Gregg, Benjamin. 2003a. *Coping in Politics with Indeterminate Norms: A Theory of Enlightened Localism*. Albany: State University of New York Press.

Gregg, Benjamin. 2003b. *Thick Moralities, Thin Politics: Social Integration Across Communities of Belief*. Durham: Duke University Press.

Gruenbaum, Ellen. 2001. *The Female Circumcision Controversy: An Anthropological Perspective*. Philadelphia: University of Pennsylvania Press.

Gutiérrez, Kris, and Barbara Rogoff. 2003. "Cultural Ways of Learning: Individual or Repertoires of Practice." *Educational Researcher* 32:19–25.

Habermas, Jürgen. 1994. "Human Rights and Popular Sovereignty." *Ratio Juris* 7:1–13.

Habermas, Jürgen. 1999. *Between Facts and Norms. Contributions to a Discourse Theory of Law and Democracy.* Cambridge: MIT Press.

Habermas, Jürgen. 2003a. *The Future of Human Nature.* Cambridge, England: Polity Press.

Habermas, Jürgen. 2003b. "Fundamentalism and Terror: A Dialogue with Jürgen Habermas," in Giovanna Borradori, *Philosophy in a Time of Terror. Dialogues with Jürgen Habermas and Jacques Derrida,* 25–43. Chicago: University of Chicago Press.

Habermas, Jürgen. 2010. "The Concept of Human Dignity and the Realistic Utopia of Human Rights." *Metaphilosophy* 41:464–480.

Hall, Peter, and Rosemary Taylor. 1996. "Political Science and the Three New Institutionalisms." *Political Studies* 44:936–957.

Hampton, Jean. 1998. *The Authority of Reason.* New York: Cambridge University Press.

Handwerker, W. Penn. 1997. "Universal Human Rights and the Problem of Unbounded Cultural Meanings." *American Anthropologist* 99:799–810.

Hartsock, Nancy. "The Feminist Standpoint," in *Discovering Reality. Feminist Perspectives on Epistemology, Metaphysics, Methodology, and Philosophy of Science,* ed. S. Harding and M. Hintikka, 283–310. Dordrecht: Kluwer.

Hashemi, Nader. 2004. "Change from Within," in Khaled Abou El Fadl, *Islam and the Challenge of Democracy,* ed. J. Cohen and D. Chasman, 49–54. Princeton: Princeton University Press.

Hashmi, Sohail. 2002. "A Conservative Legacy," in Khaled Abou El Fadl, *The Place of Tolerance in Islam,* ed. J. Cohen and I. Lague, 31–36. Boston: Beacon Press.

Hathaway, Oona. 2002. "Do Human Rights Treaties Make a Difference?" *Yale Law Journal* 111:1935–2042.

Hegel, Georg W. F. [1817] 1964. "The Proceedings of the Estates Assembly in the Kingdom of Würtemberg, 1815–1816," in *Hegel's Political Writings,* trans. T. M. Knox. Oxford: Clarendon Press.

Hegel, Georg W. F. [1821] 1970. *Grundlinien der Philosophie des Rechts,* in *Werke in zwänzig Bänden,* vol. 7, Frankfurt am Main: Suhrkamp Verlag.

Herpin, N. 2005. "Love, Careers, and Heights in France." *Economics and Human Biology* 3:420–49.

Hobbes, Thomas. [1651] 1909. *Leviathan.* Oxford: Clarendon Press.

Hogg, Michael, Deborah Terry, and Katherine White. 1995. "A Tale of Two Theories: A Critical Comparison of Identity Theory with Social Identity Theory." *Social Psychology Quarterly* 58:255–269.

Hollenbach, David. 1982. "Human Rights and Religious Faith in the Middle East: Reflections of a Christian Theologian." *Human Rights Quarterly* 4:94–109.

Horkheimer, Max, and Theodor Adorno. 1969. *Dialektik der Aufklärung.* Frankfurt am Main: S. Fischer Verlag.

Hume, David. [1751] 1966. *An Enquiry Concerning the Principles of Morals.* LaSalle: Open Court.

Hume, David. [1739–1740] 1968. *A Treatise of Human Nature,* ed. L. A. Selby-Bigge. Oxford: Clarendon.

Hunt, Lynn. 2007. *Inventing Human Rights.* New York: W.W. Norton.

Ibhawoh, Bonny. 2007. *Imperialism and Human Rights: Colonial Discourses of Rights and Liberties in African History.* Albany: State University of New York Press.

Ignatieff, Michael. 2001. *Human Rights as Politics and Idolatry.* Princeton: Princeton University Press.

Inglehart, Ronald, and Pippa Norris. 2003a. *Rising Tide: Gender Equality and Cultural Change Around the World.* Cambridge: Cambridge University Press.

Inglehart, Ronald, and Pippa Norris. 2003b. "The True Clash of Civilizations." *Foreign Affairs* 135:63–70.

Ingram, James. 2008. "What Is a 'Right to Have Rights'? Three Images of the Politics of Human Rights." *American Political Science Review* 102: 401–416.

Jackson, Jean. 1995. "Culture, Genuine and Spurious: The Politics of Indianness in the Vaupés, Columbia." *American Ethnologist* 22:3–28.

Jenkins, Richard. 1996. *Social Identity.* New York: Routledge.

Jennings, Theodore. 2005. *Reading Derrida/Thinking Paul: On Justice.* Stanford: Stanford University Press.

John XXIII (Pope). [1961] 1976. *Mater et magistra,* in *The Gospel of Peace and Justice: Catholic Social Teaching Since Pope John,* ed. J. Gremillion. Maryknoll, N.Y.: Orbis Books.

Kant, Immanuel. [1797] 1996. *The Metaphysics of Morals.* New York: Cambridge University Press.

Kant, Immanuel. [1795] 1997. *Perpetual Peace. A Philosophical Sketch,* trans. H. B. Nisbet, in *Kant: Political Writings,* ed. H. Reiss. Cambridge: Cambridge University Press.

Kant, Immanuel. [1785] 1998. *Groundwork of the Metaphysics of Morals,* trans. M. Gregor. New York: Cambridge University Press.

Karabinus, D. S. 2009. "Flow Cytometric Sorting of Human Sperm: MicroSort Clinical Trial Update." *Theriogenology* 71:74–79.

Kennedy, David. 2004. *The Dark Sides of Virtue: Reassessing International Humanitarianism.* Princeton: Princeton University Press.

Khagram, Sanjeev, James Riker, and Kathryn Sikkink. 2002. *Restructuring World Politics: Transnational Social Movements, Networks, and Norms.* Minneapolis: University of Minnesota Press.

Kierkegaard, Søren. [1849] 1980. *The Sickness unto Death,* trans. H. V. Hong and E. H. Hong. Vol. 19 of *Kierkegaard's Writings.* Princeton: Princeton University Press.

King, Martin Luther. 1967. *Where Do We Go from Here: Chaos or Community?* New York: Harper and Row.

Kohen, Ari. 2007. *In Defense of Human Rights: A Non-Religious Grounding in a Pluralistic World.* New York: Routledge.

Konstan, David. 2007. *The Emotions of the Ancient Greeks*. Toronto: University of Toronto Press.

Koskenniemi, Martti. 1991. "The Future of Statehood." *Harvard International Law Journal* 32:397–410.

Krause, Sharon. 2008. *Civil Passions: Moral Sentiment and Democratic Deliberation*. Princeton: Princeton University Press.

Kuhn, Thomas. 1970. *The Structure of Scientific Revolutions*. Chicago: University of Chicago Press.

Kurtz, Stanley. 2002. "Text and Context," in Khaled Abou El Fadl, *The Place of Tolerance in Islam*, ed. J. Cohen and I. Lague, 51–55. Boston: Beacon Press.

Kurzman, Charles, ed. 1998. *Liberal Islam: A Source Book*. New York: Oxford University Press.

La Fontaine, Jean. 1990. *Child Sexual Abuse*. Cambridge, Mass.: Basil Blackwell.

Lakoff, George. 2009. *The Political Mind*. New York: Penguin.

Landweer, Hilge. 2004. "Phänomenologie und die Grenzen des Kognitivismus." *Deutsche Zeitschrift für Philosophie* 52:467–486.

Launay, Robert. 1992. *Beyond the Stream: Islam and Society in a West African Town*. Berkeley: University of California Press.

Lefort, Claude. 1986. *The Political Forms of Modern Society: Bureaucracy, Democracy, Totalitarianism*. Cambridge, England: Polity Press.

Lettre, G. 2009. "Genetic Regulation of Adult Stature." *Current Opinion in Pediatrics* 21:515–522.

Lévi-Strauss, Claude. 1983. *Structural Anthropology*, vol. 2. New York: Basic Books.

Levine, Donald. 1991. "Simmel and Persons Reconsidered." *American Journal of Sociology* 96:1097–1116.

Liu, Y., L. Hong, K. Wakamatsu, S. Ito, B. Adhyaru, C. Y. Cheng, C. R. Bowers, and J. D. Simon. 2005. "Comparison of Structural and Chemical Properties of Black and Red Human Hair Melanosomes." *Photochemical and Photobiological Sciences* 81:135–144.

Locke, John. [1690] 1975. *An Essay Concerning Human Understanding*. Oxford: Oxford University Press.

Locke, John. [1690] 2005. *Two Treatises of Government*. Cambridge: Cambridge University Press.

Lukács, Georg. [1923] 1968. *Geschichte und Klassenbewusstsein. Studien über marxistische Dialektik*. Neuwied: Luchterhand Verlag.

Macpherson, C. B. 1962. *The Political Theory of Possessive Individualism: Hobbes to Locke*. Oxford: Clarendon Press.

Mahmood, Saba. 2004. "Is Liberalism Islam's Only Answer?," in Khaled Abou El Fadl, *Islam and the Challenge of Democracy*, ed. J. Cohen and D. Chasman, 74–77. Princeton: Princeton University Press.

Maier, Hans. 1965. *Revolution und Kirche: Studien zur Frühgeschichte der christlichen Demokratie, 1789–1901*, 2d ed. Freiburg im Breisgau: Rombach Verlag.

Mannheim, Karl. [1929] 1936. *Ideology and Utopia: An Introduction to the Sociology of Knowledge*. New York: Harvest.

Marcus, George. 2002. *The Sentimental Citizen: Emotion in Democratic Politics*. University Park: Pennsylvania State University Press.

Maritain, Jacques. 1949. "Introduction," in *Human Rights: Comments and Interpretations*, ed. UNESCO. New York: Columbia University Press.

Marx, Karl. [1843] 1967. "Toward the Critique of Hegel's Philosophy of Law," in *Writings of the Young Marx on Philosophy and Society*, ed. L. D. Easton and K. H. Guddat. Garden City, N.Y.: Doubleday.

Marx, Karl. [1845–1847] 1969. *Die Deutsche Ideologie, in Marx-Engels-Werke*, vol. 1. Berlin: Dietz Verlag.

Marx, Karl. [1852] 1975. *Der achtzehnte Brumaire des Louis Bonaparte*, in Karl Marx and Friedrich Engels, *Ausgewählte Schriften in zwei Bänden*, vol. 1. Berlin: Dietz Verlag.

Marx, Karl. [1845] 1976. "Thesen über Feuerbach," in Karl Marx and Friedrich Engels, *Ausgewählte Schriften in zwei Bänden*, vol. 2. Berlin: Dietz Verlag.

Marx, Karl, and Friedrich Engels. [1932] 1998. *The German Ideology*. Amherst: Prometheus Books.

Masters, Roger. 1994. "From Duality to Complexity in the Study of Human Nature." *Politics and the Life Sciences* 13:112–115.

Maul, Daniel. 2007. *Menschenrechte, Sozialpolitik und Dekolonisation: Die Internationale Arbeitsorganisation (IAO) 1940–1970*. Essen: Klartext Verlag.

M'Baye, Kéba. 1972/1973. "Le droit au développement comme un droit de l'homme." *Revue des Droits de l'Homme* 5:505–534.

McKeon, Richard. 1949. "The Philosophic Bases and Material Circumstances of the Rights of Man," in *Human Rights: Comments and Interpretations*, ed. UNESCO. New York: Columbia University Press.

Mead, George Herbert. [1934] 1967. *Mind, Self, and Society*. Chicago: University of Chicago Press.

Merry, Sally Engle. 2001. "Changing Rights, Changing Culture," in *Culture and Rights: Anthropological Perspectives*, ed. J. Cowan, M. Dembour, and R. Wilson, 31–55. Cambridge: Cambridge University Press.

Merry, Sally Engle. 2006. *Human Rights and Gender Violence: Translating International Law into Local Justice*. Chicago: University of Chicago Press.

Merton, Robert. 1973. "The Perspectives of Insiders and Outsiders," in Robert Merton, *The Sociology of Science. Theoretical Empirical Investigations*. Chicago: University of Chicago Press.

Meyer, John, John Boli, George Thomas, and Francisco Ramirez. 1997. "World Society and the Nation-State." *American Journal of Sociology* 103:144–181.

Meyers, Diana. 1985. *Inalienable Rights: A Defense*. New York: Columbia University Press.

Michelman, Frank. 1996. "Parsing 'A Right to Have Rights.'" *Constellations* 3:200–208.

Mill, John Stuart. [1859] 1984. "A Few Words on Non-Intervention," in *Collected Works of John Stuart Mill*, ed. J. Robson, 109–124. Toronto: University of Toronto Press.

Miller, David. 2007. *National Responsibility and Global Justice*. Oxford: Oxford University Press.

Miller, Trudi. 1993. "The Duality of Human Nature." *Politics and the Life Sciences* 12:221–241.

Moghadam, Valentine. 2003. *Modernizing Women: Gender and Social Change in the Middle East.* Boulder: Lynne Rienner.

Moltmann, Jürgen. 1977. *The Church in the Power of the Spirit: A Contribution to Messianic Ecclesiology*, trans. M. Kohl. New York: Harper & Row.

Montgomery, Heather. 2001. "Imposing Rights? A Case Study of Child Prostitution in Thailand," in *Culture and Rights: Anthropological Perspectives*, ed. J. Cowan, M. Dembour and R. Wilson, 80–101. Cambridge: Cambridge University Press.

Monroe, Kristen. 2003. "How Identity and Perspective Constrain Moral Choice." *International Political Science Review* 24:405–425.

Morsink, Johannes. 2009. *Inherent Human Rights: Philosophical Roots of the Universal Declaration.* Philadelphia: University of Pennsylvania Press.

Muntarbhorn, Vitit. 2007. *Article 34: Sexual Exploitation and Sexual Abuse of Children.* Leiden: Nijhoff Publishers.

Murphy, Jeffrie. 1988. "Afterword: Constitutionalism, Moral Skepticism, and Belief," in *Constitutionalism: The Philosophical Dimension*, ed. A. Rosenbaum. New York: Greenwood Press.

Murray, Rachel. 2004. *Human Rights in Africa: From the OAU to the African Union.* Cambridge: Cambridge University Press.

Muscroft, Sarah, ed. 1999. *Children's Rights: Reality or Rhetoric? The UN Convention on the Rights of the Child: The First Ten Years.* London: International Save the Children Alliance.

Mutua, Makau wa. 1996. "The Politics of Human Rights: Beyond the Abolitionist Paradigm in Africa." *Michigan Journal of International Law* 17:591–613.

Nickel, James. 1987. *Making Sense of Human Rights. Philosophical Reflections on the Universal Declaration of Human Rights.* Berkeley: University of California Press.

Nozick, Robert. 1974. *Anarchy, State, and Utopia.* New York: Basic Books.

Nussbaum, Martha. 1992. "Human Functioning and Social Justice: In Defense of Aristotelian Essentialism." *Political Theory* 20:202–246.

Nussbaum, Martha. 2006. *Frontiers of Justice. Disability, Nationality, Species Membership.* Cambridge: Harvard University Press.

Nylan, Michael. 2003. Review of Stephen Angle, *Human Rights and Chinese Thought. Perspectives on Politics* 1:579.

Pagden, Anthony. 2003. "Human Rights, Natural Rights, and Europe's Imperial Legacy." *Political Theory* 31:171–199.

Panksepp, Jaak. 1994. "The Role of Brain Emotional Systems in the Construction of Social Systems." *Politics and the Life Sciences* 13:116–119.

Parekh, Bhikhu. 2000. *Rethinking Multiculturalism.* Houndsmills: Macmillan.

Parkinson, Charles. 2007. *Bills of Rights and Decolonization: The Emergence of Domestic Human Rights Instruments in Britain's Overseas Territories.* New York: Oxford University Press.

Parsons, Talcott. 1951. *The Social System.* Glencoe: Free Press.

Paxton, Pamela, and Melanie Hughes. 2007. *Women, Politics and Power.* Los Angeles: Pine Forge Press.

Peek, Charles, George Lowe, and L. Susan Williams. 1991. "Gender and God's Word: Another Look at Religious Fundamentalism and Sexism." *Social Forces* 69:1205–1221.

Peirce, Charles S. 1986. "Toward a Logic Book, 1872–73," in *Writings of Charles S. Peirce. A Chronological Edition*, vol. 3, ed. C. Kloesel, 14–108. Bloomington: Indiana University Press.

Perry, James. 1997. "Antecedents of Public Service Motivation." *Journal of Public Administration Research and Theory* 7:181–197.

Perry, Michael. 2007. *Toward a Theory of Human Rights: Religion, Law, Courts*. New York. Cambridge University Press.

Pescosolido, Bernice, and Beth Rubin. 2000. "The Web of Group Affiliations Revisited." *American Sociological Review* 65:52–76.

Plessner, Helmuth. [1928] 1981. Die Stufen des Organischen und der Mensch. Einleitung in die philosophische Anthropologie, in Helmuth Plessner. *Gesammelte Schriften*, vol. 4. Frankfurt am Main: Suhrkamp Verlag.

Posner, Richard. 1999. "Emotion Versus Emotionalism in Law," in *The Passions of Law*, ed. S. Bandes, 309–329. New York: New York University Press.

Prager, Dennis, and Jonathan Glover. 1993. "Can We Be Good Without God? A Debate between Dennis Prager and Jonathan Glover at Oxford University." *Ultimate Issues* 9:3–22.

Quataert, Jean. 2009. *Advocating Dignity. Human Rights Mobilizations in Global Politics*. Philadelphia: University of Pennsylvania Press.

Quine, Willard Van Orman. 1992. *Pursuit of Truth*, rev. ed. Cambridge: Harvard University Press.

Rajagopal, Balakrishnan. 2003. *International Law from Below*. Cambridge: Cambridge University Press.

Ramadan, Tariq. 2004. *Western Muslims and the Future of Islam*. New York: Oxford University Press.

Rancière, Jacques. 2004. "Who Is the Subject of the Rights of Man?" *The South Atlantic Quarterly* 103:297–310.

Rancière, Jacques. 2006. *Hatred of Democracy*, trans. S. Corcoran. London: Verso.

Rawls, John. 1993. *Political Liberalism*. New York: Columbia University Press.

Rawls, John. 1999a. *A Theory of Justice*, rev. ed. Cambridge: Harvard University Press.

Rawls, John. 1999b. *The Law of Peoples*. Cambridge: Harvard University Press.

Renan, Ernst. 1882. *Qu'est-ce qu'une nation? Conférence faite en Sorbonne, le 11 mars 1882*. Paris: Calmann Lévy.

Renteln, Alison. 1988. "Relativism and the Search for Human Rights." *American Anthropologist* 90:56–72.

Renteln, Alison. 1990. *International Human Rights: Universalism Versus Relativism*. Newbury Park: Sage Publications.

Ricoeur, Paul. 1969. *Le conflit des interprétations; essais d'herméneutique*. Paris: Éditions du Seuil.

Rieff, David. 2002. *A Bed for the Night: Humanitarianism in Crisis*. New York: Simon & Schuster.

Rizzi, T. S., et al. 2010. "The ATXN1 and TRIM31 Genes Are Related to Intelligence in an ADHD Background: Evidence from a Large Collaborative Study Totaling 4,963 Subjects." *American Journal of Medical Genetics, Part B: Neuropsychiatric* 156:145–157.

Roberts, Dorothy. 1998. "The Meaning of Blacks' Fidelity to the Constitution," in *Constitutional Stupidities, Constitutional Tragedies*, ed. W. Eskridge and S. Levinson, 226–234. New York: New York University Press.

Rorty, Richard. 1989. *Contingency, Irony, and Solidarity*. Cambridge: Cambridge University Press.

Rorty, Richard. 1991. *Objectivity, Relativism, and Truth*. Cambridge: Cambridge University Press.

Rorty, Richard. 1993. "Human Rights, Rationality, and Sentimentality," in *On Human Rights. The Oxford Amnesty Lectures 1993*, ed. S. Shute and S. Hurley, 112–134. New York: Basic Books.

Ross, Michael. 2008. "Oil, Islam and Women." *American Political Science Review* 102:107–123.

Roth, Kenneth. 1994. "Domestic Violence as an International Human Rights Issue," in *Human Rights of Women: National and International Perspectives*, ed. R. Cook, 326–339. Philadelphia: University of Pennsylvania Press.

Runciman, W. G. 1978. "Introduction" to "The Methodology of the Social Sciences," in *Max Weber. Selections in Translation*, ed. W. G. Runciman. Cambridge: Cambridge University Press.

Said, Abdul Aziz, and Meena Sharify-Funk, eds. 2003. *Cultural Diversity and Islam*. Lanham: University Press of America.

Said, Edward. 1994. *Orientalism*. New York: Random House.

Salmon, Merrilee. 1997. "Ethical Considerations in Anthropology and Archaeology, or Relativism and Justice for All." *Journal of Anthropological Research* 53:47–63.

Sear, R., and F. W. Marlowe. 2009. "How Universal Are Human Mate Choices? Size Does Not Matter When Hadza Foragers Are Choosing a Mate." *Biology Letters* 23:606–609.

Searle, John. 1995. *The Construction of Social Reality*. New York: Free Press.

Searle, John. 2010. *Making the Social World: The Structure of Human Civilization*. Oxford: Oxford University Press.

Sen, Amartya. 1992. *Inequality Reexamined*. Cambridge: Harvard University Press.

Scanlon, Thomas. 1979. "Human Rights as a Neutral Concern," in *Human Rights and U.S. Foreign Policy*, ed. P. Brown and D. MacLean. Lexington: D.C. Heath.

Scott, W. Richard. 2001. *Institutions and Organizations*, 2d ed. Thousand Oaks: Sage Publications.

Shweder, Richard, and Jonathan Haidt. 2000. "The Culturual Psychology of the Emotions: Ancient and New," in *Handbook of Emotions*, 2d ed., eds. M. Lewis and J. Haviland-Jones, 397–416. New York: Guilford Press.

Shue, Henry. 1980. *Basic Rights. Subsistence, Affluence, and U.S. Foreign Policy*. Princeton: Princeton University Press.

Siep, Ludwig. 2002. "Moral und Gattungsethik." *Deutsche Zeitschrift für Philosophie* 50:111–120.

Simmel, Georg. 1896. "Zur Methodik der Socialwissenschaft." *Jahrbuch für Gesetzgebung, Verwaltung und Volkswirtschaft im Deutschen Reich* 20:575–585.

Simmel, Georg. [1922] 1964. *Conflict & The Web of Group-Affiliations*, ed. K. Wolff and R. Bendix. New York: Free Press.

Simmel, Georg. [1922] 1989. "Über sociale Differenzierung," in *Georg Simmel Gesamtausgabe*, vol. 2. Frankfurt am Main: Suhrkamp Verlag. Translated in Simmel (1964).

Simpson, A. W. 2001. *Human Rights and the End of Empire. Britain and the Genesis of the European Convention.* Oxford: Oxford University Press.

Sinha, Surya Prakash. 1981. "Human Rights: A Non-Western Viewpoint." *Archiv für Rechts- und Sozialphilosophie* 67:76–91.

Solomon, Robert. 1995. *A Passion for Justice: Emotions and the Origins of the Social Contract.* Lanham: Rowman & Littlefield.

Solomon, Robert. 1999. "Justice v. Vengeance: On Law and the Satisfaction of Emotion," in *Passions of Law*, ed. S. Bandes, 123–148. New York: New York University Press.

Sousa Santos, Boaventura de. 2002. "Toward a Multicultural Conception of Human Rights," in *Moral Imperialism. A Critical Anthology*, ed. B. Hernánez-Truyol. New York: New York University Press.

Spaemann, Robert. 2002. "Habermas über Bioethik." *Deutsche Zeitschrift für Philosophie* 50:105–109.

Spichenok, O., Z. M. Budimlija, A. A. Mitchell, A. Jenny, L. Kovacevic, D. Marjanovic, T. Caragine, M. Prinz, and E. Wurmbach. 2010. "Prediction of Eye and Skin Color in Diverse Populations Using Seven SNPs." *Forensic Science International: Genetics* (November 1).

Stark, Rodney. 2004. *Exploring the Religious Life.* Baltimore: Johns Hopkins Press.

Stark, Rodney, and Roger Finke. 2000. *Acts of Faith: Explaining the Human Side of Religion.* Berkeley: University of California Press.

Stout, Jeffrey. 1988. *Ethics After Babel: The Language of Morals and Their Discontents.* Boston: Beacon Press.

Strydom, Piet. 2007. "A Cartography of Contemporary Cognitive Social Theory." *European Journal of Social Theory* 10:339–356.

Sturm, R. A. 2009. "Molecular Genetics of Human Pigmentation Diversity." *Human Molecular Genetics* 18(R1):R9–R17.

Sullins, D. Paul. 2006. "Gender and Religion: Deconstructing Universality, Constructing Complexity." *American Journal of Sociology* 112:838–880.

Swidler, Ann. 1986. "Culture in Action: Symbols and Strategies." *American Sociological Review* 51:273–286.

Taylor, Charles. 1999. "Conditions for an Unforced Consensus on Human Rights," in J. Bauer and D. Bell, *The East Asian Challenge for Human Rights.* Cambridge: Cambridge University Press.

Thompson, Elizabeth. 2000. *Colonial Citizens: Republican Rights, Paternal Privilege and Gender in French Syria and Lebanon.* New York: Columbia University Press.

Thong, H. Y., S. H. Jee, C. C. Sun, and R. E. Boissy. 2003. "The Patterns of Melanosome Distribution in Keratinocytes of Human Skin as One Determining Factor of Skin Colour." *British Journal of Dermatology* 149:498–505.

Thornton, Patricia. 2004. *Markets from Culture.* Stanford: Stanford University Press.

Tomasello, Michael. 2009. *Why We Cooperate.* Cambridge: MIT Press.

Turner, Terence. 1997. "Human Rights, Human Difference." *Journal of Anthropological Research* 53:273–291.

UNESCO. 1949. *Human Rights: Comments and Interpretations: A Symposium.* Introduction by Jacques Maritain. New York: Columbia University Press.

Valadez, Jorge. 2001. *Deliberative Democracy, Political Legitimacy and Self-Determination in Multicultural Societies.* Boulder: Westview.

van den Daele, Wolfgang. 2000. "Die Natürlichkeit des Menschen als Kriterium und Schranke technischer Eingriffe." *WechselWirkung. Naturwissenchaft, Technik, Gesellschaft & Philosophie* 103–104:24–31.

Walzer, Michael. 1994. *Thick and Thin. Moral Argument at Home and Abroad.* Notre Dame: University of Notre Dame Press.

Warnock, Mary. 1987. "Do Human Cells Have Rights?" *Bioethics* 1:1–14.

Watson, J. D., and F. H. Crick. 1953. "The Structure of DNA." *Cold Spring Harbor Symposia on Quantitative Biology* 18:123–131.

Weber, Max. [1919] 1958. "Science as a Vocation," in *From Max Weber: Essays in Sociology,* ed. H. Gerth and C. W. Mills. New York: Oxford University Press.

Welzel, Christian, and Amy Alexander. 2009. "Islam's Patriarchal Effect: Spurious or Substantive?" Paper presented at the Annual Meeting of the Midwest Political Science Association, 2–5 April, Chicago, Illinois.

Westen, Drew. 2008. *The Political Brain.* New York: Public Affairs.

Wilson, Richard. 1997. "Introduction: Human Rights, Culture and Context," in *Human Rights, Culture and Context: Anthropological Perspectives,* ed. R. Wilson. London: Pluto Press.

Witkin, Herman. 1967. "A Cognitive-Style Approach to Cross-Cultural Research." *International Journal of Psychology* 2:233–250.

World Health Organization. 1999. *Female Genital Mutilation Programmes to Date: What Works and What Doesn't: A Review.* Geneva: WHO.

Young, Liane, Fiery Cushman, Marc Hauser, and Rebecca Saxe. 2007. "The Neural Basis of the Interaction Between Theory of Mind and Moral Judgment." *Proceedings of the National Academy of Sciences* 104:8235–8240.

Zerubavel, Eviatar. 1997. *Social Mindscapes: An Invitation to Cognitive Sociology.* Cambridge: Harvard University Press.

Index